RSF: The Russell Sage Foundation Journal of the Social Sciences

*Financial Reform:
Preventing the Next Crisis*

VOLUME 3 · NUMBER 1 · JANUARY 2017

RSF: The Russell Sage Foundation Journal of the Social Sciences   ISSN 2377-8261

The Russell Sage Foundation
The Russell Sage Foundation, one of the oldest of America's general purpose foundations, was established in 1907 by Mrs. Margaret Olivia Sage for "the improvement of social and living conditions in the United States." The foundation seeks to fulfill this mandate by fostering the development and dissemination of knowledge about the country's political, social, and economic problems. While the foundation endeavors to assure the accuracy and objectivity of each book it publishes, the conclusions and interpretations in Russell Sage Foundation publications are those of the authors and not of the foundation, its trustees, or its staff. Publication by Russell Sage, therefore, does not imply foundation endorsement.

Board of Trustees
Sara S. McLanahan, *Chair*
Larry M. Bartels
Karen S. Cook
W. Bowman Cutter III
Sheldon H. Danziger
Kathryn Edin
Michael Jones-Correa
Lawrence F. Katz
David Laibson
Nicholas Lemann
Martha Minow
Peter R. Orszag
Claude M. Steele
Shelley E. Taylor
Hirokazu Yoshikawa

Mission Statement
RSF: The Russell Sage Foundation Journal of the Social Sciences is a peer-reviewed, open-access journal of original empirical research articles by both established and emerging scholars. It is designed to promote cross-disciplinary collaborations on timely issues of interest to academics, policymakers, and the public at large. Each issue is thematic in nature and focuses on a specific research question or area of interest. The introduction to each issue will include an accessible, broad, and synthetic overview of the research question under consideration and the current thinking from the various social sciences.

RSF Journal Editorial Board
Elizabeth O. Ananat, Duke University
Annette Bernhardt, University of California, Berkeley
Karen S. Cook, Stanford University
Sheldon H. Danziger, RSF President
Janet C. Gornick, The CUNY Graduate Center
Jennifer Hochschild, Harvard University
Douglas S. Massey, Princeton University
Mary E. Pattillo, Northwestern University
James Sidanius, Harvard University
Mary C. Waters, Harvard University
Bruce Western, Harvard University

Copyright © 2017 by Russell Sage Foundation. All rights reserved. Printed in the United States of America. No part of this publication may be reproduced, stored in a retrieval system, or transmitted in any form or by any means, electronic, mechanical, photocopying, recording, or otherwise, without the prior written permission of the publisher. Reproduction by the United States Government in whole or in part is permitted for any purpose.

Opinions expressed in this journal are not necessarily those of the editors, editorial board, trustees, or the Russell Sage Foundation.

We invite scholars to submit proposals for potential issues through the *RSF* application portal: https://rsfjournal.onlineapplicationportal.com/. Submissions should be addressed to Suzanne Nichols, Director of Publications.

To view the complete text and additional features online please go to **www.rsfjournal.org**.

Russell Sage Foundation
112 East 64th Street
New York, NY 10065

ISSN (print):   2377-8253
ISSN (electronic): 2377-8261
ISBN: 978-0-87154-027-0

RSF: The Russell Sage Foundation
Journal of the Social Sciences

VOLUME 3 NUMBER 1
JANUARY 2017

Financial Reform: Preventing the Next Crisis

ISSUE EDITOR
Michael S. Barr, University of Michigan

CONTENTS

Part I. Introduction and Overview

Financial Reform: Making the System Safer and Fairer 2
Michael S. Barr

Part II. Financial Stability

The Impact of the Dodd-Frank Act on Financial Stability and Economic Growth 20
Martin Neil Baily, Aaron Klein, and Justin Schardin

The Resolution of Distressed Financial Conglomerates 48
Howell E. Jackson and Stephanie Massman

Part III. Consumer Protection

The Consumer Financial Protection Bureau and the Quest for Consumer Comprehension 74
Lauren E. Willis

A Public Choice Approach to the Unequal Treatment of Securities Market Participants and Home Borrowers 94
Jonathan Macey

Part IV. Market Structure

Strategic Agent-Based Modeling of Financial Markets 104
Michael P. Wellman and Elaine Wah

Part V. International Perspectives

Financial Sector Health Since 2007: A Comparative Analysis of the United States, Europe, and Asia 122
Viral V. Acharya

The European Union in International Financial Governance 138
Niamh Moloney

PART I
Introduction and Overview

Financial Reform: Making the System Safer and Fairer

MICHAEL S. BARR

In the fall of 2008, the financial crisis crushed the U.S. economy and plunged the country into the Great Recession. The crisis shuttered American businesses, cost millions of Americans their jobs, and wiped out home values and household savings. The macro effects hit hardest and were the longest lasting for those least able to bear the brunt of the crisis. It was devastating to middle-income families and perhaps even more so to low- and moderate-income households, who had little financial buffer (Barr 2012a). Financial stability, never robust for these families, dropped precipitously (Barr and Schaffa 2016). Both in the United States and globally, the crisis has led to a series of fundamental reforms. (For an early analysis, see Barr 2012b). At the same time, more needs to be done to make the financial system safer, fairer, and better harnessed to the needs of the real economy. This essay first describes the origins of the financial crisis and then outlines domestic reforms. It then turns to the need for global coordination in financial reform, and analyzes steps taken thus far, while highlighting some of the key remaining challenges ahead. Finally, it introduces other articles in this volume, produced as part of a 2014 conference on financial reform organized by the University of Michigan's Center on Finance, Law and Policy, sponsored by the Russell Sage Foundation.[1]

THE ROOTS OF THE FINANCIAL CRISIS

The financial crisis was not an act of nature, or a fluke of history. Rather, the crisis was rooted in years of unconstrained excess and failures of risk management on Wall Street, and prolonged complacency in Washington and in major financial capitals around the world. That complacency was based on a misplaced ideology: that private markets would take care of risk regulation on their own. And it was based on a misunderstanding: that somehow, since the risk of bank runs had been conquered, there was no risk to "shadow banking." Market discipline, it was believed, would force firms to engage in sound risk management. Market-based financing, it was thought, would protect taxpayers, since no federally insured deposits were at risk. But both the ideology and the understanding were deeply flawed. The costs of failure—regardless of the nature of financial intermediation or the corporate structure of the financial firm—were borne

---

Michael S. Barr is Roy F. and Jean Humphrey Proffitt Professor of Law at the University of Michigan.

Direct correspondence to: Michael S. Barr at msbarr@umich.edu, University of Michigan Law School, 625 S. State St., Ann Arbor, MI 48109.

1. I would like to acknowledge the contributions of participants in the conference "Financial Reform: Preventing the Next Crisis," at the University of Michigan Law School on October 23-24, 2014. The Russell Sage Foundation sponsored the University of Michigan's Center on Finance, Law, and Policy to host the conference. Portions of this introduction are drawn from some of my earlier articles cited in the references, including Barr 2012b and Barr 2014.

throughout society, and not fully internalized to the firms' managers, shareholders, and creditors. Indeed, government intervention to prevent even more brutal damage to the economy had the effect of helping to insulate the firms' stakeholders from full harm.

The financial sector engaged in highly leveraged, short-funded maturity transformation with too little transparency, not enough capital, and little restraint. Large firms became more interconnected. Investment banks and other financial conglomerates relied increasingly on short-term funding from money market funds, securities lenders, and securities lenders' prime brokerage business. This short-term funding was subject to runs during periods of market uncertainty, just like bank deposits before the age of deposit insurance and a lender of last resort in the form of the Federal Reserve (see, for example, Gorton and Metrick 2012). Huge amounts of risk moved outside the more regulated parts of the banking system to the unregulated markets, where it was easier to increase leverage. Legal loopholes and regulatory gaps allowed firms to evade oversight. Investment banks such as Lehman Brothers, insurance conglomerates such as AIG, and other entities performing the same market functions as banks escaped meaningful regulation because of their corporate form. Banks themselves moved activities off the balance sheet—for example, to special-purpose vehicles holding mortgage-backed securities, and outside the reach of more stringent regulation and capital rules.

Shadow banking markets were opaque and hid growing risk. Derivatives were traded in the shadows with insufficient capital to back the trades. Repo markets—short-term wholesale funding used by broker-dealers and banks—became riskier as they grew to be a larger portion of financial intermediation, and collateral shifted from treasuries to poorer-quality asset-backed securities. The lack of transparency in securitization hid the growing wedge in incentives facing different players in the system, and the system failed to require sufficient responsibility from those who made loans, or packaged them into complex instruments to be sold to investors. Synthetic products—essentially offsetting derivatives bets—multiplied risks in the securitization system and allowed the market to increase its exposure to mortgage-backed securities.

The financial sector, under the guise of innovation, piled ill-considered risk upon risk. Rapid growth in key markets hid misaligned incentives and underlying risk. Managers failed to understand new risks, or when they did, they took steps that made the system as a whole worse off. Financial institutions held increasingly inadequate capital against growing risks, and regulators failed to stop them. Managers, traders, firms, credit-rating agencies, and other gatekeepers all let short-term rewards from new financial products and rapidly growing markets blind them to the risks.

Congress and regulators weakened consumer and investor protections in the name of the free market. Households took on risk that they often did not fully understand and could ill afford. Investors bought implausibly labeled AAA securities. Mortgage fraud, securities fraud, fraudulent manipulation of key indices and currency markets—all harmed individuals and institutional investors and undermined the integrity of the market as a whole. Rising home prices helped to feed the financial system's rapid growth and to hide the declining underwriting standards for the origination and securitization of mortgage loans.

When home prices began to flatten, and then to decline, fault lines were revealed. Mortgage defaults soared and the assets based on mortgages plunged in value. The asset implosion in housing led to cascades throughout the financial system. Nonbank mortgage lenders collapsed. Investment banks could no longer borrow. Fire sales of assets, collateral calls on derivative contracts, and the tightening or closing off of repo and commercial paper markets drove firms closer to the edge. Contagion gripped the financial system, as the problems at weaker firms undermined stronger ones. Failures in the shadow banking system led to failures in more regulated parts of the banking system. Then, in the fall of 2008, credit markets froze. The overreliance on short-term financing and excessive risk taking that had produced significant profit in financial capitals in the developed economies across the world fanned a panic that nearly collapsed the global financial system.

OVERVIEW OF REFORMS

In the United States, passage of the Dodd-Frank Wall Street Reform and Consumer Protection Act of 2010 ("Dodd-Frank") ushered in comprehensive reform in key areas: enlarging the regulatory perimeter by creating the authority to regulate financial firms that pose a threat to financial stability, without regard to their corporate form; enacting a resolution authority to deal with the potential collapse of these major firms in the event of a crisis, without feeding a panic or putting taxpayers on the hook; attacking regulatory arbitrage, restricting risky activities, and beefing up banking supervision; requiring central clearing and exchange trading of standardized derivatives, and capital, margin and transparency throughout the market; improving investor protections; and establishing a new Consumer Financial Protection Bureau to look out for the interests of American households.

Today, major financial firms are subject to higher prudential standards, including higher capital and liquidity requirements, stress tests, and resolution planning through "living wills." By forcing firms to internalize more of the costs that they impose on the system, they will be incentivized to shrink and reduce their complexity, leverage, and interconnections. Should such a firm fail, there will be a bigger capital buffer to absorb losses. To stem a panic, the Dodd-Frank Act permits the Federal Deposit Insurance Corporation (FDIC) to resolve the largest and most interconnected financial companies without exposing the system to a sudden, disorderly failure that puts the economy at risk.

On the global level, the international community has put forward new rules on capital, so that there are bigger buffers in the system in the event of failures. Capital will be measured in a more conservative way, and capital levels are going up significantly. Systemically important firms will hold even higher levels of capital. There are new rules on liquidity and a global leverage limit. Derivatives reforms are proceeding, as are new approaches to dealing with the risks from repo and securities financing transactions.

Yet much more work remains to be done, and the financial sector did not leave the battlefield after their defeats in 2010. Far from it. The brutal fight over financial reform rages on, and there is serious risk that a collective amnesia about the causes and consequences of the financial crisis appears to be descending on global financial capitals that will further weaken the resolve for reform (See, for example, Coffee 2011, 2012).

COMPARING U.S. FINANCIAL REGULATION PRE-CRISIS AND POST-REFORM

Many readers may be skeptical regarding the efficacy of the reforms that have taken place thus far, either because they think they did not change the system enough, or because they think that they went too far. The following section takes the time to chart the path of reform so far, before turning to the difficulties and dangers on the road ahead.

First, before Dodd-Frank, if an entity was a bank, it had tougher regulations, more stringent capital requirements, and more robust supervision; but if an entity was an investment bank engaged in the same kind of maturity transformation, it had to abide by different rules (see Scott 2010). When U.S. investment banks needed to find a "consolidated holding company regulator" in order to meet European Union standards for doing business in Europe, the Securities and Exchange Commission set up a voluntary Consolidated Supervised Entity program which had little oversight. The SEC was not established as a prudential regulator, did not have clear supervisory power, and had little experience and few trained examiners. Moreover, the leverage ratio that served as a backstop for bank capital requirements was not applied to investment banks.

The Federal Reserve was too lax in supervising firms where it did have authority and it did not have any authority to set and enforce capital requirements on the major institutions that operated businesses outside of bank holding companies. That meant it had no supervision over investment banks, diversified financial institutions such as AIG, or the nonbank financial companies competing with banks in the mortgage, consumer credit, and business lending markets. The Office of Thrift Supervision viewed its role as supervising thrifts, not their holding companies (such as AIG). Banks and thrifts freely engaged in risky mortgage lending, and regulators did not step in until it was too late.

Today, Dodd-Frank has provided authority for clear, strong and consolidated supervision and regulation by the Federal Reserve of any financial firm—regardless of legal form—whose failure could pose a threat to financial stability. The largest investment banks that survived the financial crisis merged into or became bank holding companies subject to Fed oversight. AIG, GE Capital, Prudential, and MetLife have now been brought under Fed supervision through the Financial Stability Oversight Council (FSOC) designation. As a result of Dodd-Frank changes, thrift holding companies (including those with large insurance operations) are now supervised by the Fed. The Office of Thrift Supervision and the SEC's investment bank regime have been abolished. Thus, all bank and thrift holding companies, as well as systemically important nonbank firms, regardless of corporate form, are supervised by the Federal Reserve. We will have a single point of accountability for tougher and more consistent supervision of the largest and most interconnected financial firms.

Although the regulatory infrastructure is, to put it mildly, far from ideal, with too many divided responsibilities and too many opportunities for turf battles or regulatory gaps, Dodd-Frank created the FSOC, which is responsible for identifying threats to financial stability and dealing with them. The FSOC can recommend stricter regulatory action, and regulators must either implement such changes or explain publicly why they are not acting (see Gerson 2013). Already, this process has led the SEC to impose stricter regulation of money market funds than would otherwise have occurred (Barr 2015a). The FSOC has the potential to get information across the financial services marketplace through the Office of Financial Research (OFR), which Dodd-Frank established and empowered to collect data from any financial firm, and to develop and enforce standardization for data collection. The OFR has begun to use this authority by developing a "legal entity identifier" for financial transactions. The OFR is charged with independently assessing risks in the financial system, and can potentially serve as a counterweight to the Fed by providing independent assessments of whether the Fed is adequately supervising the largest firms and dealing with the critical issues in systemic risk. A strong OFR can serve as a check and balance for regulatory agencies, ensuring that they improve their own performance or risk being criticized (Ludwig 2012; Barr 2015a).

Dodd-Frank provides for more stringent prudential standards and higher capital and liquidity standards for the largest bank and nonbank firms. In addition to the heightened capital requirements applicable to all firms, the largest firms are subject to a capital surcharge, a leverage ratio, a toughened supplemental leverage ratio, a more stringent liquidity requirement, and capital required to pass stress tests.

Already, capital levels in the banking system have doubled, and banks' use of short-term nondeposit funding has plummeted. The annual stress tests are evaluating a firm's ability to withstand deep market contractions. There are enhanced rules on affiliate transactions and lending limits, and much stricter proposed limits on counterparty credit exposures. Deposit insurance premiums are going up on the very largest firms. The Volcker Rule prohibits banking entities from engaging in certain proprietary trading or running internal hedge funds, subject to a number of exceptions, and also helps to simplify the task of winding down major firms that are at risk of failure. Moreover, the Fed is using macro-prudential supervision as it increases its capacity to understand and mitigate risks to the financial system as a whole.

There is a healthy debate about breaking up or limiting the size of financial firms. Under the Dodd-Frank Act, major firms are subject to a concentration limit that generally prohibits a financial company from engaging in mergers or acquisitions that would result in the firm's liabilities—including wholesale funding and off-balance sheet exposures—exceeding 10 percent of the liabilities of financial companies as a whole. Dodd-Frank provides regulators with the authority to require financial institutions to restructure their activities to make it credible that they can be resolved if they are in danger of collapse; the resolution planning process has already forced firms to begin to simplify their organization form, develop "clean" holding companies, and place large amounts of capital and long-term debt in the holding company to assist with the resolution. The act also permits regulators to force firms to be broken up if they fail to submit a credible plan and thereafter fail to meet regulators' requirements to restructure themselves to make resolution credible. Such firms can also be broken up if they are found to pose a grave threat to financial stability. These enhanced prudential measures for major financial firms are likely to reduce risk in the financial system, constrain further concentration, and reduce "too big to fail" distortions.

Second, before Dodd-Frank, shadow banking markets grew dramatically with little oversight and in the absence of even regulatory or marketwide knowledge about the nature of the markets they were serving. For example, the OTC derivatives market—with a notional amount of $700 trillion at its peak—grew up in the shadows, with little oversight. Credit derivatives, which were supposed to diffuse risk, instead concentrated it. Synthetic securitization with embedded derivatives magnified failures in the real securitization market. Major financial firms used derivatives to increase their credit exposure to each other, rather than decrease it.

We should never again face a situation—such as AIG's $2 trillion derivatives portfolio—where the potential failure of a virtually unregulated, capital-deficient major player in the derivatives market can impose devastating risks on the entire system. Insufficient capital meant that major participants in the system could not reliably pay out on their obligations, and insufficient margin meant that counterparties on every transaction were more exposed to the risk of nonpayment. When the crisis began, regulators, financial firms, and investors had an insufficient understanding of the degree to which trouble at one firm spelled trouble for another, because of the opacity of the market. This lack of information magnified the contagion as the crisis intensified, causing a damaging wave of margin increases, deleveraging, and credit market breakdowns. Lack of transparency, insufficient supervision, and inadequate capital and margin left our financial system vulnerable to concentrations of risk, and to abuse.

Today, under Dodd-Frank, regulators are putting in place the tools comprehensively to regulate the OTC derivatives market for the first time. The act requires all standardized derivatives to be centrally cleared, which will substantially reduce the buildup of bilateral counterparty credit risk between major financial firms. Under Dodd-Frank rules, 75 percent of new derivative contracts were centrally cleared in 2015 as compared to only 15 percent in 2007 (Massad 2015). Central clearinghouses are subject to strong prudential supervision under the Dodd-Frank Act. Dodd-Frank requires standardized derivatives to be traded on exchanges or alternative swap execution facilities, which improves pre- and post-trade price transparency. Trading transparency will help to improve price competition as well as to improve safety and soundness, as market participants and regulators will have full access to current prices in the event of system disruptions. Even non-centrally-cleared OTC derivatives are to be reported to a trade repository, making the market far more transparent.

The act provides for prudential regulation, capital requirements, and business conduct rules for all swap dealers and major swap participants. It provides for robust capital and margin requirements for derivative transactions, and higher requirements for those that are not centrally cleared, providing a strong incentive to use central clearing and maintain a bigger buffer against losses. It also provides for regulatory and enforcement tools to go after manipulation, fraud, and other abuse.

At the same time as the act reforms derivatives markets, it provides a new framework for regulation of financial market utilities and critical payment, clearing, and settlement activities, including not only those in the derivatives markets but also those in the wholesale funding markets—securities financing transactions (such as repo and securities lending), commercial paper, and prime brokerage—that are critical to the shadow banking system.

In the lead-up to the financial crisis, major financial firms became increasingly funded not by traditional bank deposits, nor even longer-term funding in the commercial markets, but rather by overnight funding in the repo markets. An important part of that market, the triparty repo market, became increasingly concentrated in only two major clearing banks, which were themselves exposed to counterparty risk from securities firms borrowing intraday credit. As the triparty repo market became more concentrated, it also became riskier because counterparties came to accept not only Treasury securities as collateral, but also highly rated but opaque asset-backed securities. These securities in turn became riskier as credit rating agencies became increasingly willing to label as safe assets that were lower quality, including pools of securities backed only by poorly underwritten subprime and Alt-A mortgages. When the financial crisis hit, repo and commercial paper markets froze, and investors in money market funds ran, causing a massive contraction in credit not only for financial firms but also major firms in the real economy (that is, non-financial). This contraction was overcome only with massive interventions by the Fed, the FDIC, and the Treasury.

The Dodd-Frank Act provides the foundation fundamentally to reform the wholesale funding markets by providing strong authority for the Federal Reserve to regulate financial market utilities and critical payment, clearing, and settlement activities; to set new rules for capital, collateral, and margin requirements for repo and other securities financing, and other critical markets; and to establish uniform prudential standards throughout the financial system. While repo and other securities financing policies are still a work in progress, short-term financing reforms are already being reinforced by new capital and liquidity requirements, liability concentration limits under the act, and reforms to the assessment base for deposit insurance that encompass all liabilities. Once fully implemented, these reforms will have the combined effect of taxing short-term liabilities, which will force firms to internalize more of the costs of short-term funding. These steps have already reduced the use of short-term funding, and will provide incentives to manage their use more carefully even when interest rates normalize.

The act also fundamentally transforms regulation of another major element of the shadow banking system, securitization. The act requires deep transparency into the structure of securitizations, including information about assets and originators. Securitization sponsors must generally retain risk in their securitizations, unless the mortgages they pool meet guidelines as plain vanilla "qualified residential mortgages" so that incentives are better aligned among participants in the system. Capital rules will better account for risk in securitizations. Parallel changes in accounting rules will now bring the most common forms of securitization onto the balance sheet. Credit-rating agencies will be subject to heightened liability for failure to conduct ratings with integrity, with comprehensive oversight by the SEC, including policing of ratings shopping and conflicts of interest; ratings themselves will be more transparent and will include key information on rating methodology, compliance, qualitative and quantitative data, due diligence, and other protections.

Third, before Dodd-Frank, consumer protection regulation was fragmented over seven federal regulators, and prudential regulators often viewed consumer protection with hostility. Regulators lacked mission focus, marketwide coverage, and consolidated authority. Nonbanks could avoid federal supervision. Banks could choose the least restrictive consumer approach among several different banking agencies. Federal regulators pre-empted state consumer protections laws without adequately replacing these important safeguards. Fragmentation of rule writing, supervision and enforcement led to finger pointing in place of effective action.

Today, despite repeated congressional efforts to block its director, stymie its funding, overturn its structure and undermine its authority, the Consumer Financial Protection Bureau (CFPB) has been built into a strong organization. It has marketwide coverage and is setting new rules of the road for banks and nonbanks alike to police against abuses. It has strong supervisory authority over banks with at least $10 billion in assets and over broad parts of the nonbank markets. It is basing its work on an empirically grounded understanding of human behavior (see Barr, Mullainathan, and Shafir 2009), rather than abstract models and ideological assumptions. And it is already helping to end misleading sales pitches and hidden traps. Rather, it is making space for banks and nonbanks to compete vigorously for consumers on the basis of price and quality. It is strongly independent—with secure funding, policy, regulatory and enforcement authority—and strongly accountable, with regular reporting to the Congress and the public (see Barr 2015a).

The CFPB has already made significant progress in making financial services markets work better. For example, implementation of rules under the Credit Card Act of 2009 is saving consumers nearly $12 billion annually in reduced credit card fees, without increasing interest rates or undermining access (Agarwal et al. 2015). Reforms of the mortgage market are helping to eliminate some of the worst abuses such as steering low-income and minority borrowers to high-cost loans; mortgage disclosures are now both simpler and more informative; and mortgage servicing is being strongly policed. The CFPB is tackling a broad range of other critical issues, including auto, student, and payday loans; credit reporting and debt collection; and protection of military service members and their families. CFPB enforcement actions had resulted in more than $11 billion in relief to 25 million consumers as of 2015 (Cordray 2015). Key upcoming decisions include whether and how the CFPB should regulate or prohibit mandatory predispute arbitration agreements (Barr 2015b).

Fourth, before Dodd-Frank, the government did not have the authority to unwind large, highly leveraged, and substantially interconnected financial firms that failed—such as Bear Stearns, Lehman Brothers, and AIG—without disrupting the broader financial system. Firms benefitted from the perception that they were "too-big-to-fail," which reduced market discipline and encouraged excessive risk taking by firms. It provided an artificial incentive for large firms to grow and tipped the playing field in favor of the largest firms. When the financial crisis hit, the inability to resolve these firms left the government with the untenable choice between taxpayer-funded bailouts, as with AIG, or the disorderly financial collapse of a major firm, as with Lehman Brothers, the failure of which contributed to widespread financial cascades and contagion that threatened to bring down the financial system, and harmed the real economy.

Today, major bank and nonbank financial firms are subject to heightened prudential standards, including higher capital and liquidity requirements, stress tests, and "living wills." The living wills process is forcing firms to simplify their organizational forms, develop "clean" holding companies that can be resolved without disrupting their subsidiaries' functions. Firms are being required to hold sufficient capital and long-term debt at the holding company level to permit resolution. Global derivatives contracts are being rewritten to permit resolution without triggering cross-defaults and the seizure of collateral. Firms will be forced by these standards to internalize more of the costs that they might impose on the system, which will give them incentives to shrink and reduce their complexity, leverage, and interconnections. Should such a firm fail, there will be a bigger capital buffer to absorb losses. These measures will, over time, help to reduce risks in and among the largest financial institutions. In the event that such an institution fails, these actions will minimize the risk that a firm's failure will pose a danger to the stability of the financial system. But that is not enough. The government also needs the tools to respond in a crisis, to prevent financial collapse, and to protect taxpayers.

That is why Dodd-Frank permits the FDIC to resolve the largest and most interconnected financial companies, consistent with the approach long taken for bank failures. Under the Orderly Liquidation Authority, the FDIC now has the capacity to deal with the potential failure of a major financial conglomerate in an orderly fashion that limits collateral damage to the system. Shareholders and other providers of regulatory capital and long-term convertible debt to the firm will be forced to absorb any losses.

The FDIC has made significant progress in developing a strategy under the Dodd-Frank authorities, known as the "single point of entry," which would permit the holding company of a financial conglomerate to be resolved without necessarily disrupting the ability of its operating subsidiaries—bank, broker-dealer, or other parts—to function. Firms are required to hold sufficient long-term debt at the holding-company level to facilitate an orderly winding down of the holding company while permitting operating subsidiaries of the firm to continue to operate. Management can be terminated and the compensation of culpable managers can be clawed back. Critical assets and liabilities of the firm can be transferred to a bridge institution so that the firm can be resolved without causing cascading collapses in the financial system. In the event that the firm's internal capital and long-term debt are insufficient to support restructuring and ongoing operations, liquidity can be obtained through Treasury borrowing that is automatically repaid from the sale of assets of the failed firm or, if necessary, from a preauthorized, ex post assessment on the largest financial firms—not by taxpayers. In this manner, the resolution authority allows the government to resolve the financial conglomerate without exposing the system to a sudden disorderly failure that puts the whole financial sector at risk.

We need to have deep humility, however, about the ability to predict or manage the failure of a major financial firm, and even more so about the ability to deal with the failure of multiple firms during a financial crisis. Moreover, the creation of a domestic resolution authority and the broad range of domestic reforms just discussed are not enough to deal with global financial risks.

GLOBAL REFORMS: OVERVIEW

Global reforms undertaken to date have made the financial system safer, but there remain real questions about whether the financial system is safe enough. Much of the reform agenda is still a work in progress, from capital standards to regulation of derivatives and shadow banking markets, to the mechanisms necessary to wind down cross-border firms that get into financial distress. In the wake of the financial crisis, the leading economies produced a new set of institutions and institutional relationships that were more formal and more hierarchical and were designed to improve prospects for coordination. Although significant tensions still exist within this new system—particularly concerning national variation (that is, the tailoring of global standards to individual domestic landscape), extraterritorial application of national rules, and the desire for uniform global standards—the substantive outcomes to date, while imperfect, messy, and contentious, evidence a stronger commitment to meaningful, long-lasting reforms than had been in place before the financial crisis.

There is still much more substantive work to do—on capital and liquidity, resolution, and derivatives, to name a few core areas in need of action. In fact, such an approach is essential if we are to reduce the chances of another devastating global financial crisis.

Global Capital Rules

Almost immediately in the wake of the crisis, the G-20 countries began to examine the pre-crisis weaknesses in the global bank capital rules. Basel II.5, which targeted risks from off-balance-sheet assets and market risks, was developed early in 2009 and was quickly adopted by the major economies. By the G-20 summit in Pittsburgh in September 2009, U.S. Treasury Secretary Timothy Geithner had assembled a consensus in favor of higher capital standards. By late 2010, the bank regulatory standard-setting body known as the Basel Committee promulgated its "Basel III" capital standards, significantly revising the frameworks from "Basel I" and "Basel II" that had been in place prior to the crisis. Basel IV reforms are being implemented gradually across all Basel Committee member jurisdictions with full implementation set for January 1, 2019.

Basel III requires financial institutions to hold much-higher-quality capital for trading positions, securitization, and counterparty credit exposures in derivatives and secured lending transactions than its predecessor. The new capital requirements focus on common equity, significantly limiting other forms of funding that did not act as a buffer to absorb losses in a crisis. The revised rules require banks to hold Tier 1 capital in an amount no less than 6 percent of risk-weighted assets. Basel III also introduces a new Common Equity Tier 1 requirement, under which banks must hold at least 4.5 percent of risk-weighted assets in common equity. Basel III also reduces the ability of banks to rely on riskier, less-absorbent forms of regulatory capital and bars banks from including lower-quality instruments in regulatory capital. Basel III requires all firms to hold a countercyclical "capital conservation buffer," with dividends, share buybacks, or bonuses limited if Common Equity Tier I levels are within two and a half percentage points of the minimum 4.5 percent Common Equity Tier 1 level.

Basel III for the first time also imposes a global non-risk-based supplemental leverage ratio that includes firms' off-balance-sheet commitments and exposures. The leverage ratio requires banks to hold Tier 1 capital equal to 3 percent of their total exposures and is intended to supplement Basel's risk-weighted rules. Finally, firms posing the greatest risk to the financial system are required to hold even higher levels of capital—a surcharge" for systemically important financial institutions (SIFIs). All global systemically important banks (G-SIBs) will bear this surcharge, with the most systemically risky G-SIBs required to hold more capital than those with less systemic importance.

Under Basel III, minimum capital ratios are set at a level that represents a significant increase over prior rules. There are new requirements that include the creation of a capital conservation buffer above the minimums, which if breached will restrict firms' ability to pay dividends or buy back stock. The Basel Committee has put forward a graduated, risk-based, capital surcharge for the largest, most interconnected financial firms. The global rules also include new contingent capital instruments that facilitate "bail-ins"—in which privately issued debt transforms into equity under specified circumstances—to further reinforce that firms must internalize the costs of their own failure and to facilitate the resolution of globally systemically important firms. Furthermore, Basel III is instituting explicit quantitative liquidity requirements for the first time, to ensure that financial firms are better prepared for liquidity strains.

But even as some jurisdictions rightly adopt more stringent capital rules than those required under the Basel III approach, more work is needed to strengthen the global capital framework, at least for the largest firms. Risk-based capital requirements need to be made more transparent and comparable on a cross-border and institution-by-institution basis, and better substitutes need to be developed for both the discredited credit-rating agencies and the internal models of the regulated institutions. Additionally, both the global leverage ratio and the SIFI surcharge are simply too low for either to serve as an effective buffer against asset implosions or liquidity runs or to weigh effectively against any subsidies to "too big to fail" institutions. Moreover, as the countercyclical capital buffer is left to national economic circumstances and discretion, national regulators should commit to economic triggers that would increase capital requirements and use other methods to reduce leverage under specified circumstances. Furthermore, stress testing, which has served a critical role in bolstering capital oversight in the United States, is in need of further refinement, more transparency, and greater predictability.

Derivatives and Wholesale Funding Markets

G-20 leaders at the 2009 Pittsburgh summit also committed themselves to significant reforms in the OTC derivatives market. They agreed that standardized OTC derivatives should be moved onto exchange-trading platforms and should be centrally cleared. The leaders also decided that all OTC derivative trades—including those that remained purely bilateral—should be reported to trade repositories. In 2011, the G-20 further agreed that non-cleared-derivative contracts should be subject to higher margin requirements. In key jurisdictions, the statutory regimes for central clearing, exchange-based trading, and trade reporting are now in place, with the frameworks for margin requirements lagging behind. Regulatory implementation has lagged significantly behind legislation, and persistent technical, liability, and jurisdictional problems with trade reporting and trade repositories have obstructed regulators and market participants from attaining a comprehensive informational view of global derivatives markets.

Furthermore, global rules for repo and other short-term funding markets remain nascent, with most jurisdictions only in the earliest phases of proposing rules. More regulatory attention is needed on the issue of hot money, which continues to pose significant risks to systemic stability, to address weaknesses in foreign currency markets, and to restore trust and confidence to benchmark global rates such as LIBOR (London Interbank Offered Rate). In sum, much of the plumbing of the financial system is still in need of reform (see Duffie 2013).

Structural Reform and Resolution

Globally, much work remains to be done in the area of structural reform and resolution. The United States and the United Kingdom have both embraced the need for ring fencing and stronger horizontal buffers between retail deposit banks and other, riskier, financial functions, while the European Union has not adopted its expert commission's suggestions in that regard. In the Volcker Rule, the United States has adopted the strongest version of these reforms, but significant work still remains to be done on implementation in all three jurisdictions. It is particularly important, too, that ring fencing not be viewed as a panacea; structural reform will only prove effective to the extent it is integrated with broader changes in supervision, capital, and resolution mechanisms (See Barr and Vickers 2013).

Progress on structural reform is also important because of the linkages between clearer structures for financial conglomerates and ease of resolution. "Living will" requirements, such as those adopted in the United States, can help ease the process of cross-border resolution by clarifying lines of authority and aligning business risk with organizational form, but these approaches are contingent on regulators' willingness to execute along the lines of the directives of the will when most needed (see, for example, Levitin 2011). The United States and the United Kingdom have put in place a memorandum of understanding to facilitate cross-border resolution, and the single-point-of-entry approach, under which a financial conglomerate's top-tier holding company is placed in resolution while its operating subsidiaries may continue to function, may make it possible to resolve such firms even in the absence of a formal cross-border mechanism for the resolution of highly complex firms. Only time will tell.

The United States' "single-point-of-entry" model will facilitate the resolution of the largest financial conglomerates. In 2014, Europe officially adopted its Single Resolution Mechanism, which will be administered by the European Central Bank as part of its new supervisory authority over the continent's largest banks and will be funded via contributions from eligible banks, with national assessments assimilated into a communitywide fund over a number of years. The establishment of a European resolution and funding mechanism will help break the link between a national government's fiscal position and the health of domestic financial institutions—a link that exacerbated Europe's sovereign debt crisis. The crisis found many Eurozone countries unable to support troubled banks, either because the size of the bank exceeded national GDP or because public finances proved too unstable to provide any assistance.

National implementation of more effective resolution mechanisms has also been bolstered by the work of the FSB, which in 2011 released a set of best practices it considers "necessary for an effective resolution regime." The FSB is also developing a resolvability assessment process that will be used to evaluate the feasibility and credibility of national resolution mechanisms in the event of a globally systemic firm (G-SIFI) failure. Despite these significant regulatory advances, however, the orderly resolution of systemically important, highly complex cross-border firms will not be feasible without more global cooperation and a comprehensive transnational approach. Fortunately, the G-20 has recognized the important relationship between structure and resolvability. At the 2013 summit in St. Petersburg the G-20 leadership instructed the FSB, the IMF, and the OECD (Organisation for Economic Co-operation and Development) to collaborate in assessing "cross-border consistencies and global financial stability implications [of structural reforms], taking into account country-specific circumstances."

Overall, the substantive global rules developed and implemented in the post-crisis era are far more robust than their pre-crisis counterparts and provide far fewer opportunities for regulatory arbitrage and evasion. Nonetheless, significant work remains, as does the underlying question of whether the current international financial regulatory architecture is sufficient to the task of a truly sound global financial system. Achieving more organizational simplicity and clarity in the financial sector may also require new approaches altogether. For example, the United States put in place a soft cap (10 percent of total financial liabilities) on the global liabilities of U.S. firms; once the cap is hit, these firms cannot merge with or acquire other financial institutions. A tax on the wholesale liabilities of financial firms would further reinforce safety in the system by helping to constrain the size and complexity of financial conglomerates; it would also help to offset the costs to society of potential future failures, forcing firms to internalize more of those costs. The Obama administration proposed such a tax, but it never gained traction in the United States. The IMF endorsed the idea in 2010, but it has received little attention since.

Even as the post-crisis intervention of the G-20 in the global financial architecture has resulted in a harder, more formal system with a clearer hierarchy. More political accountability, and a stronger framework for generating, implementing, and monitoring cross-border rulemaking variations across domestic regulatory regimes have proliferated, with the leading economies engaged in an ambitious transnational strategy of regulatory competition. Unlike in the pre-crisis era, however, national variation and international regulatory competition to date have not resulted in widespread races to the bottom and cross-border regulatory arbitrage. Instead, the post-crisis national regulatory strategies have largely resulted in upward deviations from an already more robust global regulatory floor—a global race to the top.

This new financial architecture means that national variation alone (defined earlier as the tailoring of global standards to individual domestic landscape) can encourage this global race to the top. It also rewards first movers on a national basis, particularly as to the extraterritorial application of domestic rules. One country can take the lead in developing more robust extraterritorial standards than those required on a global level, and by doing so can effectively push other countries into the adoption of similarly stringent rules.

For instance, many countries are requiring firms to hold even more capital than the global minimum set by Basel III. In the United States, the supplemental leverage ratio for banks and thrifts is set at 6 percent, double the Basel III–required leverage ratio, and at 5 percent at the bank–holding company level. Even Switzerland, a non-G-20 nation and a traditional "offshore" banking center, has set tougher requirements than required under Basel III standards. For larger banks, Switzerland set higher capital requirements, up to 19 percent for the two largest (UBS and Credit Suisse)—the so-called "Swiss Finish," meaning a Swiss-specific addition to global standards.

In addition to regulatory variation across jurisdictions, some countries—including, most notably, the United States—have also adopted aggressive extraterritorial strategies designed to force reform upward on a global basis. For instance, the Federal Reserve Board of Governors has finalized new rules for foreign banking organizations (FBOs) operating in the United States. Under these rules, large FBOs are required to place non-branch assets under a U.S. intermediate holding company structure subject to consolidated supervision by the Federal Reserve. In many circumstances, FBOs will also now need to meet U.S. capital and liquidity rules and prudential standards with respect to their U.S. operations, in addition to the rules they must meet under their home country's laws.

These rules are prudent measures to reduce systemic risk and improve the safety and soundness of the U.S. financial system. Strong capital and liquidity rules will make these firms more robust against failure and less subject to debilitating runs in a crisis. Moreover, they help to make supervision and resolution of foreign firms operating in the United States substantially more feasible, if such resolution is required. In many ways, the rules are consistent with (or better than) the principle of national treatment, putting large FBOs and domestic banking organizations on similar footing. Nevertheless, they have also engendered significant controversy because of their extraterritorial reach, the potential to reduce the efficiency of the capital and liquidity allocation of the consolidated firm globally, and the significant structural reforms they require from firms operating in the United States that are headquartered beyond U.S. borders. It remains to be seen what effect the aggressive approach embodied in these new rules will have on the regulatory positions of foreign jurisdictions; some fear retaliation, but in my judgment, similar rulemaking by other jurisdictions would advance the aim of more effective regulation on a cross-border basis and should, ideally, contribute to an evolving global race to the top.

A similar strategy has taken hold between the United States and European Union during the development of domestic cross-border derivative regimes. The United States moved first, with strong reforms under the Dodd–Frank Act, followed by the release, by the Commodity Futures Trading Commission (CFTC), of a muscular proposed set of rules with significant extraterritorial reach. The rules drew significant criticism from foreign banking organizations, international swap dealers, and the European Commission, each of which understood the rules to effectively limit market participants who traded with U.S. parties to U.S. exchanges, in the absence of real reforms elsewhere, thus triggering significant fears over market fragmentation. As the CFTC considered these concerns and negotiated with the European Commission, in 2013 it issued an exemptive order delaying the effective date of the rules for several months. Not until the evening before this exemptive order lapsed were the CFTC and the European Commission able to agree on a "common path forward" (Barr 2014, 1014–15).

This common-path agreement embraced "equivalence," whereby the United States will consider European market participants and exchanges in compliance with both European and U.S. rules. Nevertheless, even as the CFTC's strategy of extraterritoriality has resulted in stronger European rules and reduced the potential for arbitrage, it has also increased transatlantic tensions. Ideally, implementation of extraterritorial rules would involve closer regulatory coordination between domestic and foreign jurisdictions—particularly where, as here, there is a high degree of parallelism between the European Union and the United States. Although the tensions between the United States and the European Union over cross-border derivatives rules are not likely to scuttle cooperation over other dimensions of the global-reform agenda, the possibility for transnational enmity and the need for cooperation will both grow as the global political commitment to reform wanes. The post-crisis experiences with national variation and extraterritorial strategy to date suggest that the G-20 should avoid the adoption and implementation of rigid, detailed rulemaking on a cross-border basis and should instead play the role of shepherd—working through the FSB to produce rigorous, robust prudential standards; correcting downward national deviations but otherwise encouraging strong domestic regimes that exceed minimum standards; and intervening where necessary to minimize transnational tensions.

FUTURE RISKS

Despite the enormous progress to date, we cannot afford to be complacent, and we need to keep pushing for reform. The next section focuses on five types of risk the financial system faces going forward—five ways it might fail next time. Of course, economists don't know precisely how the risk in the system will evolve. It is important to be humble about our ability to understand new risks and predict financial crises. That is why the most important step economists and policymakers can take is to build a system that is more resilient to the uncertain risks we face.

Amnesia

The first source of risk that could lead to another financial crisis is a kind of amnesia: the danger that financial institutions, regulators, lawmakers, and the public will forget the lessons of the financial crisis and let the system slip back into the practices that caused the last financial crisis. This amnesia is likely to occur as the crisis fades from memory and the financial system begins to feel safe again. No actor in the financial system is immune from such amnesia. Within financial institutions, risk managers, who are responsible for monitoring and managing a financial institution's risk, can grow complacent during good times. In addition, managers and executives may push back against risk managers who raise concerns about risky but profitable practices and activities. In the lead-up to the last crisis, some risk managers who urged firms to exercise caution or recommended that firms place limits on certain activities and investments were demoted or fired.

Regulators are also susceptible to amnesia. Regulatory discretion is essential to effective financial regulation, but it also allows regulators to soften their stance over time. We saw this before the last crisis. The public can also quickly forget the lessons of the financial crisis and the need for reform. Public attention to the financial system wanes as reporting on the financial system decreases and the fallout from the crisis fades from memory. Unfortunately, when public attention wanes, lawmakers and regulators may feel that the public will be less likely to hold them accountable in the event of a future crisis and as a result will feel less pressure to pass and implement meaningful reforms (Coffee 2011). Frankly, the financial sector can and does seek to "buy" amnesia through lobbying and campaign contributions (Roe 1996). With public pressure off, the industry can work behind the scenes—in Congress, in the federal rule-writing agencies, and in the courts—to roll back reforms and prevent any further restrictions (Coates 2015).

Although no actor in the financial system is immune from amnesia, we can take steps to ensure that institutions, regulators, and the public remain vigilant in good times. Within financial institutions we can continue to work to better align executive and managerial compensation with the time horizons of risk. For example, regulators should require that SIFIs set up compensation systems such that the senior executives of a firm would have their bonuses clawed back in the event that the firm fails to meet certain capital levels or is subject to major fines or penalties.

We can include mechanisms within the regulatory architecture designed to reduce backsliding. Several such mechanisms were included in the new regulatory infrastructure mandated by Dodd-Frank (see Barr 2015a). For example, the Financial Stability Oversight Council (FSOC) has the authority to recommend stricter actions and to require regulators to implement them, or else to explain their failure to do so to Congress and the public. Dodd-Frank imposed a similar action-forcing disclosure requirement on the Consumer Financial Protection Bureau. Twice a year the director of the CFPB is required to testify before and provide a report to Congress that includes not only a summary of the bureau's activities but also a "discussion of the significant problems faced by consumers in shopping for or obtaining consumer financial products and services," and an analysis of the complaints that the bureau has received from consumers. Dodd-Frank charged entities with competing viewpoints—the independent Office of Financial Research, the FSOC, and the Fed—to monitor and assess risks to the financial system.

Leverage and Liquidity

Concerning leverage, many ask whether the new capital levels are set high enough for the largest, most interconnected, and systemically important firms. The heightened capital requirements on these firms, known as the SIFI surcharge, require firms to have much higher levels of "total loss absorbing capacity" to meet resolution requirements; however, it is not clear that equity levels are an adequate response to the firms' systemic risks. We must keep close watch on these firms and not be afraid to adjust the surcharge up as needed.

On liquidity, firms have greatly reduced their use of short-term debt, but much more needs to be done to address the risks posed by short-term funding. As a first step, we need to implement the Basel Committee's approach to asset liquidity. In the United States, the Federal Reserve has implemented a SIFI surcharge that also takes into account liquidity risks, and such an approach should be adopted globally. Money market funds remain a source of risk in the system, even after the SEC's reforms, and I believe stable net asset value funds should hold capital against these risks. FX (foreign exchange) markets need to move toward greater transparency, while margin and collateral requirements should be improved.

Asset Bubbles

The formation of asset bubbles is a third source of risk that could lead to a future financial crisis, as it did to the last. Countercyclical prudential measures, especially countercyclical capital standards, can help risks posed by asset bubbles. Countercyclical capital standards require financial institutions to hold more capital during boom times and less capital after downturns. It is also worth thinking about whether asset-specific countercyclical rules would help limit the formation of bubbles. For example, Switzerland requires financial institutions to hold more capital against mortgage-backed assets as home values increase. Israel has adopted countercyclical mortgage lending regulations, including loan-to-value requirements. Going forward, we also need to make critical decisions about the future of Fannie Mae, Freddie Mac, and the U.S. system of housing finance. We should focus on creating a housing finance system that has broad access to affordable and sustainable mortgage credit, protects taxpayers, and provides a realistic mechanism through which the government could stem a housing crisis.

Misunderstood Innovation

A fourth risk comes from misunderstood financial innovations. Financial innovation drives economic growth by efficiently allocating capital. It lowers transaction costs, increases liquidity, and helps disperse risk. It helps ensure that the needs of market participants are fully met. At the same time, however, financial innovation can hide risk. The financial sector sometimes creates complex financial products for the purpose of exploiting uninformed consumers or investors. Financial innovations can also create risk when a product that was developed to meet the needs of a small subset of the market is offered to a broader, less-sophisticated market. We saw that happen in the mortgage market when option ARMs or "pick a pay" mortgages, designed to meet uneven cash flow experienced by a small subset of the affluent self-employed, were sold to masses of borrowers who could ill-afford the risks such products posed.

Today, we see problems with exchange-traded funds (ETFs) and high-frequency trading. ETFs are popular with investors because they provide a low-cost, tax-efficient means of investing in a diversified fund. Recently, however, innovation in the ETF market has resulted in increasingly complex and opaque funds that may pose risks to investors and to financial stability. This innovation includes the creation of synthetic, leveraged, and inverse ETFs, and runs the risks of contagions in ETF markets, when illiquidity in primary markets makes orderly investor redemptions in ETFs more difficult.

High-frequency trading uses computers and algorithms to make trades in less than a millisecond. Such high-speed trading has the potential to improve market efficiency and liquidity. But it also raises serious concerns for financial stability—high-frequency trading contributed to the "flash crash" on May 6, 2010, when stock prices inexplicably and suddenly plunged, and may undermine the fairness of financial markets. Unfortunately, regulators have been behind the curve in understanding the way such trading functions and its potential risks.

Regulating in the face of financial innovations is challenging. It is difficult to achieve the right balance between addressing the risks posed by innovation while maintaining its benefits.

I believe the solution lies in developing flexible forms of regulation that foster innovation while focusing on buffers in the system and regulatory checks and balances.

Global Risk

Last, we face the risk that global reform and recovery efforts will go off track. Sovereign risk remains real, a global mechanism to resolve ailing financial firms is still a goal rather than a reality, and the risk from lack of global coordination is great. Yet we still are building a financial architecture that relies on multiple architects and plans.

THIS VOLUME'S CONTRIBUTIONS

Scholars have developed varying approaches to assess financial reform since the crisis and no single journal issue could provide a comprehensive overview. This journal issue brings together a series of articles focused on the Dodd-Frank Act as a whole, systemic risk and resolution authority, consumer and investor protection, market structure, and global reforms. The articles were developed for a conference on the financial crisis hosted by the University of Michigan's Center on Finance, Law, and Policy.

Martin Baily, Aaron Klein, and Justin Schardin have divided Dodd-Frank's major reforms into five categories: areas that in their judgment are clear wins, clear losses, costly tradeoffs, reforms that did not go far enough, and areas where it is too soon to tell. They argue that increased capital requirements, the new single-point-of-entry resolution mechanism, and the creation of the CFPB are clear wins, and the restrictions on the government's crisis management tools in Dodd-Frank are a clear loss. They see the Volcker Rule and the Lincoln Amendment on derivatives trading as costly tradeoffs in the bill, and argue that the bill did not go far enough in consolidating the financial regulatory system. Empirical evidence will be required to test whether their initial judgments are correct.

Howell Jackson argues that the single-point-of-entry framework for the resolution of systemically important financial institutions, while it will help prevent the spread of losses through the financial system in a future crisis, nevertheless raises several concerns. First, the framework may increase moral hazard by expanding the scope of government support. Second, it may be more difficult than the FDIC anticipates for a holding company to send funding down to operating subsidiaries in a resolution. Third, there may be impediments to triggering losses of holding company creditors. Jackson suggests specific reforms that can strengthen the ability to deal with a financial firm's failure.

Lauren Willis argues for a new approach to consumer protection, moving away from mere disclosure to requiring firms to demonstrate that consumers comprehend the costs and benefits of a financial product or service before it is made available in the market. The Dodd-Frank Act directed the CFPB to promulgate rules designed to ensure that consumers understand the "costs, benefits, and risks" associated with the financial products and services they purchase. Willis argues that although mandatory disclosures may increase comprehension in lab tests, consumers take shortcuts and firms run circles around the disclosures in practice. Willis advocates for the CFPB to adopt comprehensive performance standards instead of mandating disclosures. For example, a bank imposing overdraft fees would have to prove to the CFPB, through third-party testing, that customers know how overdraft fees work under various situations.

Jonathan Macey advocates for affording home mortgage borrowers the same protections as investors in the securities market. Macey argues that adopting basic protections from securities regulation would create integral protection for consumers in the home mortgage market. For example: (1) the duty of best execution, which would require mortgage brokers to give borrowers the best deal available to them at that time, (2) the suitability requirement, which would require mortgage brokers to have reasonable grounds to believe the mortgage is suitable for the borrower, and (3) the antichurning requirement, which would prevent brokers from encouraging borrowers to refinance to collect fees.

Michael Wellman argues that researchers must evaluate the effects of trading techniques in specific contexts to understand the effects of algorithmic and high-frequency trading on financial markets. He explains the model he created that combines an agent-based market simulation with a game theoretic analysis. The model shows the effects of high-frequency trading used for latency arbitrage, which involves traders taking advantage of the time it takes information to travel from one market to another. The study found that high-frequency trading decreased overall market efficiency, even before accounting for the costs of creating the infrastructure necessary to make these trades. The model has also been used to show the effects of high-frequency trading in market making, where traders create a market for securities by maintaining offers to both buy and sell a security. Though high-frequency trading is usually thought to increase market liquidity, in many instances market efficiency decreased when liquidity was most needed.

A major post-crisis task for international finance and its regulators has been to develop better tools to measure systemic risk in the financial system. Viral Acharya suggests using a market measurement, *SRISK*, which uses a firm's size, leverage, and risk profile to measure its vulnerability to a capital shortfall in a future crisis and the health of the financial system as a whole. The *SRISK* model suggests that the U.S. financial sector has grown steadily safer since the crisis. The European financial sector grew in risk, peaking during the sovereign debt crisis of 2011, and has grown somewhat safer since then. The Asian financial sector—Chinese financial institutions in particular—has grown increasingly risky since the crisis. Acharya explains how the measure can improve regulator and market understanding of financial risk going forward.

Shedding light on one issue in global finance, Niamh Maloney argues that a fundamental shift has occurred in European financial regulation, and some fundamental new trends can be seen hidden in plain sight by the muddling, iterative, and complex regional machinations of Europe. Beneath the fractured and contentious crisis-driven negotiations lie: a strong push toward centralization; more European-level regulation of both prudential and consumer financial regulation; cross-border risk sharing by national governments; and harder law. The changes will have profound effects not only on the shape of financial regulation, but also on the continuously evolving tug between Euro-centrism and national prerogatives.

CONCLUSION

The financial system is safer, consumers and investors better protected, and taxpayers better insulated than they were before the crisis, but significant risks still remain. It will be critical to stay on the path of reform. The articles in this volume of the *RSF Journal of the Social Sciences* provide new insights into several important aspects of reform. As the volume editor I do not agree with every aspect of the analyses offered, and the same will be true for readers. But the articles provide engaging and essential reading for understanding the tradeoffs involved in policymaking, and innovative ideas for making the financial system more resilient, market structure more efficient, finance fairer for consumers and investors, and global financial regulation better coordinated and effective.

There has been progress under the Dodd-Frank Act and global reforms in tackling many of these problems, but much more work needs to be done. Dodd-Frank and global rules have increased the amount of capital the largest firms have to hold, with a higher capital surcharge. In the United States there is now a cap on the relative size of the largest firms, such that mergers or acquisitions are blocked when a firm hits the cap. New liquidation procedures under Dodd-Frank require a firm's managers, shareholders, and long-term debt holders to bear the losses of a firm's failure, not taxpayers. Living wills, structural reforms, and requirements for total loss-absorbing capacity are making it more feasible to resolve failing major financial firms, but questions remain as to who will hold the long-term debt and how knock-on effects will be managed.

Building on these reforms, we need further effective steps to regulate the shadow banking world and curb the use of "hot money," including an explicit tax on liabilities that increases with the intensity of use of short-term wholesale funding, strong collateral and margin rules for securities financing transactions, and further money market fund reform to reduce the risk that we'll experience another "bank" run or $3 trillion guarantee in that sector in the next crisis.

We must curb abusive high-frequency trading practices, bolster protections for exchange-traded funds, and make our markets more transparent and fair, by tackling conflicts of interest that too often leave regular investors exposed to unnecessary risks and fees.

We ought to require accountability at the top. Senior managers should suffer decreases of their compensation when their firms fail to meet capital standards or are hit with fines or penalties. The SEC must use its new authorities to fine credit-rating agencies that bend their analyses to meet the desires of Wall Street firms.

The Consumer Financial Protection Bureau must be strengthened and supported, not attacked at every turn. One key step is barring the kind of arbitration clauses in consumer finance contracts that prevent consumers from banding together to get their day in court (Barr 2015b). Financial innovation needs to focus on new ways to help families cope with their volatile income and expenses, and make it easier and less expensive to build a financial cushion. We also need to stop abusive small business lending practices and instead expand access to capital, skills, and business opportunities. (Barr 2015c).

The financial system is much safer and a good bit fairer than it was prior to the financial crisis, but that is not enough. We must keep fighting for a financial system that works for all of us.

REFERENCES

Agarwal, Sumit, Souphala Chomsisengphet, Neale Mahoney, and Johannes Stroebel. 2015. "Regulating Consumer Financial Products: Evidence from Credit Cards." *Quarterly Journal of Economics* 130(1): 111–64.

Barr, Michael S., Sendhil Mullainathan and Eldar Shafir. 2009. "The Case for Behaviorally Informed Regulation." In *New Perspectives on Regulation*, edited by D. Moss and J. Cisternino. Cambridge, Mass.: Tobin Project, 2009.

Barr, Michael S. 2012a. *No Slack: The Financial Lives of Low-income Americans.* Washington, D.C.: Brookings Institution.

———. 2012b. "The Financial Crisis and the Path of Reform." *Yale Journal on Regulation* 29(1): 91–119.

———. 2014. "Who's in Charge of Global Finance?" *Georgetown Journal of International Law* 45(20): 971–1027.

———. 2015a. "Accountability and Independence in Financial Regulation: Checks and Balances, Public Engagement, and Other Innovations." *Law and Contemporary Problems* 78(3): 119–28.

———. 2015b. "Mandatory Arbitration in Consumer Finance and Investor Contracts." *New York University Journal of Law and Business* 11(4): 793–817.

———. 2015c. "Minority and Women Entrepreneurs: Building Capital, Networks and Skills. Hamilton Project Discussion Paper 2015-03. Washington, D.C.: Brookings Institution.

Barr, Michael S., and Daniel Schaffa. 2016. "Nothing Left to Lose?" University of Michigan Working Paper. Ann Arbor: University of Michigan.

Barr, Michael S., and John Vickers. 2013. "Banks Need Far More Structural Reform to Be Safe." *Financial Times*, July 21, 2013.

Coates, John C., IV. 2015. "Cost-Benefit Analysis of Financial Regulation: Case Studies and Implications." *Yale Law Journal* 124(4): 882–1345.

Coffee, John C., Jr. 2011. "Systemic Risk After Dodd-Frank: Contingent Capital and the Need for Regulatory Strategies Beyond Oversight." *Columbia Law Review* 111(4): 795–821.

———. 2012. "The Political Economy of Dodd-Frank: Why Financial Reform Tends to Be Frustrated and Systemic Risk Perpetuated." *Cornell Law Review* 97(5): 1019.

Cordray, Richard. 2015. *Financial Report of the Consumer Finance Protection Bureau, Fiscal Year 2015.* November 16. Available at: http://files.consumerfinance.gov/f/201511_cfpb_report_fiscal-year-2015.pdf; accessed September 16, 2016.

Duffie, Darrell. 2013. "Replumbing Our Financial System: Uneven Progress." *International Journal of Central Banking* 9(1): 251.

Gersen, Jacob E. 2013. "Administrative Law Goes to Wall Street: The New Administrative Process." *Administrative Law Review* 65(3): 689–731.

Gorton, Gary, and Andrew Metrick. 2012. "Securitized Banking and the Run on Repo." *Journal of Financial Economics* 104(3): 425–51.

Levitin, Adam J. 2011. "In Defense of Bailouts," *Georgetown Law Journal* 99(2): 435–514.

Ludwig, Eugene A., 2012. "Assessment of Dodd-Frank Financial Regulatory Reform: Strengths, Challenges, and Opportunities for a Stronger Regulatory System." *Yale Journal on Regulation* 29(1): 181–99.

Massad, Timothy. 2015. Keynote Remarks of Chairman Timothy Massad before the Risk USA Conference, New York, October 22, 2015. Available at: http://www.cftc.gov/PressRoom/Speeches/Testimony/opamassad-31; accessed July 13, 2016.

Roe, Mark. 1996. "Chaos and Evolution in Law and Economics," *Harvard Law Review* 109: 641–68.

Scott, Hal S. 2010. "An Economy in Crisis: Law, Policy, and Morality During the Recession. Article I. Suggestions for Regulatory Reform: The Reduction of Systemic Risk in the United States Financial System." *Harvard Journal of Law and Public Policy* 33(2): 671.

PART II
Financial Stability

The Impact of the Dodd-Frank Act on Financial Stability and Economic Growth

MARTIN NEIL BAILY, AARON KLEIN, AND
JUSTIN SCHARDIN

This article assesses the benefits and costs of key provisions of the Dodd-Frank Act that strengthened regulation following the financial crisis. The provisions are placed into five groupings: clear wins, clear losses, costly tradeoffs, unfinished business, and too soon to tell. Clear wins include higher prudential standards, including for capital; the single-point-of-entry resolution authority; creation of the Consumer Financial Protection Bureau; and greater transparency and oversight of derivatives. Clear losses are restrictions on Federal Reserve emergency lending authority and forcing the Federal Deposit Insurance Corporation to obtain permission from Congress before providing temporary liquidity guarantees. Costly tradeoffs are the Volcker Rule and the Lincoln Amendment. Unfinished business includes regulatory consolidation and more independence for the Financial Stability Oversight Council and the Office of Financial Research. Too soon to tell are requirements and standards for leverage ratios, capital buffers, stress testing, and liquidity requirements.

Keywords: Dodd-Frank Act, financial regulation, benefits and costs

The Dodd-Frank Wall Street Reform and Consumer Protection Act of 2010 was designed to increase financial stability and prevent future devastation from financial crises. Dodd-Frank established the Consumer Financial Protection Bureau (CFPB), increased capital and other prudential requirements, augmented oversight of financial institutions, and created new resolution procedures to safely wind down institutions when they fail. Through these and other reforms, the financial sector is much safer today than before the crisis. A full accounting of Dodd-Frank, however, must assess how the new law has balanced improved financial stability against economic growth and other factors. Dodd-Frank has achieved much, but as with any sweeping set of reforms, there are lessons to learn from its implementation and there are corrections and adjustments that could improve its outcomes.

This article attempts to assess the benefits and costs of several key provisions of Dodd-Frank. To be clear, when discussing both economic growth and financial stability we are concerned with long-run sustainable growth and stability. Short-term boosts to economic

Martin Neil Baily is Bernard L. Schwartz Chair in Economic Policy Development and senior fellow and director of the Business and Public Policy Initiative at the Brookings Institution. **Aaron Klein** is fellow and policy director at the Business and Public Policy Initiative at the Brookings Institution. **Justin Schardin** is a director of the Financial Regulatory Reform Initiative at the Bipartisan Policy Center.

The authors would like to thank Michael Barr and the referees of this article for helpful comments. Direct correspondence to: Martin Neil Baily at mbaily@brookings.edu, Brookings Institution, 1775 Massachusetts Avenue, NW, Washington, DC 20036; Aaron Klein at aklein@brookings.edu, Bipartisan Policy Center, 1225 Eye Street, NW, Suite 1000, Washington, DC 20005; and Justin Schardin at jschardin@bipartisanpolicy.org, Bipartisan Policy Center, 1225 Eye Street, NW, Suite 1000, Washington, DC 20005.

growth that are unsustainable and require subsequent corrections are, by definition, illusory. Likewise, policies that create short-term financial stability by papering over problems promote long-term instability when those problem are eventually exposed and lead to a financial crisis or panic. Our assessments are focused on sustainable, long-run, desirable outcomes. Based on that analysis, we divide the provisions of Dodd-Frank into five categories:[1]

1. Clear wins. These are areas where Dodd-Frank has either increased both economic growth and financial stability or enhanced one of them at a minimal cost to the other. We argue that Dodd-Frank's most valuable contributions have included higher prudential standards, including for capital; the new resolution authority that has manifested in the single-point-of-entry (SPOE) strategy; creating the CFPB; and subjecting derivatives transactions to greater transparency and oversight. Higher capital requirements make institutions more resilient to financial stress events and crises. The Federal Deposit Insurance Corporation's (FDIC) SPOE approach establishes standard procedures for safely winding down a failed institution, improving financial stability and addressing the "too big to fail" issue. The CFPB consolidates oversight responsibilities, minimizes risky gaps in the regulatory infrastructure, and has improved protections for consumers. Derivatives exchange and clearing brings greater transparency to a major source of financial transactions that used to be largely unregulated. Even though these are all "clear wins" in our assessment, there is still room for improvement in all four areas.

2. Clear losses. These are areas where Dodd-Frank has either harmed both financial stability and economic growth or was detrimental to one with limited gain to the other. Two new restrictions fall into this category: requiring the Federal Reserve to make emergency loans available to an entire category of institutions rather than a single firm, and forcing the FDIC to seek and obtain a joint resolution from Congress before providing temporary liquidity guarantees on certain kinds of debt. These provisions can be expected to reduce financial stability during periods of stress with no corresponding effect of enhancing economic growth.

3. Costly trade-offs. Other provisions are harder to assess, and seem to achieve some benefits but with significant costs to efficiency and economic growth. In particular, the Volcker Rule, which bans commercial banks from engaging in proprietary trading, and the Lincoln Amendment, which prohibits entities engaged in swaps from receiving federal assistance, create costly trade-offs. Critics have complained that the Volcker Rule is complex, ambiguous, and expensive, making it difficult for banks to adhere to its requirements and for regulators to implement and oversee it. Others suggest that the Lincoln Amendment's goals can be achieved by the Volcker Rule, making the Lincoln Amendment redundant and its cost and regulatory burdens unnecessary.

4. Unfinished business. In other areas, Dodd-Frank has made some progress, but didn't go far enough. Important improvements could still be made through greater regulatory consolidation, heightened authority for the Financial Stability Oversight Council (FSOC), and more independence for the Office of Financial Research (OFR).

5. Too soon to tell: Finally, other provisions have created uncertain trade-offs between stability and economic growth, and it's too soon to accurately gauge their impact on the economy and financial system. New requirements and standards for leverage ratios, capital buffers, stress testing, liquidity, and long-term debt holdings all fall into this category.

In the coming pages we assess these provisions and their effects in more detail. We con-

---

1. Our assessment only covers areas that were addressed within the Dodd-Frank Act and not issues that it did not attempt to address, such as housing finance reform.

sider the extent to which Dodd-Frank has made the financial sector safer while we also identify weak areas that may jeopardize economic growth.

CLEAR WINS

The financial crisis revealed glaring weaknesses in the U.S. financial regulatory structure for financial reform legislation to fix. Dodd-Frank's most notable successes fall into the category of "clear wins"—measures that increased financial stability and enhanced economic growth or had a relatively low cost for one and a substantial benefit for the other. Among these successes are higher capital requirements, especially for systemically important banks and nonbanks; new authority and mechanisms to wind down failed financial institutions; the creation of the CFPB; and greater transparency for swaps and derivatives trades.

Higher Capital Requirements

Even the best regulatory regime is incapable of preventing all financial stress events and crises, and that is why financial institutions need to have enough capital to stay solvent if and when such events occur.[2] There were several reasons that levels of loss-absorbing capital proved to be too low at many such institutions going into the most recent financial crisis. Many of the assets held against regulatory standards turned out to be much riskier than commonly understood at the time, leading them to be overvalued and subject to a rapid drop in value. Starting in the 1990s, regulators added risk sensitivity and complexity to the international Basel capital standards, including allowing financial institutions to rely on their own value-at-risk models. These models relied on limited historical data, leading to assumptions that often significantly underestimated the risk to which these firms were exposed. As the Bank of England's Andrew Haldane (2012, 8) said, "The regulatory backstop had been lifted, replaced by a complex, commercial judgment. The Basel regime became, if not self-regulating, then self-calibrating." Other regulatory measures set up what have been called perverse incentives, such as the 1996 Market Risk Amendment, which provided better capital treatment for assets held in trading accounts versus as long-term investments (Financial Crisis Inquiry Commission 2011, 196).

The financial crisis led to greater regulatory scrutiny on capital levels. Figure 1 shows the significant increase in Tier 1 capital—a bank's core capital, consisting largely of its equity capital and disclosed cash reserves—of the six largest U.S. bank holding companies since the crisis. During the 2000s leading up to 2008, this measure fluctuated between 8 and 9 percent of risk-weighted assets before dropping below 8 percent late in 2007. Since 2010, it has generally been between 12 and 14 percent.[3]

Dodd-Frank attempted to find long-term solutions to these pre-crisis problems by instituting higher prudential standards, including for capital, for all bank holding companies with more than $50 billion in assets. The Federal Reserve has based its requirements for these entities, which it oversees, on the global Basel III capital standards. Basel III tries as well to solve several pre-crisis problems in part by increasing required capital levels, especially for the largest global banks; defining more strictly what counts toward fulfilling regulatory capital requirements; and mandating additional capital buffers. Basel III's requirements will be phased in gradually until they are fully implemented by January 1, 2019 (Bank for International Settlements 2014). Figure 2 shows the phase-in schedule.

U.S. regulators have in some cases mandated standards that go beyond Basel III, including measures like bank stress testing and additional capital for the largest U.S. bank holding companies. In addition, global regulators have agreed on a minimum level of unsecured long-term debt that can be converted to equity in case of the failure of one of the large bank holding companies that must hold it. (This will be discussed in greater detail in the following section, about failure resolution.)

---

2. In essence, capital is the percentage of a bank's assets it can lose and still be solvent.

3. The figure is based on the definition of Tier 1 capital specified in Basel II. This is not the same definition that is used in Basel III. The figure likely overstates the level of Tier 1 capital with the new definition.

Figure 1. "Big Six" Average Tier 1 Capital Ratio

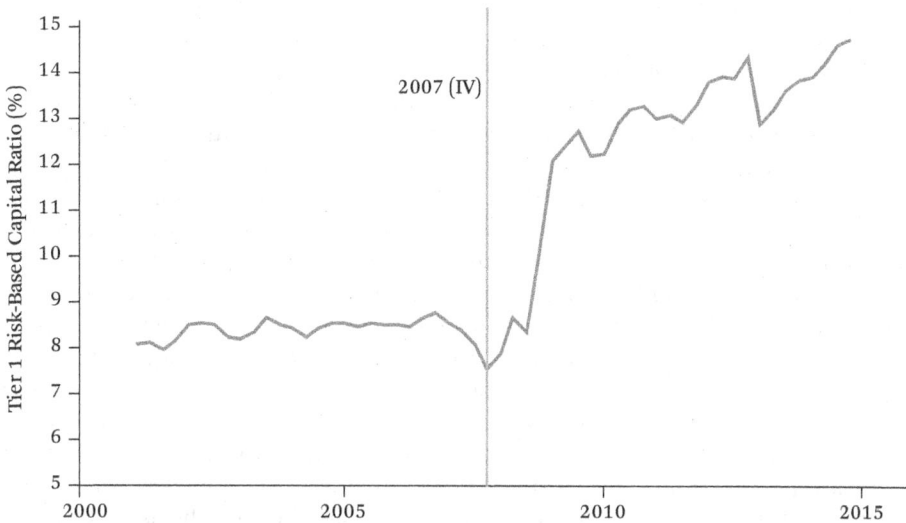

Source: Federal Reserve Board, n.d.
Note: Unweighted average of the Tier 1 risk-based capital ratios of JPMorgan, Citi, Bank of America, Wells Fargo, Goldman Sachs, and Morgan Stanley; Goldman Sachs and Morgan Stanley only began reporting in 2009.

Figure 2. Schedule of the Basel III Capital Phase-In

	2014	2015	2016	2017	2018	2019
CET1/RWA						
Minimum	4.0	**4.5**	**4.5**	**4.5**	**4.5**	**4.5**
Plus buffers:						
Capital conservation			0.625	1.25	1.875	**2.5**
G-SIBs[a]			0.625	1.25	1.875	**2.5**
Tier 1						
Minimum (ratio to RWA)	5.5	**6.0**	**6.0**	**6.0**	**6.0**	**6.0**
Leverage ratio (to exposure measure)	Observation	Disclosure	Disclosure	Disclosure	Migration to Pillar 1	Migration to Pillar 1

Source: Bank for International Settlements 2014.
Note: Entries in bold denote full strength of each Basel III standard (in terms of the capital ratio). The corresponding definitions of eligible capital become fully effective in 2022.
[a]Refers to the maximum buffer, as applicable.

Gauging the impacts of any single factor on economic growth is difficult. There is some evidence, however, that the improved stability from increased capital requirements has not had a significant negative impact on the economy. Recent research by Stephen G. Cecchetti and Kermit L. Schoenholtz, for example, found that most banks were able to increase their capital levels by accepting a smaller return on assets, cutting their net interest margins, and reducing their operating costs. Further, they argue that "predictions that higher capital requirements would drive up interest margins and reduce credit volumes are at odds with the evidence of smaller spreads and increased lending. Insofar as there was any aggregate macroeconomic impact, it appears to have been limited or inconsequential" (Cecchetti and Schoenholtz 2014).

There is no settled economic consensus on the point at which increasing capital requirements will be outweighed by the economic costs of doing so. As we have said, we think that so far the increases in required capital have been justified by the increased safety they have brought. There are anecdotal reports that financial activities have been moving out of banks and into the nonbank sector, but the large and regional banks are now profitable and doing well (Kroszner 2015; Financial Stability Board 2015b).[4] At some point that dynamic would change if capital levels are pushed up more and more, and defections of people and activities from the regulated banking sector in the United States take off. In a later section we explore whether or not the combination of multiple different capital requirements now being proposed would create problems of this kind.

New Failure Resolution for Large Systemically Important Institutions: The Problem Created by Troubled Large Institutions

During the financial crisis, many large financial institutions faced losses that threatened their viability.[5] Because of the interconnections among institutions and the market climate associated with a financial panic, the failure of one or more such institutions might cause the failure of others. The revelation that several institutions held portfolios of troubled assets increased the probability in the minds of market participants that many more institutions might also hold such troubled assets and their viability might be threatened. As a result the interbank funding market shut down, putting the whole U.S. financial system in danger, a danger that spread globally. U.S. policymakers were faced with an extraordinary dilemma: bail out the troubled institutions, thereby giving taxpayer support to private companies, or let the troubled institutions fail, potentially resulting in systemic collapse and depression.

A determination to avoid the same dilemma in a future crisis has spurred innovation in financial regulatory policy. Dodd-Frank instituted a new failure-resolution regime that seeks to ensure that the losses resulting from bad decisions by managers will be borne by equity and debt holders of that company, while at the same time greatly reducing the risk of financial collapse.

Overview of Single Point of Entry
Prior to the passage of Title II of the Dodd-Frank Act, the FDIC's resolution powers were limited to federally insured banks and thrifts. The lack of authority to place the holding company of an insured depository institution or any other nonbank financial entity into FDIC receivership served as a major source of instability during the crisis. Regulators lacked an important tool to resolve these entities in an orderly manner and help stem contagious panics and runs that can result from such failures. As the U.S. Bankruptcy Code proved inadequate for containing the distinct risks generated by the failure of systemically important financial institutions (SIFIs) and lacking the authority to place those firms under FDIC receivership, the government was left with the unfortunate choice of either extending taxpayer-funded bailouts or allowing the institutions to undergo disorderly bankruptcies, potentially at the risk of broader financial instability.

Dodd-Frank took several steps to address

---

4. Randall S. Kroszner (2015) showed data indicating that the liabilities of the shadow banking sector had fallen, whereas the liabilities of the banking sector had increased. The Financial Stability Board issued a report on global shadow banking that showed strong growth in this sector globally, but in line with Kroszner's data this report showed a decline in shadow sector assets as a percent of total financial assets in the United States (Financial Stability Board 2015b, 59).

5. This section was drafted by William Bekker of the Brookings Institution.

the need for a formal procedure to deal with the failure of systemically important financial institutions in the future.[6] Title I of the act requires all SIFIs to prepare resolution plans that formally demonstrate how, in the event of a business failure, they could be resolved under the Bankruptcy Code in an orderly manner. However, to deal with the possibility that a SIFI may not be resolvable under the Bankruptcy Code without threatening financial stability, Title II of Dodd-Frank set forth an Orderly Liquidation Authority (OLA) for the FDIC to resolve systemically important institutions (Federal Deposit Insurance Corporation 2013b).

In order to implement its new authorities under Title II, the FDIC has been developing SPOE, which aims to resolve large and complex financial institutions that are insolvent by placing the top-tier holding company of the organization under FDIC receivership: the FDIC enters the company at the holding company level, the "single point." SIFIs are generally organized under a holding company structure with a top-tier parent managing hundreds, if not thousands, of legal entities spanning a wide swath of regulatory and legal jurisdictions. Since these entities are highly interconnected, often providing support services to one another and sharing funding as needs arise, it can be difficult to conduct an orderly resolution of one part of the company without jeopardizing other entities in the structure. SPOE seeks to address this issue by providing a mechanism where the failing holding company is removed but the subsidiaries are placed under the control of a newly created bridge holding company whose managers and directors are appointed by the FDIC. The equity and long-term unsecured debt that had been issued by the old holding company are removed and are no longer considered liabilities of the bridge company or the subsidiaries it has taken over. Because these liabilities have been removed, the new bridge holding company is solvent and it has been effectively recapitalized without requiring taxpayer funds.

Dodd-Frank created the OLA and an Orderly Liquidation Fund (OLF) as a backup source of temporary liquidity (but not capital) for the bridge holding company if other sources of liquidity cannot be secured in the interim. The new well-capitalized parent, the bridge company, would be able to smooth over funding frictions that arise for subsidiaries as a result of a financial distress occurring in other parts of the organization. In such a way, SPOE enables the company as a whole to remain operational and capable of serving markets during resolution proceedings. This preserves the franchise value of the institution and avoids the systemic risk effects of an organizationwide collapse. (For a more detailed discussion of how the bridge company is capitalized, see Jackson and Massman, this volume). In developing SPOE, the FDIC strove to create an insolvency regime that would promote market discipline by ensuring that the costs of the failed or failing SIFI fell exclusively on the shareholders and the unsecured creditors of the top-tier holding company. To achieve this end while preserving financial stability, SPOE is designed so that the assets from the receivership, primarily consisting of investments in and loans to subsidiaries, would be transferred to a bridge financial holding company organized by the FDIC. Certain liabilities would be transferred to the bridge company as well. These include claims of secured creditors, which would be transferred to prevent the spillover effects of creditors liquidating collateral en masse, and liabilities that are vital to facilitating company operations, such as obligations to vendors that provide essential services. All claims of equity holders and unsecured creditors, however, would remain in the receivership with losses being apportioned according to the statutory order of priority.

After the bridge financial company's assets have been valued, SPOE provides for the payment of creditors' claims in the receivership through the issuance of securities by the bridge financial company in a securities-for-claims exchange. This process involves the issuance and distribution of new debt and equity

---

6. A "SIFI" designation refers to both banks with over $50 billion in assets that are automatically subject to enhanced prudential standards as well as non-banks designated as SIFIs by FSOC.

Figure 3. Total Loss Absorbing Capacity Final Rule

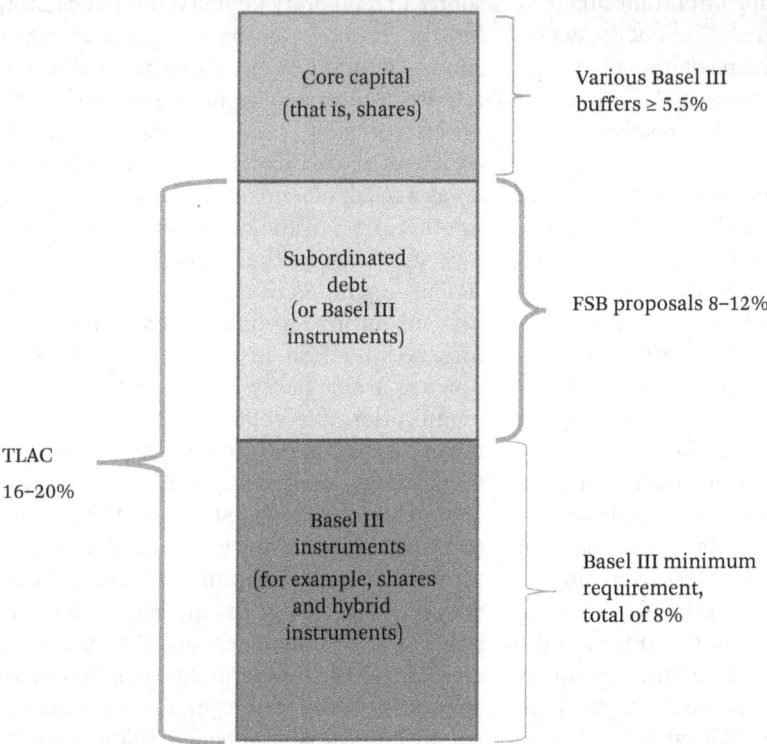

Source: De Nederlandsche Bank 2014.

to be exchanged for claims in the receivership on a pro rata basis.[7]

In order for this to work, the holding company must have an adequate cushion of equity and unsecured debt in order to absorb the losses. To this end, U.S. regulators have made progress on assessing the appropriate levels of debt and equity required to successfully implement a SPOE resolution. At the international level the Financial Stability Board (FSB), a group of regulators currently headed by Mark Carney, governor of the Bank of England, has agreed on a framework for the "total loss absorbing capacity" (TLAC) that banks must hold (Financial Stability Board 2015a). This proposal was endorsed by the G-20 at its November 2015 meeting in Antalya, Turkey (see figure 3). Its provisions are consistent with the SPOE approach to failure resolution, although this does not mean all members of the G-20 are on board with SPOE.

Following the execution of the securities-for-claims exchange, the charter of the bridge financial company would be terminated and supplanted by the charter(s) of a new holding company or several holding companies. The newly created financial company would be required to meet or exceed all regulatory capital requirements. Before turning operations over to the private sector, however, the FDIC would require the board of directors and management of the bridge company to prepare a restructuring plan under which the new company could be resolved under the Bankruptcy Code without serious adverse effects on the U.S. financial system.

7. In addition to the issuance of debt and equity, contingent securities, such as warrants and options, in the new financial company that will succeed the bridge company may be issued. These contingent securities would enable claimants in lower-priority classes, namely, unsecured creditors and shareholders, to recoup value in the event that the final valuation of the bridge company was lower than its true market value.

Although the FDIC anticipates that the funding needs of a bridge company would be effectively fulfilled by private markets, particularly since the bridge company would have a strong balance sheet as well as public backing during the resolution process, Title II also provides for an OLF to serve as a backup source of liquidity support in case the new company cannot access private capital. The OLF would be available on a fully secured basis and is intended to function as a short-term source of liquidity to be repaid immediately once the bridge company could access customary sources of private market funding. In the event that the bridge company was unable to fully repay its OLF funds, the FDIC would impose risk-based assessments on other SIFIs to ensure against taxpayer losses.

Benefits of SPOE

The lack of infrastructure for resolving SIFIs prior to Title II served as a major source of instability during the crisis. The uncertainty over which firms would be rescued by bailouts not only served to amplify market panic but also raised a host of political issues as government officials were left with the poor choice of either rescuing firms considered "too-big-to-fail" (TBTF) or risking a wholesale collapse of the financial system.[8] In setting forth a predictable and preannounced regime for resolving SIFIs in the future, the SPOE approach takes a major step toward ending a highly problematic source of risk in the financial system.

Beyond addressing the uncertainty surrounding TBTF, the SPOE approach offers a structured means of ensuring that losses are absorbed by shareholders and long-term creditors while still enabling the organization to remain operational as an ongoing concern. This strategy offers the benefit of allowing the holding company's operating subsidiaries to continue serving markets, thereby reducing the likelihood of contagion, and preserves the organization's franchise value. Further, by isolating the parent of the troubled institution along with its debt and equity liabilities and providing for a rapid recapitalization of the banking group as a whole, SPOE mitigates the risks of liquidity runs and fire sales as short-term creditors would no longer have an incentive to withdraw liquidity from subsidiaries. Furthermore, ensuring that losses are imposed on shareholders and creditors should promote market discipline, diminish the potential for SIFIs to receive funding advantages in markets, and reduce the moral hazard created by the prospect of government bailouts.

The SPOE recapitalization strategy also makes the issue of resolving a global bank with foreign subsidiaries more manageable. Many SIFIs operate on a global scale that makes orderly resolution in the absence of a coordinated international effort difficult. In particular, the possibility of host countries isolating the operations of a nondomestic bank by restricting the ability of that bank to transfer assets or funds to operations outside of the country, a practice known as ring fencing, is a major risk involved in resolving global SIFIs (Institute of International Bankers 2014). Although guidelines on how to resolve banks whose operations span territories with differing laws and regulatory practices have been issued by the Basel Committee on Banking Supervision, the risk remains that foreign regulators, in order to safeguard local interests, will engage in ring fencing when a SIFI exhibits signs of financial distress.

The FSB's TLAC proposal tried to address the concern about the ring-fencing problem by saying that adequate loss absorbing capacity must be held in each country where a multinational institution operates. Thus the proposal reassures countries that they do not need to mandate ring fencing because the operations of domestic subsidiaries are protected. One can question the FSB's proposal, since it could be said to require ring fencing as a way of avoiding ring fencing, but the rationale is to provide a predictable level of protection for national markets while still preserving adequate flexibility for a bridge holding company to restructure the troubled institution and keep all essential subsidiaries open. And so, although SPOE does not fully resolve this issue, by set-

---

8. The term "TBTF" refers to all firms that pose systemic risks. Size is only one of a number of factors, such as complexity or interconnectedness, that may make a firm systemically important.

ting forth a strategy for recapitalizing the holding company while keeping subsidiaries and branches operational, it should reduce foreign regulators' incentives to disrupt the resolution process because depositors can be assured that their funds are safe and markets will be able to continue conducting operations with the company. Finding methods to resolve large global institutions remains a work in progress; in its latest consultation on SPOE the FDIC welcomed comments on this issue.

Concerns and Outstanding Issues

Some believe the standard for determining when the OLA may be used, namely when private bankruptcy threatens financial stability, is too subjective. The government is given broad discretion for determining when to apply SPOE, although application requires a high hurdle with agreement by super majorities of the FDIC and the Federal Reserve Board, combined with approval by the administration.[9] In addition to the criticism of potentially serving as a source of instability in the critical early moments when a systemically important institution exhibits signs of material financial distress, the subjectivity of the determination process has been criticized for being inconsistent with the general approach for bankruptcy. This concern, however, does not necessarily undermine the SPOE approach and can be addressed with further public guidance. For instance, Randall Guynn (2014, 288) suggests that a policy statement or a statutory mandate expressing a commitment to resolving all complex and global SIFIs under SPOE would substantially reduce the uncertainty of the determination process.

There is a lack of alignment between Titles I and II of the Dodd-Frank Act. Title II outlines a plan to resolve large institutions under FDIC direction, while Title I requires all covered institutions to submit resolution plans, or living wills, to the Federal Reserve and the FDIC, outlining a strategy for resolution under the Bankruptcy Code. Devising a resolution strategy can be a costly undertaking for banks, particularly for large and complex institutions (Herring 2010). Yet while complying with the living will requirement, these institutions also must prepare for the very different resolution contingency via SPOE set forth in Title II. These dual and conflicting rules for how large and complex institutions must prepare for failure place an unnecessary and costly regulatory burden on the institutions (Baily and Elliott 2014, 190). This is not to argue that living wills are unnecessary—there is at least some anecdotal evidence that the process of developing living wills helps financial institutions and regulators better understand their operations and prepare for potential future stress events—but rather that a convergence between Title I and Title II, for example, by requiring institutions to create living wills that describe resolution plans under SPOE, would create a more realistic planning scenario. This convergence is possible because the essential elements of the SPOE approach could be applied in a bankruptcy proceeding provided that there are adjustments to the Bankruptcy Code. David Skeel has discussed the potential for using SPOE with a revised bankruptcy code (Skeel 2014). There is some progress on this front, as the public portions of the 2015 living wills of most of the largest bank holding companies assume the use of SPOE for resolution, something that was not true in earlier versions of the living wills.

Finally, some concerns have been raised

---

9. As summarized in the FDIC's December 2013 Notice on SPOE, the determination process is as follows: In order for a SIFI to be resolved under Title II, two-thirds of the Federal Reserve Board and the Board of Directors of the FDIC must make a determination as to whether private bankruptcy for a failed institution poses a threat to financial stability, and then must draw up recommendations for resolving the institution under SPOE for approval by the secretary of the treasury and the president. If the company or its largest subsidiary is a broker-dealer or insurance company, then the role of the FDIC would be replaced by the SEC and the Federal Insurance Office, respectively, with the FDIC still being consulted in the determination process. Following executive approval, a twenty-four-hour judicial review process is initiated, and only after review has been completed may the FDIC initiate the resolution process.

that the OLF provision in Title II is tantamount to a formal sanctioning of bailouts by the public sector. The OLF, however, exclusively serves as a source of fully secured liquidity and may not be used by the bridge company as a source of capital. That distinction—between fully secured liquidity and capital injections—is the distinction between acceptable, short-term, publicly funded liquidity solutions and the type of government bailouts that were part of the government's 2008 crisis response. Furthermore, Dodd-Frank expressly prohibits taxpayer losses from the use of the Title II authority, and provides for several mechanisms, such as the ex-post charges on SIFIs in the event that the bridge company cannot fully repay OLF funds, to ensure that this end is met.

Conclusion on SPOE
There is no way to be certain how the new failure resolution provisions in Dodd-Frank would have impacted the unfolding of the financial crisis. It is hard to imagine, however, that the failure of Lehman Brothers, for example, would not have been easier to manage if regulators had been able to use orderly liquidation authority under SPOE and had had a backup source of temporary liquidity available to them, holding aside the benefits of having a living will for the company in place.

The SPOE strategy has received extensive support from a wide range of financial industry groups, think tanks, rating agencies, foreign regulators, and other stakeholders (Guynn 2014, 281–86). Since first being announced, SPOE has gained acceptance as a viable strategy for resolving systemically important institutions. By taking steps to end the TBTF issue, the SPOE strategy addresses a profound source of instability in the previous regulatory regime. Although there are still obstacles that will need to be overcome and areas in which improvements can be achieved, as the FDIC continues to implement its authorities under Title II, SPOE represents progress toward a safer financial system.

Creation of the CFPB
Housing was at the heart of the 2008 financial crisis. Poorly underwritten mortgages, predatory and misleading lending practices, and overly complex mortgage products served to inflate the asset bubble that ultimately created the financial crisis. Such products and practices were allowed to proliferate in part because oversight was fragmented among several regulatory agencies, leading to "significant gaps and weaknesses" in supervision (U.S. Department of the Treasury 2009, 7). In some cases, these agencies did not have the authority to regulate nonbank consumer products, which effectively prevented them from protecting consumers who had been subjected to predatory lending practices by nonbank mortgage providers. In other cases, financial regulators did not have the will to act on the authority granted by Congress. For example, the Federal Reserve waited fourteen years to adopt new rules under the Home Ownership and Equity Protection Act of 1994, by which time that law's ability to limit abuses of consumers was too late to help prevent or mitigate the impacts of the crisis (Financial Crisis Inquiry Commission 2011, 22).

The idea for a freestanding agency to correct these problems is generally credited to then professor Elizabeth Warren, now a senator from Massachusetts, who first proposed such an agency in 2007 (Warren 2007). This idea gained bipartisan support when the Treasury Department under Secretary Henry Paulson offered a similar proposal for a business conduct regulator in its "Blueprint for a Modernized Financial Regulatory Structure" released in 2008 (U.S. Department of the Treasury 2008). The blueprint stated that business conduct "is fundamentally linked to consumer protection" (170) and that centralizing such regulation in a single body "leads to greater consistency in the treatment of products, eliminates disputes among regulatory agencies, and reduces gaps in regulation and supervision" (14).

By consolidating the oversight responsibilities of seven different agencies under a single roof with a unified focus, the creation of the CFPB was a significant achievement for consumer protection (Bianco 2013, 1, 4). Dodd-Frank provided the bureau with the jurisdictional scope to cover most major consumer financial products, thereby leaving fewer gaps in the regulatory infrastructure.[10] Since it was created, the CFPB has engaged with both bank and nonbank lenders, industry participants, consumer groups, and policymakers, and has been active in making substantive policy decisions almost from its inception. It has taken actions to remove misleading financial products from the marketplace and has promulgated rules on qualified mortgages and money transfers. It has shown flexibility in responding to comments on initial drafts of its rules. It is difficult to think of another new regulatory agency that has established itself as quickly and has had as much impact in its first few years.

Of course, even if gaps are filled, quality regulations and a will by regulatory agencies to implement them is also essential. Agencies sometimes have the necessary authority to address a problem but either choose not to use it or simply fail to identify or understand the problem. In addition, agencies with multiple mandates, such as ensuring both safety and soundness and consumer protection, can have a difficult time prioritizing among them. Dodd-Frank addressed these issues as well by creating a CFPB with a single priority of protecting consumers. That does not guarantee the CFPB's success, but it does give the agency a better chance to achieve its goals.

Like any agency (particularly a new agency) the CFPB is not perfect and can be improved. The Government Accountability Office (GAO) found a number of areas where the bureau can improve its supervisory process, and the Bipartisan Policy Center (BPC) found that the quality of the new agency's decisionmaking has been better when it has used an open process for rule making and other activities (Fischer and Rodriguez 2013, 19). In addition, the CFPB and the federal prudential regulatory agencies are still working to coordinate their efforts, with prudential regulators at times struggling to integrate the bureau's findings and examination timelines into their own existing examination processes. Some tension between the bureau and prudential agencies is healthy since different criteria should be used to judge whether financial institutions are achieving safety-and-soundness goals as opposed to whether their products, activities, and practices are within appropriate boundaries from the perspective of consumers. Cooperation is, however, essential, to avoid regulatory gaps.

Despite prominent early support from both sides of the aisle, the CFPB has turned out to be perhaps the most controversial provision of Dodd-Frank.[11] Critics have charged that the bureau is an unaccountable bureaucracy that adds a regulatory burden on firms while harming those it is supposed to protect by raising prices for, and limiting choice in, financial products (Katz 2013; Winkler, Gitis, and Batkins 2014). Our judgment, however, is that the CFPB has done a remarkable job in a short time in providing much-needed protection to consumers. This enhanced protection will lead to greater financial stability by reducing the likelihood that dangerous products, activities, and practices will proliferate and threaten financial stability. In the long run, to the extent that the bureau is able to efficiently root out illegal financial practices that harm consumers, and that Congress adopts sensible legal measures, it may potentially increase economic growth.

Derivatives and Transparency

The derivatives market, particularly for those traded over the counter (that is, privately ne-

---

10. Some exemptions from the CFPB's authority were granted, such as oversight over the extension of credit provided through auto dealers.

11. Several of the more controversial elements of the CFPB's creation include its existence as an independent agency within another independent agency (the Federal Reserve), its being headed by a single director as opposed to a board or a commission, and its reliance on funding from the Federal Reserve as opposed to from the congressional appropriations process. It is worth noting that the two newest financial regulatory agencies Congress created, the CFPB during President Barack Obama's tenure and the Federal Housing Finance Agency (FHFA) during President George W. Bush's tenure, were structured as single-headed agencies. However, Congress has had difficulty confirming directors to lead both agencies.

gotiated), amplified risks to the financial system that built up during the crisis. Derivatives are not inherently dangerous and are a useful tool for managing risk. According to the International Swaps and Derivatives Association (ISDA), of the total notional outstanding value of over-the-counter (OTC) derivatives as of June 30, 2013, about 95 percent were either interest rate or foreign exchange derivatives (International Swaps and Derivatives Association 2014a, 4), which generally performed well during the crisis. An oft-cited example of using another kind of derivative, a commodity derivative, is when airlines buy financial instruments to lock in a price for fuel oil, a major cost of doing business for them. This protects these airlines from sudden spikes in oil prices, but also removes the ability for them to profit from drops in prices such as the ones seen in the latter half of 2014. A derivative of this type transfers the risk of future price changes from airlines to investors, who will realize the related profits or losses. In the right circumstances, derivatives are a tool to transfer risk from those who want to be rid of it to those best able to assume it.

Unfortunately, risk is sometimes instead transferred to those who least understand it rather than to those most able to bear it. The market for OTC derivatives exists in large part because companies often demand instruments tailored to their specific risks and circumstances, which makes it difficult to standardize products. OTC derivatives, however, were largely unregulated before the crisis. Little information was disclosed about them and over time they became more complex and difficult to understand, both as individual instruments and in the way they affected markets in aggregate. Credit default swaps (CDS) were used as insurance against the default of debt securities,[12] which grew increasingly complex themselves, leading to sellers of CDS—notably AIG—to drastically underprice these instruments because they, similarly, underestimated the true risk of default. As if by magic, debt securities with marginal credit ratings were broken apart and repackaged into new securities with a large tranche rated as very safe. The complicated nature of many of these products and the lack of transparency surrounding them made such sleight of hand appear more plausible at the time.

While some aspects of its implementation have been controversial, Title VII of Dodd-Frank made real progress by subjecting swap dealers to greater oversight and requiring most derivatives to trade on open exchanges and be centrally cleared. The ISDA estimates that eventually 70 percent or more of even OTC derivatives trades will be cleared (International Swaps and Derivatives Association 2013, 3). Adding much-needed oversight and transparency to such a large and consequential market is another clear win for Dodd-Frank.

CLEAR LOSSES

As we emphasized in the beginning of this article, we believe that the financial system is much safer because of changes made as a result of Dodd-Frank. However, we judge a few provisions of the act as clear losses, providing little or no increase in stability. The first example actually reduces stability.

Restrictions on Federal Reserve and FDIC Crisis Authority

The U.S. government's actions to contain the financial crisis were unpopular from the beginning and remain so. Public polls have consistently shown that Americans opposed providing money to financial firms that were in danger during that time. As the BPC's report on systemic risk explained, the public believes that government policy mostly helped large banks and companies and the wealthy; that emergency assistance amounted to giveaways to bail out otherwise insolvent institutions; and that the government's actions have not made the economy more secure (Dugan, Fisher, and Muckenfuss 2014, 31). According to Gallup, confidence in the Federal Reserve is

---

12. A swap is a derivative in which two or more parties agree to exchange the cash flows resulting from two or more different financial instruments. In the case of a CDS, the buyer owes one or more payments to the seller as with an insurance premium, while the buyer receives a payment if the underlying security being insured defaults.

now lower than it was before the crisis (Kohn 2014, 3).

Anger at the Federal Reserve for not preventing the crisis and for its unpopular actions during the crisis influenced the debate on Dodd-Frank, which included a provision to ban the Fed from providing emergency loans to a single firm, as it did in 2008 with AIG and Bear Stearns. Instead, these loans must be offered through programs with "broad-based eligibility"—that is, they must be made available to a category of institutions rather than on a one-off basis to a single company. This provision is intended to prevent future bailouts of financial institutions and, by extension, to reduce the moral hazard created by industry expectations of future bailouts. These are laudable goals, but the new restriction in Dodd-Frank on the Fed's lending authority is potentially a threat to financial stability and could, perversely, exacerbate moral hazard issues.

To understand why, it is necessary to differentiate between providing temporary liquidity to an otherwise solvent institution in a crisis and providing capital to save an insolvent institution. The latter constitutes a bailout. The former has been one of the primary responsibilities of central banks for many years: to be the lender of last resort. When a financial crisis starts, creditors have an incentive to run, or quickly withdraw their funding by refusing to roll over existing debt. Account holders have an incentive to quickly withdraw funds from institutions that market participants fear are or may soon be insolvent. Such runs can lead to panics and crises, which can greatly damage the real economy.

It is far less expensive to prevent runs before they occur. For many years, the Federal Reserve, through its discount window, has provided loans to firms experiencing temporary liquidity problems. During the crisis, the agency set up a number of programmatic facilities to inject temporary liquidity into other major segments of the financial system, such as broker-dealers and money market mutual funds. Taken together, these actions by the Federal Reserve involved committing huge government resources to prevent much greater potential damage to the economy. Prohibiting the Federal Reserve from making emergency loans until it can justify making them to an entire class of institutions forces the agency either to wait to lend until a financial stress event has gotten worse or to evade the spirit of the law by effectively lending, as before, to a single firm under cover of a tortured definition of "broad-based" class of firms. The Federal Reserve should not be forced to make such a decision.

This is not to imply that there should be no restrictions on the Federal Reserve's emergency lending authority. Appropriate thresholds should be in place to ensure that loans are made only when truly necessary, and only to otherwise solvent firms at a penalty rate and with high-quality collateral. The Federal Reserve's emergency lending also should be made transparent after a reasonable time period. In fact, Dodd-Frank and the Emergency Economic Stabilization Act of 2008 (EESA, more popularly known for establishing TARP, the Troubled Asset Relief Program) amended the Federal Reserve Act to address these issues with a series of new requirements (Federal Reserve Act, 12 U.S.C. Section 343 [3] [B–D]), which augmented restrictions already in place prior to the crisis and codified additional transparency mechanisms. The additional transparency regarding emergency lending by the Fed imposed in EESA do not appear to have limited the Federal Reserve's ability to do what it thought was necessary while providing greater public accountability.

Further, contrary to post-crisis conventional wisdom, prohibiting the Federal Reserve from making emergency loans to single institutions can make moral hazard worse. The BPC's paper on systemic risk explains how:

> Take, for example, a hypothetical case in which two major companies originate most of the auto loans in the United States. Company A has made high-risk investments in assets that have gone bad, causing Company A to become insolvent and threatening to put the entire financial system at risk. Company B is well managed and solvent but faces short-term liquidity problems because the market is nervous about lending to any auto

loan originators due to the actions of Company A. Under Dodd-Frank's new provisions, the Federal Reserve is unable to extend credit to Company B while letting Company A fail, because such lending must be conducted through programs with "broad-based eligibility"—that is, be offered to both companies A and B. In so doing, the new provisions make it more difficult to punish Company A's shareholders and management, who have not done their jobs well, without also punishing the stakeholders in Company B. In this way, the new lending provisions can actually create moral hazard.

We recognize that these views are controversial. One of the referees for this essay argued that there was no additional moral hazard with a broad-based lending program as long as the Federal Reserve follows the Bagehot dictum and only lends to solvent institutions at a penalty rate with appropriate collateral. This point is well taken, but we recall that in the last financial crisis serious problems occurred in AIG, an insurance company that no one thought ahead of time would have needed emergency intervention from the Federal Reserve. It would have been hard to create a broad facility available to all insurance companies in the time frame needed to deal with the crisis. We do not know what the next crisis will look like and what institutions may be in trouble, and so we judge that the Federal Reserve needs the discretion to lend to individual institutions when necessary.

In a post on his blog at the Brookings Institution website, Ben Bernanke, the former Federal Reserve Board chairman, also took a different view from the one given here (Bernanke 2015). He said that the new restrictions were ones the Federal Reserve could live with and they represented a workable compromise between Congress, which wants more control over Federal Reserve actions, and the need for quick and decisive actions in a crisis. He did, however, express concern over disclosure requirements. He argues that institutions will postpone going to the Federal Reserve for help because of the stigma attached to such borrowing—specifically, a fear that other lenders will quickly take their money out of the institution, creating a run. Under current law, Federal Reserve emergency lending must be disclosed immediately to Congress but may be kept secret from the public for two years at the request of the chair of the Federal Reserve Board. However, financial institutions may not believe Congress will abide by the two-year rule and the information will leak out. Hence, some institutions that should be borrowing might not do so. (Senators David Vitter (R-La.) and Elizabeth Warren (D-Mass.) have proposed making Federal Reserve emergency lending public immediately).[13]

These points, too, are well taken, and the three authors of this article are not in complete agreement on the disclosure issue. There are situations where transparency can be harmful, but there have also been situations where the Federal Reserve needed to be more transparent in its actions and at least keep Congress informed.

On balance, our judgment is that, although the Federal Reserve made mistakes before and during the financial crisis, its use of its lender-of-last-resort authority to provide temporary liquidity to financial institutions was perhaps its greatest success. It is important that the Federal Reserve retains the ability to fight a future crisis with the same success.

Dodd-Frank also made changes to the FDIC's crisis authority, with mixed results. The law recognized the value of actions taken during the crisis by the FDIC—such as through the Temporary Liquidity Guarantee Program (TLGP)—to guarantee debt issued by healthy insured depository institutions. One study found that the TLGP reduced yields on bank-issued debt, promoted liquidity in fixed income markets, and made it cheaper for banks to borrow at a time when that ability was more important (Ambrose, Cheng, and King 2013). In addition, the program achieved these results while also realizing a $9.3 billion gain for the Deposit Insurance Fund (Federal Deposit Insurance Corporation 2013a). In response,

---

13. See Bailout Prevention Act of 2015, S. 1320, 114th Cong., 2015.

Congress laid out an explicit process whereby the FDIC can use such authority in the future, subject to several reasonable limitations (Dodd-Frank Wall Street Reform and Consumer Protection Act).[14]

Unfortunately, Congress required that the FDIC seek and obtain a joint resolution from Congress before it can issue such guarantees. Naturally Congress should thoroughly review actions taken by regulators, but time is compressed in a crisis. Destabilizing runs can begin and spread, threatening the entire financial system, within days or even hours. The longer responses are delayed, the greater the potential damage to the financial system and the economy. Having to wait for Congress to pass a resolution that may be unpopular, though necessary, would subject crisis response to an unnecessary and potentially costly delay or, in extreme circumstances, block debt guarantee authority entirely. Recall that despite pleas from the president, the treasury secretary, the chairman of the Federal Reserve, the Speaker of the House and the minority leader of the House, the full House of Representatives voted down the first TARP proposal. That vote precipitated the largest single-day point drop in the history of the Dow Jones Industrial Average. It is not always easy to get Congress to act quickly during a crisis.

It was inevitable that government intervention on a massive scale to save the financial sector would prove unpopular, but that unpopularity is not based on an accurate perception of what the direct costs were to taxpayers. The big "bailout" fund was the TARP, which was used primarily to inject capital into banks. Other government assistance took the form of loans to and investments in financial institutions. In aggregate these actions returned a significant profit to taxpayers.[15] When bailouts occur, it is because they are thought by regulators and other government officials to be the least-bad option available. Financial crises are inherently unexpected to most relevant decision-makers, who would otherwise have acted to prevent them. Thus, we do not know what the source of the next crisis will be, nor what specific form it will take. Because of the massive damage that financial crises can cause to the real economy, it is vital that regulators have the necessary flexibility to respond quickly to unexpected circumstances to mitigate and prevent damage. The actions taken during the crisis by the Federal Reserve and the FDIC were paradoxically both unpopular and, on the whole, highly successful. Further, the Federal Reserve had had this extraordinary authority available to it since the 1930s but had not used it to any significant degree for more than seventy years, until the financial crisis. In short, the authority was used judiciously as well as effectively. Dodd-Frank's restrictions on this authority are a clear loss for financial stability.

COSTLY TRADE-OFFS

Assessing Dodd-Frank beyond its clear wins and losses is more difficult. Certain provisions in the new law achieve some benefits, but likely at an even greater cost. Most prominent are the controversial Volcker Rule and the swaps push-out rule, otherwise known as the Lincoln Amendment.

The Volcker Rule

A popular narrative in recent years is that the repeal of key sections of the Banking Act of 1933, otherwise known as Glass-Steagall, contributed significantly to the crisis. The provisions in Glass-Steagall that separated commercial banking and securities activities were repealed in pieces during the 1980s and 1990s as part of an effort to modernize financial regulation, which resulted in the creation of large financial holding companies that included banks and other financial activities such as insurance companies and broker-dealers under a single roof. This allowed newly diversified banks to engage in proprietary trading. Opponents of these changes have argued that they

---

14. See Dodd-Frank Wall Street Reform and Consumer Protection Act, Pub. L. No. 111-203, 111th Cong. Available at: www.gpo.gov/fdsys/pkg/PLAW-111publ203/html/PLAW-111publ203.htm; accessed July 11, 2016.

15. The Treasury has received more back than it disbursed to banks and to AIG. See the TARP Tracker, available at: https://www.treasury.gov/initiatives/financial-stability/reports/Pages/TARP-Tracker.aspx; accessed July 27, 2016.

set up potential conflicts of interest with banks' clients and increase moral hazard and reduce financial stability because these banks hold taxpayer-insured deposits and have the ability to access government liquidity through the Federal Reserve's discount window. Proponents have argued that diversified financial institutions are made safer by being able to rely on a wider range of revenue streams. There is merit in each of these arguments.

Whether or not repealing Glass-Steagall was good policy, there is little evidence that proprietary trading was a direct and major contributor to the most recent crisis. The problem was not trading per se, but the fact that financial institutions bought and held asset-backed securities for which the underlying risk was badly mispriced by the market as a whole. In effect, they purchased bad loans. Traditional banking involves taking deposits and using the funds to make loans to families or small and medium-sized businesses. This is something policymakers want banks to do in order to help people buy houses and companies create jobs, but such lending has always been risky. Individual loans are risky indeed and even a more diversified portfolio of loans can be risky in a local or a national downturn. For generations, bank failures have resulted from banks making bad loans and the recent crisis had much in common with this historical pattern, although the complex financial engineering made the problem bigger and more difficult to rectify than previous events. The Volcker Rule as written in Dodd-Frank bans proprietary trading by banks that is not done at the behest of their clients and it also limits banks' ownership of, and relationship to, "covered funds," which include hedge funds and private equity funds (Dodd-Frank Wall Street Reform and Consumer Protection Act, section 619). The rule's primary congressional sponsors, Senators Jeff Merkley (D-Ore.) and Carl Levin (D-Mich.) intended the rule to "put a strong firewall between banks and hedge fund–style high-risk trading" and thereby "change the culture and practices at our nation's largest financial firms, to prevent Wall Street and the big banks from making swing-for-the-fences bets that put depositors and taxpayers at risk" (Merkley and Levin 2013). The former Federal Reserve chairman Paul Volcker, for whom the rule is named, envisioned a simple, clear ban on proprietary trading (Stewart 2011). The rule that was finalized by five regulatory agencies is highly complex and includes exceptions for market-making and hedging activities. As BPC's report on the Volcker Rule and the Lincoln Amendment explained (Cox, Macey, and Nazareth 2013, 11):

> Judging the intent of a trade in real-world situations is not an easy task. For example, for the purposes of market-making, a financial institution may buy securities that it reasonably expects its clients will want to purchase. If market conditions change or the institution simply misjudges, those securities may go unsold for longer than expected, which could resemble proprietary trading. A trade that starts as a hedge may later look speculative as the result of other trades within a portfolio. Some trades are even made for more than one purpose at a time.

This is not to argue against nuanced oversight. Given that the Volcker Rule is the law, regulators should do what they can to get it right. That means taking an iterative, phased-in approach to gathering data, finding trading patterns, and identifying proprietary trading in a way that differentiates among different activities and asset classes. There are benefits to be achieved for financial stability if the Volcker regulations are properly implemented and regularly adjusted based on changing market conditions.

The question is how many of these benefits can be realized, and at what cost. A 2014 Office of the Comptroller of the Currency (OCC) study estimated that initial compliance would cost the banking industry $4.3 billion (Miedema 2014). If the cost and complexity of regulations end up limiting legitimate market-making and hedging activity, or force providers of such services from the market, it could raise prices and reduce liquidity to the extent of outweighing the benefits realized. The Volcker Rule only went into full effect in July 2015 and we do not know what its impact will be. When the Federal Reserve issued the draft version of the rule, some of the comment letters expressed concern that medium-sized enterprises would find it more costly or more difficult to issue new debt with the rule in place. The final Volcker regulations also require banks to divest themselves of existing assets such as collateralized loan obligations within a specified time period, as opposed to banning purchases of assets of this type and allowing ownership of existing assets to wind down over time, which creates the prospect of banks' being forced to sell at fire-sale prices. Perhaps acknowledging this problem, the Federal Reserve and other regulators have repeatedly granted one- and two-year extensions for these legacy assets, the most recent lasting until July 2017.

The Lincoln Amendment

Another provision in Dodd-Frank meant to separate securities and commercial banking activities was the swaps push-out rule, or Lincoln Amendment. Added by Senator Blanche Lincoln (D-Ariz.), the provision attempts to protect taxpayers from subsidizing trading activity, derivatives activity in particular, by prohibiting insured depository institutions with access to Federal Reserve liquidity facilities from engaging in certain derivatives trading activities.

However, prominent regulators such as Volcker and Sheila Bair, a former FDIC chairman, suggested that the goals of the push-out rule are already achieved by the Volcker Rule (Bair 2010; Volker 2010). In light of this, keeping the push-out rule in place adds additional cost for both regulators and industry without realizing additional benefits.

It is also unclear how implementation of the Lincoln Amendment would work in relation to the proposed SPOE resolution regime. If a holding company needs to recapitalize a troubled swaps dealer subsidiary that has been pushed out of the subsidiary bank, then the damage caused would appear to be the same whether the problems were inside or outside one specific subsidiary. Put another way, under an SPOE failure system, it is unclear what the benefit to taxpayers is of having separated the swaps dealer.

There were also concerns raised about how the implementation of this push-out would affect the unwinding of derivatives contracts in the event of failure. In October 2014, subsequent to passage of the Lincoln Amendment and as part of the financial regulators' work to improve the failure resolution regime, the ISDA announced that eighteen major global banks had agreed on a new "stay protocol" in which these banks waive their cross-default and early termination rights "to give regulators time to facilitate an orderly resolution" if one of the eighteen enters failure resolution (International Swaps and Derivatives Association 2014b). Whether these changes fully address the earlier concerns is not clear, but the changes were a step in the right direction.

Finally, it is important to note that for the Lincoln Amendment to achieve its goals, regulators would have to be willing to allow the pushed-out swaps dealer to fail, if it were in trouble, without any consequence to the insured depository institution. Early on in the last financial crisis, regulators faced a somewhat similar choice with regard to certain structured investment vehicles (SIVs). These SIVs were not swaps dealers, but were legally separate investment vehicles that some large financial institutions had created and sold investments in to some of their largest clients. When some of these SIVs got into early trouble, several financial firms took them onto their balance sheets or provided them with substantial financial support. These firms argued that doing so, with the approval of their regulator, was necessary to avoid reputational risk. The lesson is that even if something is considered "pushed-out" and "off the books" during good times, it may still be "pulled back in" during a crisis or panic.

The BPC proposed to indefinitely suspend implementation of the Lincoln Amendment pending implementation of the Volcker Rule. Since then, Congress has substantially changed the law, effectively rolling back large sections of the Lincoln Amendment as part of an omnibus spending bill. This legislation created considerable backlash, owing in part to substantive disagreements and in part to concerns about the process for adding the provision to this bill. However, Congress passed and the president signed the legislation, effectively ending the costly trade-off of the Lincoln Amendment.

Figure 4. Fragmented U.S. Regulatory Structure Prior to Dodd-Frank Act

Depository and Lending Activity	Federal Reserve	OCC	FDIC	OTS	State Banking Supervisors
Consumer Financial Products	Federal Reserve	OCC	FDIC	OTS	State Banking Supervisors
Securities and Bonds Products	SEC				
Derivatives Products Exchange Based	CFTC				
Derivatives Products Over-the-Counter Based					
Insurance Products	State Insurance Regulators				

Source: Neiman and Olson 2014, 49–50.

UNFINISHED BUSINESS

We put in a separate category areas where Dodd-Frank made progress but did not go far enough. Most prominent in this category of unfinished business is inadequate streamlining of the U.S. financial regulatory architecture and too little authority and independence for the new macro-prudential agencies that Dodd-Frank created.

Regulatory Consolidation

The high level of fragmentation and overlap found in the U.S. financial regulatory structure contributed to the financial crisis. A 2014 BPC report (Neiman and Olson 2014, 60–64) identified three prominent examples for which this was the case:

1. The lack of understanding of regulators of the risks associated with complex new financial products that undergirded the complicated system of mortgage originations and securitizations
2. The inability of regulators to exercise jurisdiction over derivatives markets due to congressional action
3. Ineffective oversight of thrift holding companies—such as AIG—that resulted from structural opportunities for regulatory arbitrage and capture, and ineffective coordination among federal regulatory agencies with overlapping jurisdictions

Since no single agency was responsible for taking an overall view of the financial system, in the years leading up to the crisis significant gaps developed and regulators did not see the broad risks that were building up in the system in the 2000s. A lack of common financial data standards was a related and substantial impediment to understanding market risk. Overlapping jurisdiction for both bank prudential and capital markets regulatory agencies created interagency friction, inefficient use of supervisory and regulatory resources, duplicative requests and compliance responsibilities for financial institutions, and opportunities for regulatory arbitrage as institutions had incentives to play off one agency against another under the threat of "charter shopping." The regulatory system as it was prior to Dodd-Frank is shown in figure 4, by activity and product.

Dodd-Frank made some progress in addressing the problem of overlapping jurisdictions. It created a new supercouncil of regulators, the FSOC, to keep an eye on risk in the financial system as a whole and to better coordinate among agencies. It also created the OFR to support the FSOC, develop common finan-

Figure 5. Somewhat Improved U.S. Regulatory Structure After Dodd-Frank Act

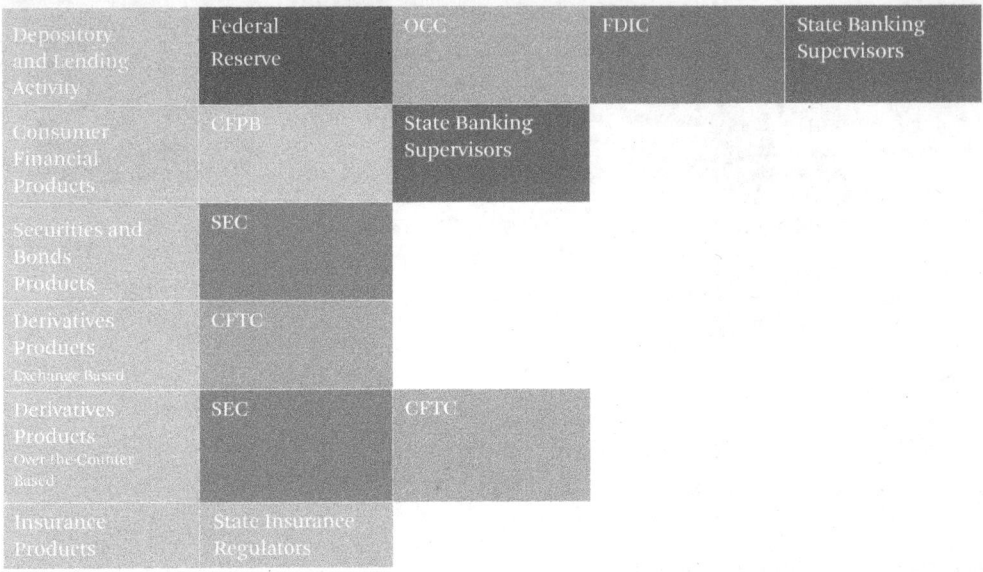

Source: Neiman and Olson 2014, 49–50.

cial data standards, and analyze threats to financial stability. As detailed earlier, Dodd-Frank created the CFPB to consolidate federal oversight of consumer financial products in a single agency, and it closed a major gap by bringing derivatives products under the jurisdiction of the Commodity Futures Trading Commission (CFTC) and the SEC. The act also eliminated the Office of Thrift Supervision (OTS), which had been responsible for overseeing many of the financial institutions engaged in the riskiest practices prior to the crisis, and moved its previous responsibilities to several other agencies, particularly the OCC. These were all positive steps.

As after previous crises, however, Congress found it much easier to create new agencies than to consolidate existing ones. Figure 5 shows the progress that was made and also the overlap and fragmentation that remains. Jurisdictional issues in Congress prevented a merger of the CFTC and the SEC, something that has been recommended numerous times over the years. Prudential bank regulation is still divided among three federal agencies. And since there is no federal insurance charter or regulatory agency, insurance companies that are designated by the FSOC as systemically important are regulated by the Federal Reserve. To date three of the four companies designated by the FSOC have been insurance companies and it is not yet clear whether the Federal Reserve has the expertise and the proper framework to effectively regulate these institutions. Further, Dodd-Frank's attempt to improve coordination by assigning multiple agencies to jointly write rules and regulations has seen mixed results at best: many congressionally mandated deadlines have been missed and there has been friction between and among agencies.

There is no single "best" approach to financial regulatory architecture, but the current U.S. system remains more fragmented and less efficient than it should be. The BPC's 2014 report, "Dodd-Frank's Missed Opportunity: A Road Map for a More Effective Regulatory Architecture," made a series of recommendations to build on what Dodd-Frank began, including the following recommendations (Neiman and Olson 2014, 5–10):

- Create a consolidated examination force that would leverage resources, expertise, and knowledge from each of the prudential bank regulators and result in a single set of

Figure 6. Proposed Bipartisan Solution: Streamlining Regulation

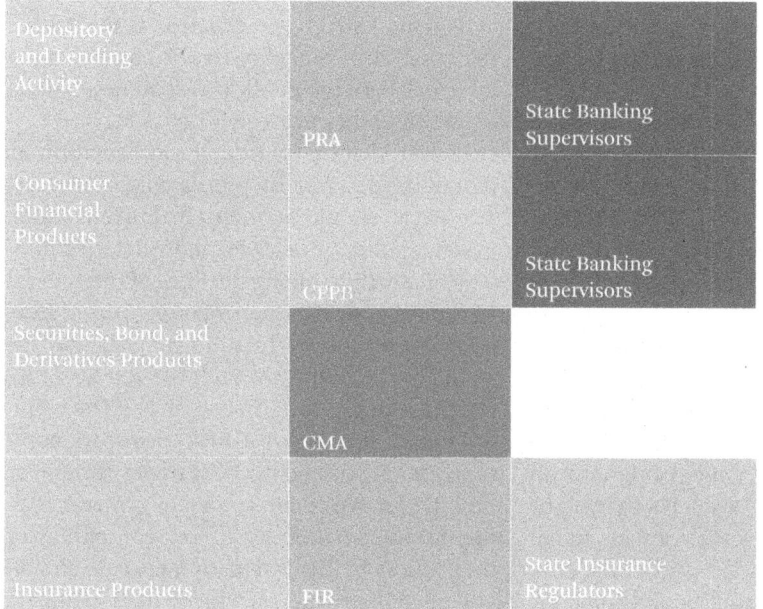

Source: Neiman and Olson 2014, 49–50.

supervisory questions and a single examination report.

- Build on this exam force by eventually eliminating the OCC and vesting all bank and bank holding company supervision and regulation within a single Prudential Regulatory Authority (PRA).
- Merge the CFTC and the SEC into a single capital markets authority.
- Create a new federal insurance charter and Federal Insurance Regulator (FIR) to ensure that insurance companies, products, and practices are overseen by an entity that is expert in the business of insurance.
- Phase out the federal thrift charter in favor of a single, modern federal banking charter.
- Ensure that all independent financial regulatory agencies can rely on funding independent of congressional appropriations.

The BPC plan would result in a more streamlined structure, as shown in figure 6.

There will always be significant hurdles to such major changes, but policymakers should not wait until the next financial crisis proves once again that they are necessary.

The Financial Stability Oversight Council

As previously stated, Dodd-Frank took a positive step forward by creating the FSOC and the OFR as macro-prudential regulators. Such systemic oversight was a major gap in pre-crisis regulation, and the agencies were also assigned the jobs of plugging gaps in financial data and improving coordination among FSOC member agencies.

Congress, however, left the FSOC without the necessary authority to carry out all of its duties. The FSOC's major power is to designate nonbanks as SIFIs, thereby subjecting them to oversight by the Federal Reserve Board. This, though, is a binary power that does not allow federal regulators to exercise much oversight of nonbanks unless they are designated as SIFIs. In addition, the process is controversial, with particular friction around the FSOC's track record of assigning the SIFI designation to large insurance companies.

The lack of authority held by the FSOC is

most evident in its inability to force cooperation among member agencies or to force an agency to change its behavior. The FSOC may make recommendations to its member agencies to address threats to financial stability, but it cannot compel them to act even if there is a supermajority vote of the full membership. Similarly, although it provides a valuable forum for member agencies to meet and discuss issues, the council does not have the authority to force improved coordination on activities such as joint rule writing.

BPC's Responding to Systematic Risk report recommended that the FSOC be given additional authority to address these issues (Dugan, Fisher, and Muckenfuss 2014, 48–52). The council would be able to issue regulations on its own when two or more agencies charged by Congress to jointly write such regulations fail to complete them within 180 days of the congressionally mandated deadline for doing so. In addition, the FSOC would have the authority to issue its own regulations when it finds them necessary to deal with a grave threat to financial stability.[16]

With power comes accountability. The FSOC has been criticized for its lack of openness despite having instituted a transparency policy in May 2014 (Financial Stability Oversight Council 2014). Bills have been introduced in Congress to allow members of boards and commissions represented on the council, members of Congress who sit on FSOC oversight committees, and FSOC member agency staff to be able to attend council meetings. Other legislation would subject the FSOC to the transparency and open-process provisions of the Government in the Sunshine Act, the Federal Advisory Committee Act, and the Administrative Procedures Act. Companies under review for possible SIFI designation believe that they should be better informed at all stages of that process and be given better and earlier opportunities to provide materials and feedback to the council, review the council's findings, and learn exactly what risks the council believes they pose to financial stability, which is a precursor to designation as a SIFI.

For the FSOC to be effective, it must have the trust of its stakeholders. A balance must be struck between public transparency and the council's ability to freely discuss sensitive issues and analyze proprietary information as part of the designation process and otherwise. The FSOC should augment its current transparency policy by releasing more detailed minutes of meetings, along the lines of the Federal Reserve's Federal Open Market Committee, which provides useful information and insights to the public through the release of its minutes subject to a three-week lag. The council would also be wise to improve its communication with companies under review for designation while continuing to protect confidential information. Notifying companies of their status in the designation process and allowing them to interact with council members at all stages would improve the process and lead to better outcomes. In February 2015, the FSOC addressed some of these suggestions in a series of amendments to its designation process (Financial Stability Oversight Council 2015).

The Office of Financial Research

Dodd-Frank created the OFR and charged it with supporting the FSOC, identifying potential sources of systemic risk, and improving the quality and standardization of financial data. An ideal OFR would be free enough of political constraints to "ring the alarm bell" about systemic threats it identifies, and would seize upon its data mission in order to close data gaps and improve the data used by all financial regulators. The new agency has contributed in several areas, but its progress overall has been disappointing. Although the OFR was set up as an office within the Treasury Department, it was given the ability to act much more independently than other Treasury offices, something the OCC has long done. The OFR has instead chosen to focus on supporting the

---

16. The recommendation in the PPC's report "Dodd-Frank's Missed Opportunity" would allow the FSOC to impose heightened standards and safeguards, while the recommendation in "Responding to Systemic Risk" would allow the council to issue its own regulations, but only when a member agency has failed to act.

FSOC and the Treasury, which limits its ability to be an independent voice, a tremendous missed opportunity. The agency would also gain short-term influence and long-term effectiveness by focusing a greater share of its energy on its data quality and standardization mission.

TOO SOON TO TELL

Earlier, we argued that increasing bank capital requirements is a clear win for Dodd-Frank and global financial reform. Increasing capital is not free, but it is worth the cost in the contribution it makes by improving the stability of individual institutions and the financial system as a whole. New prudential requirements, though, do not only affect the mandated level of Tier 1 capital at banks. Dodd-Frank, Basel, and work by the G-20 also specify requirements or standards for leverage ratios, additional capital buffers, stress testing, liquidity, and long-term debt holdings.

Leverage Ratio

Basel III includes a minimum leverage ratio—calculated as Tier 1 capital divided by total consolidated assets—of 3 percent. The ratio acts as a backstop to risk-weighted capital metrics by measuring assets without risk weighting. In September 2014, the Federal Reserve, the FDIC, and the OCC finalized a rule for an enhanced supplementary leverage ratio for banks with over $700 billion in assets (Board of Governors of the Federal Reserve System, Federal Deposit Insurance Corporation, and Office of the Comptroller of the Currency 2014). The ratio is 5 percent for U.S.-based global systemically important bank holding companies and 6 percent for their insured banks. Below these levels, institutions will be subject to regulatory limitations on capital distributions and discretionary bonus payments.

Capital Buffers

Basel III includes provisions for a capital conservation buffer at 2.5 percent of risk-weighted assets. It is intended to augment Tier 1 capital by further building up capital buffers during healthy operating periods that can be drawn upon during stress events. A countercyclical capital buffer of between 0 and 2.5 percent of risk-weighted assets provides another buffer that is intended to vary, rising in periods when regulators are concerned that credit growth is excessive.

Stress Tests

Dodd-Frank requires annual stress tests for all bank SIFIs. Stress tests assess the ability of banks to weather extreme stress events and have become a central tool of Federal Reserve supervision since they were first used extensively in early 2009. They have proved valuable to both banks and regulators, but are also complex and costly. Further, flawed assumptions can cause stress tests to fail to predict important gaps and problems in the same way that flawed assumptions about risk can lead to inaccurate risk-weighting of assets.

Liquidity

Basel III instituted two new measures of liquidity: the Liquidity Coverage Ratio (LCR) and the Net Stable Funding Ratio (NSFR). LCR dictates that banks must hold enough high-quality liquid assets (cash, excess reserves held at the Federal Reserve, and U.S. treasuries) to cover their cash needs for a scenario in which they would be unable to access capital markets for a thirty-day period. NSFR is intended to promote the use of more stable, longer-term sources of funding by requiring that a firm's stable funding (deposits, equity, and long-term wholesale funding) is greater than its weighted long-term assets.

Taken together, LCR and NSFR are intended to ensure that firms can meet their liquidity needs during stress events. There is some risk, though, in predicting future liquidity. U.S. treasuries are considered one of the safest and most liquid assets in the world and are included in LCR calculations for that reason. That assessment could change drastically if a future crisis were triggered by the U.S. government defaulting on its debt, something that was conceivable during the debt-ceiling crises of 2011 and 2013. Municipal debt provides another example. Because state and local governments rarely default, their debt is considered very safe. However, because much of their debt is held by retail investors and many municipalities have small issuances,

Figure 7. Basel III, Quantitative Impact

$$\uparrow \text{Capital ratio} = \frac{\text{Eligible capital} \downarrow}{\text{Risk-weighted assets} \uparrow}$$

$$\text{Leverage ratio} = \frac{\text{Tier 1 capital}}{\text{Total exposure}} \geq 3\%$$

$$\text{Liquidity coverage ratio} = \frac{\text{High-quality liquid assets}}{\text{Total net cash outflows over the next 30 calendar days}} \geq 100\%$$

$$\text{Net stable funding ratio} = \frac{\text{Available stable funding}}{\text{Required stable funding}} \geq 100\%$$

Source: Basel Committee on Banking Supervision 2012, slide 11.

they may not trade frequently. Often the securities that trade the most frequently, and hence are the most liquid, are those of the small number of troubled state or local governments. For example, three of the five and ten of the top seventeen most frequently traded municipal securities over a ninety-day period in late 2014 were issued by Puerto Rico, whose government continues to face serious potential default risk as of this writing.[17] If liquidity is not properly defined, it can skew demand for both safe and risky assets. Further, what is liquid one day can suddenly become illiquid in a crisis, such as happened with asset- and mortgage-backed securities during the most recent crisis.

Long-Term Unsecured Debt

In November 2015, the G-20 endorsed an FSB proposal for a framework for TLAC that goes beyond the minimum capital requirements in Basel III for the largest global banks (Klein and Ryan 2014). The FSB proposed a new global minimum standard of 16 to 20 percent of risk-weighted assets that each of these institutions would need to meet in TLAC, which would be a combination of equity and debt at the holding company level that can either be written down or converted to equity in the event of significant losses or failure.

It is not clear how these rules taken in combination (see figure 7) will affect financial stability, nor how they will affect the operations, lending decisions, and adjustments to asset holdings of banks. Getting the balance right will require proper weighting of risk, accurate prediction of liquidity, and global coordination, along with good judgment and flexibility on the part of regulators and market participants.

CONCLUSIONS

The analysis in this article leads us to a few overarching conclusions about the impact of financial reform and the state of the financial system today.

---

17. Date range October 20 to December 23, 2014; see Bondview.com, "Most Active Bonds," www.bondview.com/trends/most-active-bonds/sector/All%20Sectors/state/All%20States/min_yield/5/min_volume/0/start_date/10-20-2014/end_date/12-23-2014/taxable/all; accessed June 6, 2016.

1. The financial sector is much safer today than before the crisis. Some provisions have been "clear wins" for Dodd-Frank. They have improved stability without seriously harming efficiency and economic growth. These provisions include higher capital requirements, the SPOE resolution approach, and the CFPB.

2. We are on the right path to ending "too-big-to-fail," thanks in large part to the SPOE strategy. The SPOE approach successfully minimizes uncertainty about which firms could expect to be rescued in case of financial distress. By offering clear procedures for resolving failed institutions, the SPOE strategy removes a major source of risk from the financial sector.

3. Consumers are better protected now. The CFPB has quickly increased the safeguards for consumers by taking steps to remove misleading financial products from the market place and crafting rules on qualified mortgages and money transfers. However, the agency can and should improve, particularly in the areas of supervision and interagency cooperation.

4. Financial stability must be balanced with economic growth. The system must be safe, but this should be achieved in a way that does not excessively constrain efficiency and economic growth. Policymakers must be careful to encourage financial stability without discouraging healthy economic activity.

5. Corrections and adjustments to Dodd-Frank would improve its performance. Although Dodd-Frank has been largely successful in stabilizing the financial sector, it still needs to be fine-tuned. Stronger efforts should be made in the areas of regulatory consolidation, FSOC authority, and OFR independence. The Volcker Rule requirements should be clarified for banks to make implementation easier and more efficient. The new limitations on Federal Reserve and FDIC crisis authority should be eliminated for the sake of financial stability. The subjectivity surrounding SPOE and firm expectations should be rectified and the tensions between living will requirements and the SPOE approach should be resolved. Finally, regulators should carefully monitor areas where it is "too soon to tell" what the effects of changes are, so they can react swiftly and appropriately to new developments.

APPENDIX

In 2013, the Bipartisan Policy Center conducted an informal survey of selected thought leaders with regulatory, industry, consumer advocacy, and academic backgrounds.[18] BPC asked them which provisions in Dodd-Frank were most likely to reduce or raise systemic risk. A summary of their responses is shown in figure A1.

---

18. Although the survey was sent to a broad range of respondents from varying backgrounds, it was not conducted using a random or scientific sample nor were its findings reweighted.

Figure A1. Results of BPC Survey Regarding Effectiveness of Dodd-Frank to Reduce Systemic Risk

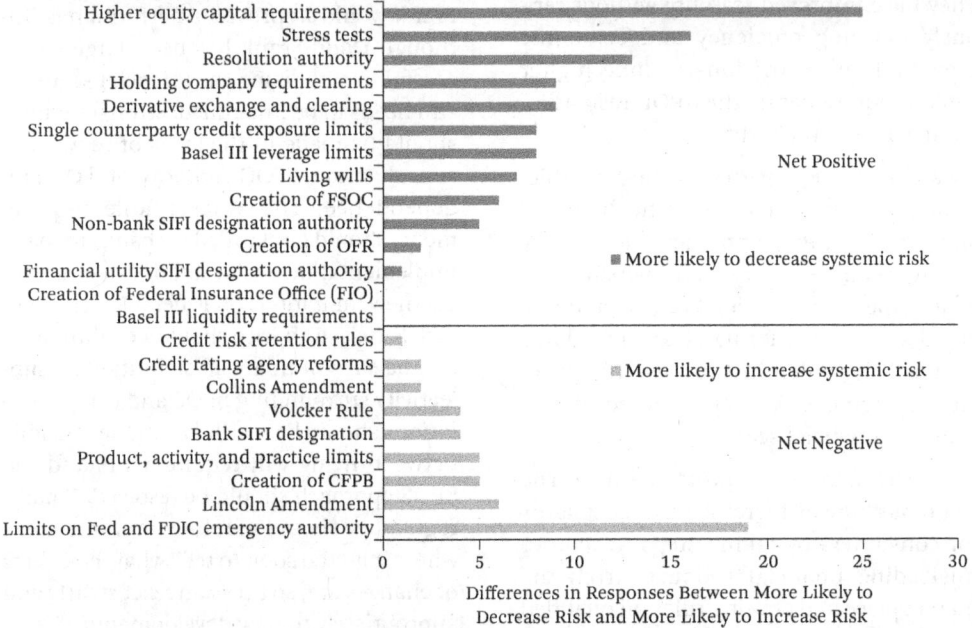

Source: Dugan, Fisher, and Muckenfuss 2014.

REFERENCES

Ambrose, Brent W., Yiying Cheng, and Tao-Hsien Dolly King. 2013. "Financial Crisis and Temporary Liquidity Guarantee Program: Their Impact on Fixed-Income Markets." *Journal of Fixed Income* 23(2). Available at: http://ssrn.com/abstract=2240018; accessed July 11, 2016.

Baily, Martin Neil, and Doug Elliott. 2014. "How Is the System Safer? What More Is Needed?" In *Across the Great Divide: New Perspectives on the Financial Crisis*, edited by Martin Neil Baily and John Taylor. Stanford, CA: Hoover Institution Press.

Bair, Sheila C. April 30, 2010. "Comments on Senate Agriculture Committee's OTC Derivatives Bill." Congressional Record Online through the Government Publishing Office. Available at: www.gpo.gov/fdsys/pkg/CREC-2010-05-04/html/CREC-2010-05-04-pt1-PgS3065-2.htm; accessed June 27, 2016.

Bank for International Settlements. 2014. "The Financial System at a Crossroads." Available at: http://www.bis.org/publ/arpdf/ar2014e6.htm; accessed June 27, 2016.

Basel Committee on Banking Supervision. 2012. "Basel III Capital Adequacy Accord." Slide presentation. Available at: www.slideshare.net/pankajbaid17/basel-iii-capital-adequacy-accord; accessed June 27, 2016.

Bernanke, Ben S. 2015. "Fed Emergency Lending." *Ben Bernanke's Blog*, December 3, 2015. Available at: www.brookings.edu/blogs/ben-bernanke/posts/2015/12/03-fed-emergency-lending; accessed June 6, 2016.

Bianco, Katalina M. 2013. "Consumer Financial Protection Bureau: Evolution of a New Agency with Emerging Regulatory Framework." Alphen aan den Rijn, The Netherlands: Wolters Kluwer. Pp. 1, 4. Available at: http://news.wolterskluwerlb.com/media/CFPB-White-Paper.pdf; accessed June 6, 2016.

Board of Governors of the Federal Reserve System, Federal Deposit Insurance Corporation, and Office of the Comptroller of the Currency. 2014. "Agencies Adopt Enhanced Supplementary Leverage Ratio Final Rule and Issue Supplementary Leverage Ratio Notice of Proposed Rulemaking." Press release. Available at: www.occ.gov/news-issuances/news-releases/2014/nr-ia-2014-54.html; accessed June 27, 2016.

Cecchetti, Stephen G. and Kermit L. Schoenholtz. 2014. "Higher Capital Requirements Didn't Slow the Economy." *Money and Banking*, December 15. Available at: www.moneyandbanking.com/commentary/2014/12/15/higher-capital-requirements-didnt-slow-the-economy; accessed June 27, 2016.

Cox, James D., Jonathan R. Macey, and Annette L. Nazareth. 2013. "A Better Path Forward on the Volcker Rule and the Lincoln Amendment." Stanford, Calif.: Hoover Institution, Bipartisan Policy Center. Available at: http://bipartisanpolicy.org/wp-content/uploads/sites/default/files/files/A%20Better%20Path%20Forward%20on%20the%20Volcker%20Rule%20and%20the%20Lincoln%20Amendment_Final.pdf; accessed June 6, 2016.

De Nederlandsche Bank. 2014. "TLAC Reduces Risks of Global Systemic Banks." DNBulletin. Available at: www.dnb.nl/en/news/news-and-archive/dnbulletin-2014/dnb315049.jsp; accessed June 27, 2016.

Dugan, John C., Peter R. Fisher, and Cantwell F. Muckenfuss III. September 2014. "Responding to Systemic Risk: Restoring the Balance." Washington, DC: Bipartisan Policy Center. Available at: http://cdn.bipartisanpolicy.org/wp-content/uploads/sites/default/files/BPC%20Responding%20to%20Systemic%20Risk.pdf; accessed June 27, 2016.

Federal Deposit Insurance Corporation. 2013a. "Temporary Liquidity Guarantee Program." Available at: https://www.fdic.gov/regulations/resources/TLGP/index.html; accessed June 27, 2016.

Federal Deposit Insurance Corporation. 2013b. "The Resolution of Systemically Important Financial Institutions: The Single Point of Entry Strategy." *Federal Register* 78(243): 76614. Available at: www.fdic.gov/news/board/2013/2013-12-10_notice_dis-b_fr.pdf; accessed June 6, 2016.

Federal Reserve Board. n.d. "Reporting forms: Y-9C." Available at: www.federalreserve.gov/apps/reportforms/reporthistory.aspx?sOoYJ+5BzDal8cbqnRxZRg==; accessed June 6, 2016.

Financial Crisis Inquiry Commission. 2011. *The Financial Crisis Inquiry Report: Final Report of the National Commission on the Causes of the Financial and Economic Crisis in the United States*, p. 196. Available at: http://www.gpo.gov/fdsys/pkg/GPO-FCIC/pdf/GPO-FCIC.pdf; accessed June 27, 2016.

Financial Stability Board. 2015a. FSB Issues Final Total Loss-Absorbing Capacity Standard for Global Systemically Important Banks." Press release. Available at: www.financialstabilityboard.org/wp-content/uploads/20151106-TLAC-Press-Release.pdf; accessed June 27, 2016.

Financial Stability Board. 2015b. "Global Shadow Banking Monitoring Report 2015." Available at: http://www.fsb.org/wp-content/uploads/global-shadow-banking-monitoring-report-2015.pdf, accessed July 11, 2016.

Financial Stability Oversight Council. 2014. "Transparency Policy for the Financial Stability Oversight Council." Available at: www.treasury.gov/initiatives/Documents/FSOCtransparencypolicy.pdf; accessed June 27, 2016.

———. 2015. "Supplemental Procedures Relating to Nonbank Financial Company Determinations." Available at: www.treasury.gov/initiatives/fsoc/designations/Documents/Supplemental%20Procedures%20Related%20to%20Nonbank%20Financial%20Company%20Determinations%20-%20February%202015.pdf; accessed June 27, 2016.

Fischer, Rick, and Eric Rodriguez. 2013. "The Consumer Financial Protection Bureau: Measuring the Progress of a New Agency." Washington, D.C.: Bipartisan Policy Center. Available at: http://bipartisanpolicy.org/wp-content/uploads/sites/default/files/BPC%20Consumer%20Financial%20Protection%20Bureau%20Report.pdf; accessed June 27, 2016.

Guynn, Randall. 2014. "Framing the TBTF Problem: The Path to a Solution." In *Across the Great Divide: New Perspectives on the Financial Crisis*, edited by Martin Neil Baily and John Taylor. Stanford, Calif.: Hoover Institution Press.

Haldane, Andrew G. 2012. "The Dog and the Frisbee." Speech given at the Federal Reserve Bank of Kansas City's Thirty-Sixth Economic Policy Symposium, "The Changing Policy Landscape." Jackson Hole, Wyoming (August 31). Available at: https://www.kansascityfed.org/publicat/sympos/2012/ah.pdf; accessed June 27, 2016.

Herring, Richard. 2010. "Wind-Down Plans as an Alternative." In *Ending Government Bailouts as We Know Them*, edited by Kenneth Scott, George Shultz, and John Taylor. Stanford, Calif.: Hoover Institution Press.

Institute of International Bankers. 2014. "Re: FDIC's Notice and Request for Comments on the Resolution of Systemically Important Financial Institutions: The Single Point of Entry Strategy." Comment letter to the Federal Direct Insurance Corporation (FR Docket No. 2013-30057). Available at: www.fdic.gov/regulations/laws/federal/2013/2013-single-point-entry-c_13.pdf; accessed June 27, 2016.

International Swaps and Derivatives Association. 2013. "Non-Cleared OTC Derivatives: Their Importance to the Global Economy." Available at: www2.isda.org/attachment/NTM2OA==/Non-Cleared%20OTC%20Derivatives%20Paper.pdf; accessed June 27, 2016.

International Swaps and Derivatives Association. 2014a. "The Value of Derivatives." Available at: www2.isda.org/attachment/NjQ3Mw==/ISDA%20FINAL%202014.pdf; accessed June 27, 2016.

International Swaps and Derivatives Association. 2014b. "Major Banks Agree to Sign ISDA Resolution Stay Protocol." Available at: www2.isda.org/news/major-banks-agree-to-sign-isda-resolution-stay-protocol; accessed June 27, 2016.

Jackson, Howell E., and Stephanie Massman. 2017. "The Resolution of Distressed Financial Conglomerates." *RSF: The Russell Sage Journal of the Social Sciences* 3(1). doi: 10.7758/RSF.2017.3.1.03.

Katz, Diane. 2013. "The CFPB in Action: Consumer Bureau Harms Those It Claims to Protect." Washington, D.C.: Heritage Foundation. Available at: www.heritage.org/research/reports/2013/01/the-cfpb-in-action-consumer-bureau-harms-those-it-claims-to-protect; accessed June 27, 2016.

Klein, Aaron, and Peter Ryan. 2014. "What to Watch for: The G20 Brisbane Summit and Putting an End to Too-Big-to-Fail." Stanford, Calif.: Hoover Institution, Bipartisan Policy Center. Available at: http://bipartisanpolicy.org/blog/what-to-watch-for-the-g20-brisbane-summit-and-putting-an-end-to-too-big-to-fail; accessed June 27, 2016.

Kohn, Donald. 2014. "Federal Reserve Independence in the Aftermath of the Financial Crisis: Should We Be Worried?" Washington, D.C.: Brookings Institution, Hutchins Center on Fiscal and Monetary Policy. Available at: www.brookings.edu/~/media/research/files/papers/2014/01/16%20federal%20reserve%20independence%20financial%20crisis%20kohn/16%20federal%20reserve%20independence%20financial%20crisis%20kohn.pdf; accessed June 27, 2016.

Kroszner, Randall S. 2015. "Future of Banks: Will Commercial Banks Remain Central to the Financial System?" Paper presented at the Atlanta Federal Reserve's Twentieth Annual Financial Markets Conference, "Central Banking in the Shadows: Monetary Policy and Financial Stability Postcrisis." Atlanta (March 30 to April 1, 2015). Available at: https://www.frbatlanta.org/-/media/Documents/news/conferences/2015/0330-financial-markets/papers/kroszner-randall.pdf; accessed June 27, 2016.

Merkley, Jeff, and Carl Levin. 2013. "Merkley and Levin Statement on Final Volcker Rule." Available at: http://www.merkley.senate.gov/news/press-releases/merkley-and-levin-statement-on-final-volcker-rule; accessed June 27, 2016.

Miedema, Douwe. 2014. "US Regulator Estimates Volcker Rule's Cost for Bank." Reuters, March 20. Available at: www.reuters.com/article/2014/03/20/us-banks-volcker-costs-idUSBREA2J25O20140320; accessed June 27, 2016.

Neiman, Richard H., and Mark Olson. 2014. "Dodd-Frank's Missed Opportunity: A Road Map for a More Effective Regulatory Architecture." Washington, D.C.: Bipartisan Policy Center. Available at: http://bipartisanpolicy.org/wp-content/uploads/2014/12/BPC-FRRI-Dodd-Franks-Missed-Opportunity-April-2014.pdf#page=60; accessed June 27, 2016.

Skeel, David A., Jr. 2014. "Single Point of Entry and the Bankruptcy Alternative." In *Across the Great Divide: New Perspectives on the Financial Crisis*, edited by Martin Neil Baily and John B. Taylor. Stanford, Calif.: Hoover Institution Press.

Stewart, James B. 2011. "Volcker Rule, Once Simple, Now Boggles." *New York Times*, October 21.

U.S. Department of the Treasury. 2008. "Blueprint for a Modernized Financial Regulatory Structure." Available at: www.treasury.gov/press-center/press-releases/Documents/Blueprint.pdf; accessed June 27, 2016.

——. 2009. "Financial Regulatory Reform, a New Foundation: Rebuilding Financial Supervision and Regulation." Available at: www.treasury.gov/initiatives/Documents/FinalReport_web.pdf; accessed June 27, 2016.

Volcker, Paul A. 2010. "Volcker Letter to Lawmakers Opposing Amendments to Audit the Fed." *Wall Street Journal*, May 6.

Warren, Elizabeth. 2007. "Unsafe at Any Rate." *Democracy: A Journal of Ideas*, no. 5 (Summer). Available at: www.democracyjournal.org/5/6528.php?page=all; accessed June 27, 2016.

Winkler, Andy, Ben Gitis, and Sam Batkins. 2014. "Dodd-Frank at 4: More Regulation, More Regulators, and a Sluggish Housing Market." Washington, D.C.: American Action Forum. Available at: http://americanactionforum.org/research/dodd-frank-at-4-more-regulation-more-regulators-and-a-sluggish-housing-mark; accessed June 6, 2016.

The Resolution of Distressed Financial Conglomerates

HOWELL E. JACKSON AND STEPHANIE MASSMAN

One of the most elegant legal innovations to emerge from the Dodd-Frank Wall Street Reform and Consumer Protection Act of 2010 is the FDIC's single-point-of-entry (SPOE) initiative, whereby regulatory authorities will be in a position to resolve the failure of large financial conglomerates (corporate groups with regulated financial entities as subsidiaries) by seizing a top-tier holding company, downstreaming holding-company resources to distressed subsidiaries, wiping out holding-company shareholders while simultaneously imposing additional losses on holding-company creditors, and allowing the government to resolve the entire group without disrupting the business operations of operating subsidiaries (even those operating overseas) or risking systemic consequences for the broader economy.

Although there is much to admire in the creativity underlying SPOE, the approach's design also raises a host of novel and challenging questions of implementation. This chapter explores a number of these questions and elaborates upon the following points. First, in contrast to traditional approaches to resolving financial conglomerates, SPOE is premised on the continued support of all material operating subsidiaries, thereby potentially extending the scope of government support and thus posing the possibility of mission creep and expanded moral hazard. Second, SPOE contemplates the automatic downstreaming of resources to operating subsidiaries in distress, but effecting that support is likely to be more difficult than commonly understood. If too much support is positioned in advance, there may be inadequate reserves at the top level to support a single subsidiary that gets into an unexpectedly large amount of trouble. Alternatively, if too many reserves are retained at the holding-company level, commitments of subsidiary support may not be credible (especially to foreign authorities) and it may become difficult legally and practically to deploy those resources in times of distress.

SPOE is most easy to envision operating in conjunction with the FDIC's expanded authority under its Orderly Liquidation Authority (OLA) established under Title II of the Dodd-Frank Act. However, the act's preferred regime for resolving failed financial conglomerates is the U.S. Bankruptcy Code (where Lehman was resolved) and not OLA. Several complexities could arise were a bankruptcy court today called upon to implement an SPOE resolution plan. While many legal experts are working on legislative proposals to amend the Bankruptcy Code to facilitate SPOE resolutions, there are a number of legal levers that federal authorities could deploy under current law to increase the likelihood that the SPOE strategy could be effected through traditional bankruptcy procedures. The task would be challenging and would require considerable advanced planning. But there are substantial benefits to be had from taking steps now to increase the likelihood that the bankruptcy option represents a viable and credible alternative for effecting SPOE transactions without resort to OLA and Title II of the Dodd-Frank Act.

Keywords: financial conglomerates, single point of entry, orderly liquidation, authority, Dodd-Frank Act, financial regulation

Howell E. Jackson is James S. Reid, Jr., Professor of Law at Harvard University. **Stephanie Massman** received her J.D. from Harvard Law School in 2015.

In writing this chapter, we benefitted from helpful comments and suggestions from Michael Barr, Donald Bernstein, Mark Roe, David Skeel, Margaret Tahyar, Paul Tucker, Eli Vonnegut, and two anonymous referees. Direct correspondence to: Howell E. Jackson at hjackson@law.harvard.edu, Griswold 510, Harvard Law School, Cambridge, MA 02138; and Stephanie Massman at smassman@jd15.law.harvard.edu.

If a regulatory Rip Van Winkle had wandered up into the Catskill Mountains in the summer of 1996 only to emerge again twenty years later, in 2016, much of the supervisory landscape would appear strange and unfamiliar: stress tests and centralized clearing of derivatives; new regulatory actors in the form of the Financial Stability Oversight Council and the Consumer Financial Protection Bureau; and billion-dollar enforcement settlements with major financial conglomerates announced with startling frequency. But one of today's leading regulatory challenges, the resolution of financial conglomerates, would strike a familiar note for our latter-day Knickerbocker. That topic was also a source of intense controversy in policy circles back in the 1990s, and one that echoes (albeit imperfectly) in today's debates over regulatory reform and the resolution of financial conglomerates.

The problem of failed financial conglomerates emerged on the national stage back in 1984, when the Federal Deposit Insurance Corporation (FDIC) intervened with an investment in the Continental Illinois holding company. Although shareholders of the holding company were largely wiped out, the FDIC's action saved holding-company bondholders from suffering losses and prompted scathing criticisms that the FDIC had overstepped its statutory mandate to protect insured depositors. A few years later, the Federal Reserve Board raised industry hackles in advancing a new "source-of-strength" doctrine under which bank holding companies might be called upon to infuse capital into failing bank subsidiaries, undermining (in the view of industry opponents) principles of limited liability and corporate separateness within financial groups. Statutory amendments adopted through the Federal Deposit Insurance Corporation Improvement Act (FDICIA) of 1991 partially codified the source-of-strength doctrine and when the Bank of New England failed in the early 1990s, the FDIC was able to invoke these new FDICIA provisions to lay claim to conglomerate-wide resources to reduce the corporations' resolution costs.[1]

To a person steeped in banking policy debates of the 1990s, the emerging policy debates over the Orderly Liquidation Authority (OLA) of Title II of the Dodd-Frank Act along with the FDIC's single-Point-of-entry (SPOE) proposal would seem eerily familiar.[2] Under this new resolution strategy, the FDIC is to be appointed receiver of the top-tier U.S. holding company of a systemically important financial institution (SIFI).[3] As contemplated under SPOE, the receivership would absorb losses incurred by all material operating subsidiaries and then recapitalize those subsidiaries as needed with a combination of holding company reserves and the conversion of pre-positioned intracorporate loans. Federal authorities would then organize a new bridge holding company to receive assets from the receivership estate. As envisioned, these transferred assets would consist primarily of the receivership's investments in recapitalized downstream subsidiaries and other healthy affiliates. The equity holders' and unsecured creditors' claims of the old holding company would remain in the receivership, bearing losses according to their priority. These claims would either be wiped out or satisfied through a securities-for-claims exchange, giving these claimants equity in the new bridge holding company. In theory, this approach would ensure that the original holding company's stockholders and debt holders will absorb all losses of the consolidated company while transferring support down to operating subsidiaries to allow operations (most significant, their systemically

---

1. The source-of-strength doctrine was ultimately fully codified in the Dodd-Frank Act. For an analysis of these doctrinal developments in the 1990s, see Jackson 1994. For more recent and comprehensive work tracing the history of the source-of-strength doctrine through the Dodd-Frank Act, see Lee 2012a and Lee 2012b.

2. See sections 201–14 of the Dodd-Frank Wall Street Reform and Consumer Protection Act of 2010. For an overview of OLA and the ways in which it differs from traditional bankruptcy procedures, see Massman 2015.

3. Request for Comments regarding Resolution of Systemically Important Financial Institutions: The Single Point of Entry Strategy, 78 Fed. Reg. 76,614, 76,616 (December 18, 2013). There is an extensive literature on SPOE from early articulations in Guynn 2012 through more complete accounts such as Bovenzi, Guynn, and Jackson 2013, PwC 2015, and Skeel 2014. For a critical perspective, see Kupiec and Wallison 2014.

important operations) to continue uninterrupted during the course of resolution.

The downstreaming of holding-company resources to cover losses in failing subsidiaries in the first phase of SPOE is just what the Federal Reserve Board's original source-of-strength doctrine was designed to accomplish. And to the extent that the SPOE proposal would pass those losses along to holding-company creditors, that is also consistent with the Fed's original source-of-strength approach in that the assignment of losses to holding company creditors corrects the most widely criticized aspects of the FDIC's bailout of Continental Illinois bondholders.

To be sure, the logic underlying OLA and SPOE is not exactly the same as the original source-of-strength doctrine and related innovations of the 1990s. There are two key differences: First, those earlier interventions were primarily aimed at reducing resolution costs and solving a moral-hazard problem. To the extent that holding companies allowed their subsidiaries to take on financial risks and incur financial losses, the source-of-strength doctrine forced the holding companies to internalize those losses, thereby correcting incentives and diminishing moral hazard concerns. While OLA-SPOE also has these salutary incentive effects, the structure is centrally designed to address systemic risk concerns (whether of contagion or interconnectedness) by creating a structure that permits the downstream subsidiaries of financial conglomerates to remain in business and honor their creditors (especially runnable short-term creditors). Although fear of subsidiary creditors' losses had clearly been a concern underlying the FDIC's intervention in Continental Illinois, avoiding losses to subsidiary creditors was not central to other major bank-holding company failures following the Continental Illinois failure (such as MCorp or Bank of New England), where the principal operating subsidiaries were clearly insolvent and were headed into receivership and supervisory mergers. The primary government concern in both cases was to pass along the cost of those failures to holding-company creditors so as to minimize government losses and establish appropriate incentives for the future.

Another key difference between the FDIC's new SPOE approach and its pre–Dodd-Frank Act precursors is the extent to which regulatory authorities are doing extensive advanced planning to facilitate orderly resolution in times of financial crisis. Although in former times financial holding companies, at least in the United States, were subject to consolidated capital requirements and activities restrictions, little else was required to ensure that these holding companies would retain adequate additional reserves to come to the assistance of their banking subsidiaries in times of distress. The source-of-strength doctrine was largely limited to the assets that happened to be available when subsidiary banks failed, and little regulatory attention was given to making sure that a financial conglomerate organized itself in a manner that would facilitate downstreaming value to insured banks when crises rose. In the wake of Dodd-Frank, however, considerable advanced planning is required. In particular, systemically important financial institutions are required to develop acceptable living wills (resolution plans) with considerable attention to precise steps that will be taken to resolve the firm in an orderly manner, should financial difficulties arise. (Barr, Jackson, and Tahyar 2016, ch. 9.3.)

Drawing on insights into the regulation of financial conglomerates developed in the debates of the 1990s, this chapter explores a series of questions about the evolving SPOE strategy that U.S. authorities are currently developing. Our goal is to highlight several important challenges to successful implementation of the SPOE strategy, as well as a handful of possible solutions available under existing statutory standards. This entails some discussion of technical issues of banking regulation and bankruptcy law, but we attempt to keep these technical references to a minimum and to stress the overarching policy issues. We also do not attempt to replicate an excellent growing literature proposing ways in which the federal Bankruptcy Code could be amended to accommodate SPOE resolutions.[4]

---

4. See Skeel 2014; Huertus 2015; Jackson 2015; Lee 2015; and Skeel 2016.

The article has four main parts. The first part explores a series of design challenges in the SPOE approach to resolving financial conglomerates, challenges that the emerging literature on the subject (much of it quite illuminating) has failed to examine adequately. The second section sketches out what is emerging as a complex choice architecture for the resolution of financial conglomerates, a choice architecture that is built around a statutory presumption that financial conglomerates will be resolved through traditional bankruptcy procedures and not the highly publicized OLA procedures established in Title II of the Dodd-Frank Act. The third part focuses on a central, but potentially problematic, resolution alternative: application of SPOE resolution under the existing federal Bankruptcy Code. Here we flag several key difficulties and suggest potential workarounds under current law. In the last section we conclude with some preliminary thoughts on deeper issues of regulatory philosophy underlying emerging approaches to the resolution of financial conglomerates.

DESIGN CHALLENGES OF IMPLEMENTING SPOE

One of the striking features of the SPOE approach is the extent to which it expands the scope of holding-company support obligations beyond what was contemplated in prior holding-company resolution strategies under the original source-of-strength doctrine and related policies (Baer 2014; Kupiec 2015). This point is illustrated in figure 1. The diagram on the top highlights the direction of financial support envisioned in the resolution of financial conglomerates in the 1990s. At that time, the sole recipient of capital contributions was the failing commercial bank within a corporate group. Support could be drawn from the holding company (under the sources-of-strength doctrine) or from healthy FDIC-insured depository institutions (via the cross-guarantee provisions of FDICIA). But the beneficiary was invariably an FDIC-insured banking subsidiary.

Under SPOE, however, the scope of coverage is potentially much broader. With its emphasis on preserving the going-concern value of all material operating affiliates, SPOE contemplates support being given to insolvent affiliates other than FDIC-insured depositories. Reflecting the runs, similar to bank runs, experienced at Lehman Brothers and Bear Stearns as well as the systemically destabilizing difficulties of AIG's financial affiliates operating out of London, SPOE contemplates a much wider umbrella of support, as illustrated by the diagram on the bottom of figure 1. The credibility of providing this support is especially important for distressed affiliates located offshore, as it is this commitment that is necessary to dissuade foreign authorities from seizing the assets of impaired foreign affiliates in order to protect creditors in local markets. Indeed, one of the major advantages of SPOE is that the approach is designed to centralize resolution efforts in the home country of internationally active financial firms, where the holding company will presumably be located, and to forestall the dissipation of going-concern value that took place in the aftermath of the Lehman Brothers failure, when innumerable local receiverships were declared.[5]

The Pre-Positioning Dilemma

The expansive scope of SPOE support obligations, combined with the importance of making credible commitments to foreign authorities, generates a "pre-positioning" dilemma for regulatory authorities. To appreciate this dilemma, one must consider the intracorporate connections between financial holding companies and their downstream subsidiaries. Figure 2 illustrates these relationships. As contemplated under SPOE, holding companies are to have three kinds of assets: direct equity investments in subsidiaries, loans to subsidiaries, and reserves of some sort (presumably

---

5. Among the early proponents of the SPOE approach were senior officials at the Bank of England who recognized the potential value of the strategy for the successful resolution of global firms. See Tucker 2014. For additional background on collaborations between the FDIC and Bank of England officials as early as 2012, see Skeel 2016.

Figure 1. Comparison of Prior Resolution Strategies and SPOE

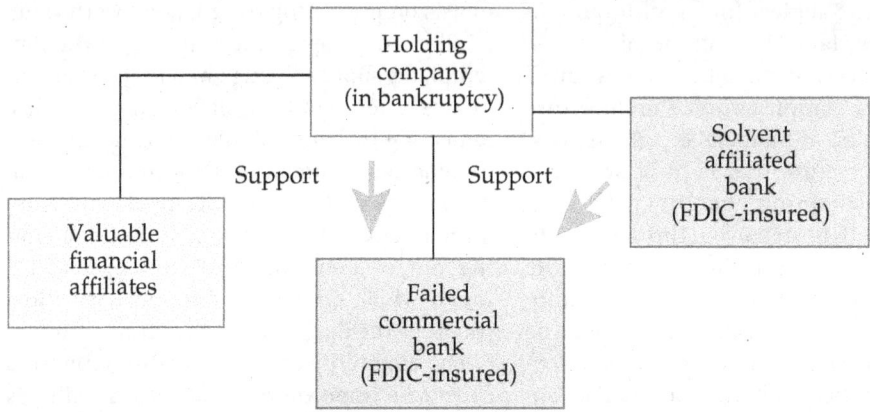

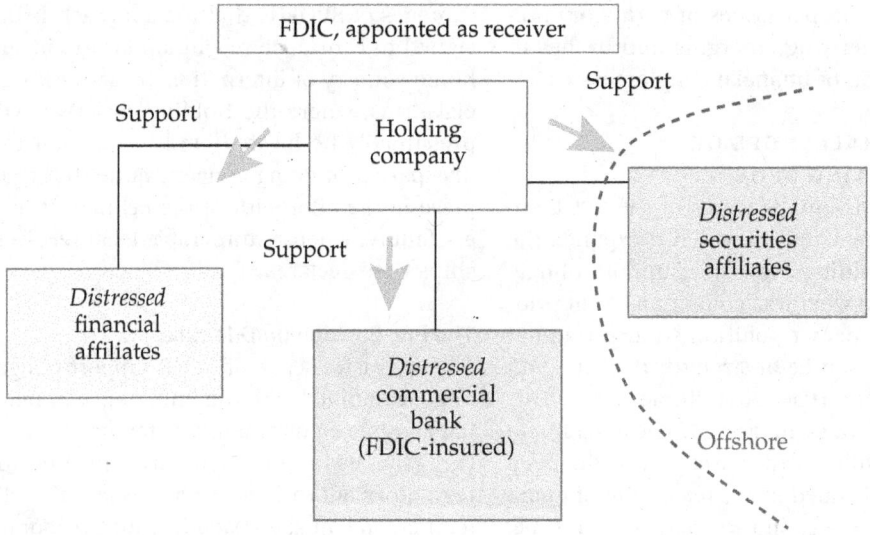

Source: Authors' compilation.

marketable securities or cash equivalents).[6] When a subsidiary suffers serious losses, holding-company equity in that subsidiary will immediately be written down. To recapitalize the subsidiary, the holding company (or perhaps receiver for the holding company) will

---

6. This intracorporate support—whether equity, loans, or holding company reserves—is commonly called internal total loss-absorbing capital (or internal TLAC) and is distinguished from external TLAC, which consists of both equity and potentially loss-absorbing debt, mostly commonly, at least for U.S. financial conglomerates, to be issued at the holding-company level. See Federal Reserve Board Notice of Proposed Rulemaking on Total Loss-Absorbing Capacity, 80 Fed. Reg. 24,926 (November 30, 2015). See also Financial Stability Board 2014. For additional insights on TLAC, see Gordon and Ringe 2015.

Figure 2. Intracorporate Connections Under SPOE

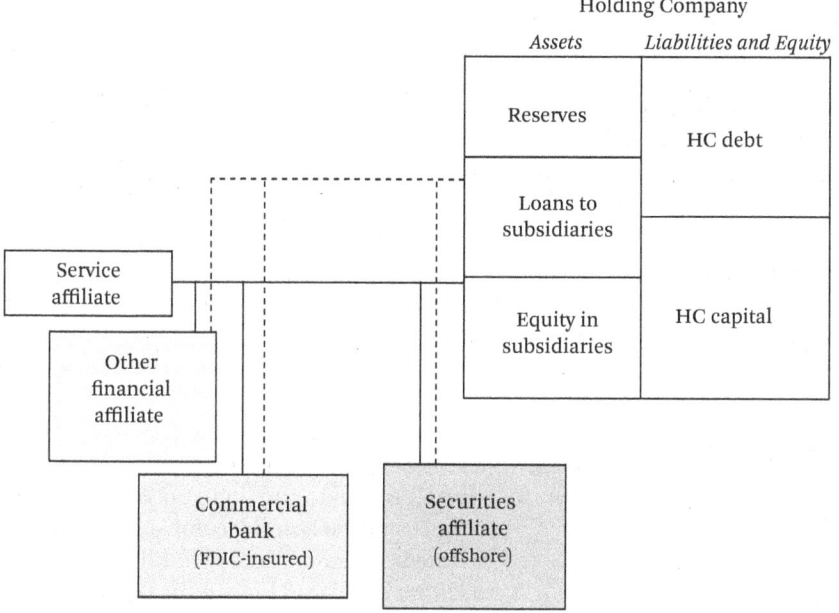

Source: Authors' compilation.

convert some or all of the holding company's intracorporate loans to the subsidiary into equity and, if necessary, also make additional contributions to the subsidiary from holding company reserves. In that manner, the holding company will downstream value to distressed subsidiaries, effectively recapitalizing the subsidiaries and transferring the subsidiary losses to holding company shareholders and debt holders.

Developing effective design standards for these intracorporate connections poses numerous challenges. One, which has already received considerable attention, is figuring out how much additional funding capacity financial conglomerates should maintain at the holding company level. In the parlance of figure 2, that means how large the reserves and loans to subsidiaries must be to ensure that the holding company has the financial wherewithal to absorb subsidiaries' losses in times of financial distress. (The whole purpose of the SPOE exercise is to provide for the automatic recapitalization of operating subsidiaries without resort to new capital raising in the midst of a financial crisis). But a separate and related design question for SPOE concerns how much holding-company capacity should be "pre-positioned" into operating subsidiaries in the form of loans or similar forms of intracorporate indebtedness.[7] The advantage of the pre-positioning through loans is that pre-positioned assets are potentially more credible commitments with a higher degree of automaticity. Indeed, the goal of the pre-positioning is to provide foreign regulators with ex ante assurance that the holding company will indeed bear losses (Tucker 2014). But the drawback is that pre-positioned assets reduce holding-company flexibility in times of financial stress. If, as is almost always the case, losses are not evenly distributed across operating subsidiaries, an SPOE based on fully pre-positioned financial assets may not be effec-

---

7. From a theoretical perspective, it might seem irrelevant whether reserves are held at the holding-company level or downstream in the form of a loan that will be forgiven in the event of subsidiary losses, but there are important differences in terms of credibility, especially when the subsidiary is located in other jurisdictions. Reserves that must be downstreamed in times of crisis have less "automaticity" than do loans that are automatically forgiven upon the occurrence of some predetermined trigger.

tive.[8] On the other hand, an SPOE strategy with 100 percent of holding-company resources held in reserve may not provide a credible commitment to subsidiary creditors or foreign regulators supervising offshore affiliates.[9] Recognizing the multitude of potential problems associated with each of the foregoing strategies, the Federal Reserve Board and the FDIC have advocated for a mixed approach, noting that firms should "not rely exclusively on either full pre-positioning or [assets held by] the parent" and that they "should not assume that a net liquidity surplus at one material entity can be moved to meet net liquidity deficits at other material entities or to augment parent resources" (Bank of America 2016, 7; see also Morgan Stanley 2016, 7 and JPMorgan Chase 2016, 8, for substantially similar language).

Anticipating Uncooperative Holding Company Creditors

Whatever share of holding-company resources are pre-positioned in operating subsidiaries, the execution of the SPOE strategy is quite possibly going to prompt hostile and aggressive reactions from holding-company creditors. (One of the lessons of prior experiences with the source-of-strength doctrine is that holding-company creditors invariably resist the downstreaming of value to failed subsidiaries, and bankruptcy courts, oriented as they are toward the protection of creditors rights, have been surprisingly hostile to intracorporate transfers of value to distressed subsidiaries in manners inconsistent with ordinary principles of limited liability [Lee 2012a, 2012b].) At the very least, resistance of this sort is something that authorities need to consider carefully in their review of living wills designed to facilitate resolutions under SPOE.

To understand the perspective of creditors in such situations, consider again the relationships illustrated above in figure 2. Even with a total loss of the holding company's equity investment in subsidiaries, holding-company creditors could still look to the company's reserves and loans to subsidiaries as sources of repayment if the holding company were to go into receivership. Those creditors may well be better off if the holding-company receiver de-

---

8. Creative lawyering could no doubt come up with potential solutions for the pre-positioning dilemma. One possible solution, to be used only in times of financial crisis, might be to allow holding companies to use intracorporate loans made to healthy subsidiaries as an asset that the holding companies could contribute to unhealthy subsidiaries with higher-than-anticipated losses. Assuming regulatory authorities would allow for such a transfer, this approach would increase the available resources that the holding company could transfer to unhealthy subsidiaries and diminish some of the rigidity of pre-positioning. Whether foreign officials would find such a capital contribution (with its intracorporate exposures) as credible as a cash infusion or the forgiveness of parent-to-subsidiary debt is an open question. Consider, for example, if serious losses occurred at a London affiliate of a major U.S. insurance company. How much confidence would it give a Bank of England official to be told that the loan subsidiary was to be recapitalized with a loan to an affiliate in Nebraska (which, as far as the BoE official knows, may also be facing serious losses)? Furthermore, there is the risk that defensive "ring-fencing" by foreign jurisdictions could prevent the free flow of assets from an affiliate in one jurisdiction to an affiliate in another jurisdiction in times of financial distress. In their review of 2015 living wills, the Federal Reserve Board and the FDIC specifically identified ring-fencing as a significant threat to a successful SPOE bankruptcy strategy. See JPMorgan Chase 2016, 6. See also Morgan Stanley 2016, 5; Bank of America 2016, 6.

9. One measure that has been suggested to enhance the credibility of unfunded commitments to shore up foreign affiliates would be to provide some sort of security for the commitment, likely in the form of pledging marketable securities held at the holding-company level. Putting to one side the question of whether such pledges could be enforced efficiently in the midst of financial stress, this approach is really a variant of pre-positioning, with the actual downstreaming of assets to be executed at the very last minute. One issue that would need to be sorted out is how rights under such pledge agreements would be shared, if at all, among different affiliates. And if shared, the question to consider is whether such sharing would constitute a credible commitment for foreign authorities likely operating under the fog of market instability. As discussed in note 11, one advantage of providing security to subsidiary-support commitments is that it diminishes the likelihood that other holding-company creditors could object to the holding company's honoring commitments in times of financial stress.

clined to downstream reserves to distressed subsidiaries or converted loans into equity investments as the SPOE strategy contemplates.[10] If the past is any guide, counsel for those creditors might easily characterize efforts to downstream value to distressed subsidiaries as fraudulent conveyances or possibly improper preferences in violation of traditional bankruptcy principles.[11] Even though objections of this sort may not prove persuasive to the FDIC acting as receiver under OLA as established by Title II of the Dodd-Frank Act, the arguments may be much more compelling to a bankruptcy court judge coming to the transaction with a quite different professional orientation (with a focus on protecting creditor rights).

As is explored in more detail below, Congress amended the Bankruptcy Code back in 1990 to clarify the rights of the Federal Reserve Board to enforce its source-of-strength doctrine against bankruptcy estates, creating with section 365(o) of the Bankruptcy Code a priority for capital commitments to FDIC-insured bank subsidiaries. Even with this priority in place, federal authorities have not always been able to prevail against objections of holding-company creditors in bankruptcy proceedings (Lee 2012b). Moreover, nothing in the Dodd-Frank Act created similar privileges for obligations to support nonbanking affiliates of failing financial conglomerates, as contemplated under SPOE. Accordingly, it does not seem to be much of a stretch to predict that holding-company creditors may contest efforts to downstream value within failing financial conglomerates to the extent that those transactions diminish the returns to creditors.

Reorienting Regulators from the Right-Hand Side of the Holding Company Balance Sheet

A third and more subtle reorientation of the SPOE strategy is a shift in regulatory attention away from the right-hand side of the holding-company balance sheet. As described earlier, the source-of-strength doctrine was primarily intended to solve a moral-hazard problem by imposing losses on holding-company creditors and shareholders. The idea was that enhanced financial obligations of financial conglomerates would force holding-company stakeholders to monitor more carefully the activities of the entire corporate group, especially FDIC-insured bank subsidiaries. For conglomerates that did not credibly rein in the riskiness of their activities, the capital market would impose an ex ante penalty in the form of higher interest charges and costs of capital. But the work was being done, by and large, on the right-hand side of the holding-company balance sheets.

The SPOE strategy retains this logic, but also imposes considerable attention on the left-hand side of the holding-company balance sheet. One of the manifestations of this change is our earlier discussion of pre-positioning assets in intracorporate loans. Among other things, the SPOE strategy requires regulatory authorities to consider how holding-company reserves will be deployed. But SPOE's interventions into the left-hand side of holding-company balance sheets go considerably be-

---

10. To be sure, the inverse may also be true. There may well be circumstances where the holding company (and its creditors) will be better off if the holding company downstreams value to a subsidiary in difficulty. Preservation of going-concern value in the subsidiary's business may warrant additional investments, and in some cases the holding company may have guaranteed the debt of subsidiaries such that the financial fate of the two entities is already bound together. Effective supervision of subsidiary activities and higher subsidiary capital requirements will also make it more likely that preservation of the subsidiary is in the best interest of holding-company creditors. The interesting case, however, and the case that has occurred with some frequency in the past is when the subsidiary really is a black hole and holding-company creditors would much prefer to cut off support and retain assets at the holding-company level.

11. Note that if holding-company commitments were secured by marketable assets at the holding-company level (see note 9), these concerns would be much diminished. The characterization of downstream transfers as a preference could also be resisted if there were no preexisting commitment to make those transfers. But, as discussed earlier (see note 7), precommitments to support material subsidiaries, particularly those located in foreign jurisdictions, are central to the SPOE strategy.

yond pre-positioning (Jarque and Price 2015). The entire exercise of drafting and reviewing resolution plans for systemically important financial conglomerates is based on the assumption that regulatory authorities should have a say in the organization of financial conglomerates, including which activities should be located in which legal entities and the degree of complexity permitted in intracorporate servicing arrangements.[12] To be sure, this analysis and preparation is well intended: its goal is to make financial conglomerates more resolvable in times of financial stress. This advanced planning may be essential to the operation of a workable SPOE strategy. But it takes regulatory authorities substantially deeper into the business decisions of financial groups than was ever the case with old-fashioned—that is, pre–Dodd-Frank Act—limitations on permissible holding-company activities under the Bank Holding Company Act of 1956. This expansion of the regulatory perimeter also carries with it risks of its own, including both additional costs from regulatory oversight and the potential that supervisors may be fostering identical business strategies and hence correlated risks across the financial services sector.[13]

MULTIPLICITY OF RESOLUTION ALTERNATIVES AND COMPLEXITY OF CHOICE ARCHITECTURE

One of the somewhat surprising artifacts of the Dodd-Frank Act reforms is that the United States now has in place a multiplicity of resolution alternatives for financial conglomerates. The United States now maintains at least three basic systems for resolving large financial groups, each with a distinctive structure (see table 1).

The traditional approach to the failure of a financial group ("option C" in table 1), contemplates the primary resolution's being conducted at the level of the regulated subsidiary by financial supervisors, and the holding-company liquidation being handled separately under the federal Bankruptcy Code. This is how the FDIC deals with routine failures of banks and thrifts, with the regulated depository typically being taken over by another bank through a purchase-and-assumption transaction or some other form of deposit transfer. Although a holding-company bankruptcy may also occur, it traditionally has been of only marginal importance unless the holding company happens to have substantial resources, which banking authorities might try to claim in a source-of-strength proceeding to mitigate FDIC losses. Prior to the Dodd-Frank Act, option C was the only resolution approach available and it was the manner in which the Lehman resolution was handled: SIPC dealt with the receivership of the firm's flagship broker-dealer and the bankruptcy court handled the holding-company bankruptcy. Option C remains available today, and is, as a practical matter, the only alternative available for small bank holding companies (those with less than $50 billion in assets) and is, at least in our view, the presumptive approach even for bank holding companies above the $50 billion asset level but beneath the threshold of a major regional with more than $100 billion of assets.

Title II of the Dodd-Frank Act creates a new resolution alternative, the Orderly Liquidation Authority (OLA), for large financial conglomerates (Massman 2015). As implemented under the FDIC's SPOE approach and as outlined earlier in this paper, the alternative (option A in table 1) envisions the appointment of the FDIC as receiver of the holding company and the continued conduct of business without formal receivership proceeds of major operating subsidiaries. Thus, in contrast with option C, this alternative has no receiverships imposed at the subsidiary level. Rather, the resolution is con-

---

12. Many of the of the FDIC and Federal Reserve Board's objections to recent living wills relate to concerns that the firms in questions had not sufficiently simplified their organizational structures. See Board of Governors of the Federal Reserve System and Federal Deposit Insurance Corporation 2016.

13. The impact of adopting credible living wills comes, of course, on top of many substantive changes in legal requirements, many required by the Dodd-Frank Act, that also increase the cost of operations, require the maintenance of greater liquidity reserves and capital cushions, and potentially reduce further variations in business strategies across financial conglomerates.

Table 1. Overview of Resolution Alternatives and Their (Presumptive) Application

	Resolution Alternatives		
	Option A	Option B	Option C
Type of Institution	Orderly Liquidation Authority Under Applied with Respect to Holding Company Under SPOE Approach via Title II of DFA	SPOE-Like Resolution of Holding Company Under Bankruptcy Code	Primary Resolution Through Receiverships of Regulated Subsidiaries with Holding Companies Resolved Under Bankruptcy Code, as Needed
Bank holding companies			
G-SIBs	Possible	Supposedly presumptive	Unlikely
Major regional BHCs	Possible	Supposedly presumptive	Conceivable
BHCs with assets less than $50 billion	Unlikely	Possibly, but unlikely	Presumptive
Nonbank SIFIs designated by FSOC	Possible	Supposedly presumptive	Unlikely
Other large undesignated financial firms	Available, but unlikely	Available, but unlikely	Presumptive

Source: Authors' compilation, based on Dodd-Frank Act reform.

ducted at the holding-company level. Under the Dodd-Frank Act, OLA is technically available for all bank holding companies, as well as nonbank SIFIs previously designated by FSOC under Title I of the Dodd-Frank Act and certain other large undesignated financial firms meeting statutory standards. The procedures are not available unless determinations of systemic risk are made by the secretary of the treasury, a supermajority of the board of governors of the Federal Reserve, and a qualifying vote of one other body (either the FDIC, SEC, or FIO, depending on the financial conglomerate in question).

Located somewhat awkwardly between options A and C is an SPOE-like resolution of a financial holding company under the federal Bankruptcy Code. Unlike option A, this approach does not contemplate the use of OLA and Title II of the Dodd-Frank Act. Unlike option C it does not contemplate the appointment of receivers for regulated subsidiaries. Rather, option B envisions the use of an SPOE resolution but under the federal Bankruptcy Code, with bankruptcy judges presiding, as opposed to the FDIC under OLA.[14] But unlike option A resolutions, this resolution approach is not governed by the special receivership pow-

14. Opinions as to the viability of option B have evolved over time, but many experts working in the field seem now to be squarely of the view that such resolutions are possible. See, for example, Guynn 2014, who states, "Whether it is possible to execute SPOE recapitalization under the Bankruptcy Code was once an open question. It is now understood to be possible" (296). Considerable attention, however, is also being devoted to amending the Bankruptcy Code to make it easier to implement SPOE resolutions. See sources cited in note 4. As a practical matter, SIFIs and their counsel are under considerable pressure to characterize their Option B plans as credible, as that is a statutory requirement for such plans under the Dodd-Frank Act. See next note.

ers of Title II and does not have access to the sort of debtor-in-possession financing (DIP financing) that the Orderly Liquidation Fund (OLF) provides for OLA proceedings.

Although option B is something of an ungainly creature, it is the resolution alternative that the Dodd-Frank Act establishes as statutorily presumptive for most major financial conglomerates in the United States. In preparing the living wills that Title I of the Dodd-Frank Act requires of all major bank holding companies (those with more than $50 billion in assets) and FSOC-designated nonbank SIFIs (such as AIG, Prudential Insurance, and GE Capital), firms are called upon to make representations that the resolution plans could be credibly executed under the federal Bankruptcy Code.[15] These plans, which would also provide a blueprint for the FDIC were it to resolve the firm under OLA in a Title II (option A) proceeding, contemplate an SPOE approach with resolution at the holding-company level and the continued conduct of business at the operating-subsidiary level.[16]

To summarize, the U.S. legal system currently allows for three quite different approaches to the resolution of financial conglomerates. The law does not offer clear guidance as to which approach to take in which circumstances, but we believe that one can discern presumptive approaches with more and less plausible alternatives for different classes of firms. Our interpretation of this logic (summarized in table 1) proceeds as follows.

Start with the smaller bank holding companies defined as systemically important under the Dodd-Frank Act: those with more than $50 billion in assets but falling beneath the level of a major regional. These firms are subject to the living will requirements of Title I of the Dodd Frank Act and enhanced supervision of various sorts, yet their failure is unlikely to pose systemic risk concerns of the sort required for designation under option A or even the SPOE-treatment associated with option B. Our presumption therefore is that these kinds of institutions would be treated with the FDIC's traditional bank resolution procedures under option C. If these firms get into trouble, absent dire market conditions, there will be no grounds for taking the somewhat extraordinary and costly steps associated with holding-company resolution procedures rather than simply disposing of regulated subsidiaries through sale to other acquiring firms in standard purchase-and-assumption transactions.[17]

Another group of firms that we would presumptively locate in option C are large financial conglomerates that lack bank affiliates (and hence bank-holding company status) and that also have not been previously designated as systemically important by the FSOC. Although these firms could theoretically qualify for resolution under OLA, our suspicion is that federal authorities would be extremely reluc-

---

15. See section 165(d)(4)(B) of the Dodd-Frank Act: "[Each SIFI] shall resubmit [a] resolution plan within a time frame determined by the Board of Governors and the Corporation, with revisions demonstrating that the plan is credible and would result in an orderly resolution under title 11, United States Code, including any proposed changes in business operations and corporate structure to facilitate implementation of the plan." In their most recent assessments of living wills for a number of prominent systemically important firms, federal authorities expressly identified bankruptcy resolution plans as failing this credibility standard. See Board of Governors of the Federal Reserve System and Federal Deposit Insurance Corporation 2016. The precise bases of these findings have not been made public; the problems we identify and discuss in this chapter may well be part of the reasoning.

16. For an overview of how the FDIC might have made use of living wills in the application of an option A resolution of the Lehman Brothers collapse (if the Dodd-Frank Act had been in effect at the time), see Federal Deposit Insurance Corporation 2011.

17. There have, apparently, been some limited examples of traditional bank failures that have been resolved at the holding-company level through section 363 transactions and prepackaged reorganizations. See Christiansen et al. 2014. Arguably, these approaches represent an option D, holding-company resolution outside of SPOE. Interestingly, at least two major conglomerates—Wells Fargo and Bank of New York Mellon—have submitted living wills contemplating option C resolutions. See PwC 2015.

tant to invoke Title II of the Dodd-Frank Act without the preparations associated with FSOC designations under Title I. These firms would not have submitted living wills or otherwise provided regulatory authorities with the kinds of information on corporate structures and resolution plans required of other designated nonbank SIFIs. They would, moreover, not have the capital structures or intracorporate connections required to effect an SPOE disposition. And, just as these firms would not be prepared for option A's resolution under OLA, they would be unprepared for option B's SPOE-like resolution under the federal Bankruptcy Code, making option C their default alternative and presumptive approach. To be sure, should a truly large financial firm not designated as an SIFI—perhaps a firm on the scale of Berkshire Hathaway—encounter sudden and unexpected financial distress, one could imagine federal authorities attempting option A or option B on the fly, but it would be a treacherous path to negotiate and one likely to end in a messy ditch.

What remains then are a core group of systemically important institutions, already subject to enhanced prudential oversight by the Federal Reserve Board with resolution plans already prepared and reviewed by regulatory authorities. These firms are also the ones with potential systemic consequences in the event of failure. Under the Dodd-Frank Act, resolution of this group is, in theory, presumed to take place under option B, but these entities are also the firms for which Title II was created and it is at least conceivable that they would be resolved under option A. It is also possible, at least for the major regionals, that federal authorities might conclude that systemic risks were not at issue and traditional resolution procedures (that is, option C) would be appropriate. This decision would be largely in the hands of the FDIC, which has the power to force option C by imposing a receivership on FDIC-insured bank subsidiaries that become insolvent. And the imposition of such a receivership would (absent extraordinary efforts) violate the principles of SPOE and render both option A and option B unavailable.

The more interesting decision point, however, is between the use of option A or option B for a bank holding company that was arguably systemically important or a nonbank SIFI previously designated by the FSOC. A number of factors could militate against invoking the much-publicized OLA powers of Title II for even these firms. To begin with, there are numerous congressional statements indicating that OLA should be used only as a resolution alternative of last resort. The sentiments underlying these statements resonate with ongoing concerns in some quarters that OLA resolutions are synonymous with federal bailouts (presumably as a result of the availability of federal funding via the OLF).[18] Conceivably such concerns could lead critical officials, perhaps a new secretary of the treasury acting on campaign commitments to address issues regarding "too big to fail" entities, not to turn one of the keys necessary to invoke OLA. But even less dogmatic government officials might choose not to invoke option A if the failure in question was seen as idiosyncratic and not as the consequence of widespread market disruptions. Certainly, there would be advantages in demonstrating that option B offered a feasible

---

18. The authors of the Dodd-Frank Act went to considerable lengths to structure OLF funding so as to limit its use to liquidity funding and to minimize the risk of losses to the federal government. In extreme cases, the measures could include special assessments on other financial institutions to prevent any costs being passed on to taxpayers. See Massman 2015. However well intended those measures may be, there remains some risk that regulatory authorities in the future will underestimate the losses of a failing firm in times of financial stress and choose not to invoke recoupment options (possibly out of legitimate fears of pro-cyclical effects). Commentators have widely different assessments of the likelihood of OLF funding being deployed in such a manner as to constitute a shareholder or creditor bailout at the expense of taxpayers. Nevertheless, invoking Title II and tapping into the OLF clearly pose some degree of political risk, even if federal funds are ultimately repaid and all losses are imposed on private parties. In addition, legal challenges to Title II procedures remain a possibility. See Merrill and Merrill 2014. Together these factors along with other considerations noted in the main text could steer government officials away from option A and toward option B if the path forward seemed clear.

means to resolve large financial firms in a nondisruptive, SPOE-like manner under the ordinary rules of bankruptcy and without reliance on OLA's special rules and access to federal funds. While one might imagine a failing conglomerate preferring to have its resolution assigned to the more robust regime that OLA creates, public authorities might well conclude that invoking option B in appropriate cases would generate fewer moral-hazard concerns and less political backlash down the road. It is, moreover, possible for regulatory authorities to begin an SPOE-like resolution under the federal Bankruptcy Code and then transfer it to OLA if difficulties arise as the proceedings develop. Accordingly, at least when financial markets are not in the midst of a September 2008–style freefall, option B may well turn out to be the resolution alternative of choice, even for systemically important firms. That is, of course, if option B can be turned into a viable alternative, the topic to which we now turn.

LIMITS OF THE EXISTING BANKRUPTCY CODE AND SOME PARTIAL SOLUTIONS (IN THE ABSENCE OF STATUTORY REFORM)

Resort to federal bankruptcy courts for the resolution of distressed financial companies in an SPOE-like transaction presents a number of potential challenges, many of which have been discussed in the rich body of literature on resolution planning under the Dodd-Frank Act. In our view, there are three critical issues as well as a larger background concern about the capacity of regulatory officials, notably the FDIC, to control resolution strategies in bankruptcy courts. We will begin with a summary of each of these issues and then offer a set of regulatory solutions, all of which entail significant advance planning on the part of regulatory authorities, some of which is already under way. In general, what we suggest in the following pages is the creative, but hopefully not implausible, invocation of existing regulatory authority on the part of the FDIC and Federal Reserve Board to prepare financial conglomerates for SPOE-like resolution under the Bankruptcy Code. Critically, none of these solutions relies upon the amendment of current law and therefore do not depend upon the vagaries of current legislative processes in the United States. But they do necessitate careful attention to how living wills and other resolutions plans are structured well before a firm encounters financial difficulties.

Cross-Defaults on Qualified Financial Contracts with Affiliated Entities

An initial and significant problem in resolving financial conglomerates under the Bankruptcy Code is the possibility that counterparts on derivatives contracts and other qualified financial contracts (QFCs) will exercise existing contractual rights to close out their transactions with affiliated entities, precipitating a run on the corporate group and dissipating going-concern value that the SPOE approach is designed to preserve. The Dodd-Frank Act addressed this problem, at least in part, by staying such actions with respect to counterparties of affiliates of conglomerates being resolved under OLA proceedings. The Dodd-Frank Act stay, however, does not extend to firms being resolved under the Bankruptcy Code, that is, to the option B alternative (Roe and Adams 2015). Moreover, there exists a separate concern that the Dodd-Frank Act stay may not be enforced by courts in foreign jurisdictions. Over the past few years, federal authorities have attempted to address both of these issues by encouraging amendments to the International Swaps and Derivatives Association (ISDA) master agreements.[19] But the ISDA reforms represent an imperfect solution, being of a voluntary nature and not necessarily covering all QFCs that could run in the face of financial distress. Accordingly, under current law there is a risk that federal authorities may not be able to prevent a run by the derivatives counterparties of affiliates of holding companies that are resolved under the federal Bankruptcy Code. Thus, the

---

19. For an overview of these reforms, see Geen et al. 2015 and Sidley Austin LLP 2015. While the revisions of the ISDA master agreements were clearly taken with the encouragement of regulatory authorities, the reforms were not the product of a legal requirement and, as is explored in note 20, do not necessarily cover all contexts or counterparties that regulatory authorities would want to stay in the face of an Option B resolution.

risk of QFC runs with an option B resolution is potentially substantial.

Resistance by Holding-Company Creditors and Bankruptcy Courts to the Recapitalization of Operating Subsidiaries

As explained, one of the lessons of regulatory efforts to enforce the source-of-strength doctrine has been persistent resistance of holding-company creditors and bankruptcy courts to transactions that recapitalize downstream subsidiaries but impair the value of holding-company creditors. Under plausible interpretations of the Bankruptcy Code, downstreaming reserves or converting intracorporate loans into equity can be characterized as impermissible preferences or fraudulent conveyances. The FDIC and the Federal Reserve Board identified problems in the resolution plans of all six firms submitting SPOE-based 2015 resolution plans. For future plans, those firms were directed to "include a detailed legal analysis of the potential state law and bankruptcy law challenges and mitigants to the planned provision of [capital and liquidity to subsidiaries prior to bankruptcy] . . . In identifying appropriate mitigants, [the firms were directed to] . . . consider the effectiveness, alone or in combination, of a contractually binding mechanism, pre-positioning of financial resources in material entities, and the creation of an intermediate holding company" (Bank of America 2016, 12; see also State Street 2016, 13; Morgan Stanley 2016, 10; Citigroup 2016, 7; Goldman Sachs 2016, 10–11; and JPMorgan Chase 2016, 17–18 [all substantially similar language]).

Even though comparable issues theoretically arise with financial conglomerates resolved under OLA proceedings of Title II, a critical difference is that the FDIC will exercise considerable control over the operation of OLA receiverships, whereas the bankruptcy court will preside over option B resolutions. While a bankruptcy court judge might ultimately accept the downstream of holding-company value that SPOE strategy contemplates, experience with the source-of-strength doctrine suggests the process will not be easy, adding another mark against the bankruptcy court alternative as opposed to OLA under Title II.[20]

Lack of DIP Financing

The third commonly cited concern with bankruptcy court resolutions for financial conglomerates is the lack of an obvious source of DIP financing. Whereas, with OLA, the FDIC receiver has statutory authority to tap into the Treasury's OLF with ample sources of liquidity, there is no comparable source of public financing for financial conglomerates resolved under the federal Bankruptcy Code. This is, indeed, a critical distinction between the two processes and is one of the reasons that OLA is denominated by some as a form of federal bailout, whereas resolution under the federal Bankruptcy Code is not. As set forth in the margins, this characterization of OLA can be understood in a number of ways,[21] but for current purposes what is important to note is that the OLF is not available to financial conglomerates resolved under option B, and many informed experts are concerned that private sources of DIP financing would be either unavailable or at least inadequate for major financial conglomerates forced into a bankruptcy under the federal Bankruptcy Code.[22] Even if runs by counterpar-

---

20. For a review of legal challenges to the source-of-strength doctrine, see Lee 2012b. Conceivably, the courts would be less resistant to the doctrine in light of the Dodd-Frank Act's statutory codification, but that remains a source of uncertainty.

21. As discussed in note 18, one characterization is based on an assessment that, notwithstanding statutory restrictions, OFL funds might ultimately be used to support shareholders and creditors at the expense of taxpayers. Another and more extreme position characterizes the use of any sort of government funding, even for liquidity purposes on terms that would satisfy traditional lender-of-last-resort support, as constituting a form of government bailout. Those adopting the latter position implicitly object to any sort of government financing for financial firms in periods of financial stress, even perhaps access to the discount window or traditional lender-of-last resort activities.

22. For a thorough discussion of this issue, see Skeel 2015. It is telling that all six of the firms submitting SPOE-based 2015 resolution plans faced either deficiency or shortcoming notices with regard to their models and

ties on derivative transactions with affiliates were somehow addressed, financial conglomerates in bankruptcy could still encounter the runoff of substantial amounts of other short-term liabilities and would require substantial liquidity support at the holding-company level, support that would be difficult to obtain from private sources, especially in periods of financial distress.

Lack of Expertise in and Advanced Planning by Bankruptcy Courts
A final and more generalized concern about reliance on bankruptcy courts to resolve financial conglomerates sounds in institutional competence. The best articulation of this perspective comes from a paper by FDIC officials several years ago explaining why OLA procedures would have been much more effective in dealing with the insolvency of Lehman Brothers in September of 2008 than the bankruptcy court actually was. Among other differences, "The Orderly Liquidation of Lehman Brothers Holdings Inc. under the Dodd-Frank Act" (Federal Deposit Insurance Corporation 2011) focused on the bankruptcy court's very limited understanding of Lehman when the company was forced into bankruptcy and on the incapacity of the parties to line up immediate DIP financing to stabilize operations and retain control over foreign affiliates. As portrayed in the article, the bankruptcy court lacked both the knowledge and the tools to move quickly enough to resolve a distressed firm on the scale of Lehman Brothers in a timely and orderly manner.

We will now sketch out a series of proposed solutions to these problems, starting with the general point about bankruptcy court capabilities and then working through the three more technical concerns summarized earlier. Our analysis here is necessarily skeletal, but it offers what might be seen as a more muscular regulatory posture that could, in our view, respond to the major limitations of bankruptcy resolution for financial conglomerates. A recurring theme in this discussion is the importance of federal authorities' deploying, well in advance of financial crises, a range of supervisory tools to shape the structure of resolution plans so as to maximize the likelihood of successful option B resolutions.

Proactive Planning for Option B Resolutions with an Option C Stick in the Closet

We start with a few preliminary points about the ability of federal regulators—most particularly the FDIC and Federal Reserve Board—to prepare in advance for the resolution of a major financial conglomerate in bankruptcy. In stark contrast with the actual Lehman filing, financial regulators in the post–Dodd-Frank Act environment will have done immeasurably more advanced planning than was possible in 2008. As long as the financial conglomerate either is regulated as a major bank holding company or has been designated by FSOC as systemically important, the firm will have produced—and both the FDIC and Federal Reserve Board will have critiqued and reviewed—a resolution plan with a detailed analysis of how the entity might be resolved in a bankruptcy proceeding. This should provide authorities with an in-depth understanding of the firm's operations and material subsidiaries as well as a game plan for resolving the firm through an SPOE-type resolution.[23]

---

processes for estimating liquidity needs for material operating entities during a resolution period. Only three firms faced problems with regard to the adequacy of their planned liquidity sources; however, it is possible that better modeling will demonstrate adequacy failures at the other firms as well.

23. The Federal Reserve Board and the FDIC have stressed bankruptcy preparedness in a firm's resolution plan by requiring governance mechanisms that provide for, among other things, the "timely execution of a bankruptcy filing and related pre-filing actions," including "any emergency motion[s] required to be decided on the first day of the firm's bankruptcy." See, for example, JPMorgan 2016, 17. Furthermore, the agencies have also encouraged firms to complete draft emergency motions and proposed forms of order. See, for example, Goldman Sachs 2016, 12 (draft emergency motion for continued stay relief under ISDA Resolution Stay Protocol). Such advanced planning for bankruptcy filings will likely allow firms to submit to the bankruptcy court the best information

Whereas Lehman Brothers entered bankruptcy in a chaotic environment with negligible advance planning and much uncertainty, future transactions of this sort will come after much groundwork has been laid. Indeed, if federal authorities choose to attempt option B—that is, if they impose an SPOE-like resolution in bankruptcy—they will be coming with a prepackaged plan to transfer valuable holding-company assets to a bridge holding company in something not too different from the increasingly popular section 363 transactions now routinely used in ordinary corporate reorganizations.[24] So, whereas the Lehman Brother's filing presented the bankruptcy courts with a very big headache, which has taken years to resolve, a future bankruptcy filing of a financial conglomerate will, if properly prepared, arrive as a neatly wrapped package, courtesy of the FDIC and Federal Reserve Board staff operating under powers granted them under Title I of the Dodd-Frank Act.

In addition, federal authorities will come with a fairly big stick with which to constrain holding-company creditors inclined to resist their prepackaged plan. If, as will almost always be the case, the distressed conglomerate includes a troubled regulated entity, an FDIC-insured bank or an SEC-registered broker-dealer or a major insurance company, authorities have the power to seize that subsidiary through nonbankruptcy processes, effectively moving resolution to option C. Federal authorities may not want to go down that route for reasons of systemic risk; option C will also be an extremely unattractive choice for holding-company creditors as it will likely dissipate going-concern value and further impair the interests of holding company creditors. As discussed in the next section, additional steps should be taken to weaken legal arguments that holding-company creditors might raise to resist option B resolution plans. The power of regulatory authorities to threaten subsidiary seizures should a bankruptcy court delay in approving a prepackaged resolution plan greatly enhances the ability of the FDIC and Federal Reserve Board to shape the course of an option B resolution. Their control is not formally the same as in OLA under option A, but in practice the differences may not be material.

Taking a More Muscular Approach to Cross-Defaults on QFCs

We now turn to technical challenges in resolving financial conglomerates through bankruptcy proceedings, starting first with the problem of cross-defaults on QFCs with holding-company affiliates. Recall that the problem here is twofold. First, the stay provisions written into Title II of the Dodd-Frank Act do not extend to firms being resolved in bankruptcy. Second, federal authorities' current approach to addressing the residual cross-default problems depends on voluntary adjustments to ISDA agreements, which entail a complicated process of negotiation among private parties, are not mandatory, and as currently drafted do not deal with all potential problems that could arise should a large and global financial conglomerate become financially distressed.

There is, however, a straightforward regulatory solution to the problem, which would solve all cross-default problems for both OLA and bankruptcy. Under section 165(b) of the Dodd-Frank Act, the board of governors can adopt "such other prudential standards as the Board of Governors ... determines are appropriate" for systemically important financial

---

possible as quickly as possible. Moreover, to the extent such drafts are made public, it would be both possible and beneficial for bankruptcy judges to familiarize themselves with such draft filings prior to an actual financial conglomerate's bankruptcy filing.

24. Arguably, the transfer would be even simpler than typical section 363 transfers because in an option B resolution it is contemplated that subsidiaries would be transferred to a new bridge holding company that would be controlled by a fiduciary for the sole benefit of the bankruptcy estate of the bankrupt holding company. There would arguably be no need to value the business as would be required if the sale were being made for consideration to a third party.

conglomerates.[25] The board of governors, could, in our view, use this authority to adopt a regulation that prohibits any affiliate of a systemically important financial conglomerate to enter into a QFC that grants counterparties authority to exercise any sort of right of acceleration or collateral call for a limited number of days following the filing of a resolution plan under either OLA or the federal Bankruptcy Code. These requirements need not be limited to the stay provisions of Title II of the Dodd-Frank Act and could be designed with an eye toward improving the viability of both option A and option B resolution alternatives. To be sure, the board would need to justify the terms of this requirement in its proposal and adopting release, but its legal authority is sufficient to prohibit any QFC terms that would impair the ability of federal authorities to use the resolution technique of their choice.[26]

In a similar vein, the Federal Reserve and the FDIC could use their authority to review and assess the credibility of resolution plans under section 165(d) of the Dodd-Frank Act to police the QFCs and other contractual commitments of systemically important financial conglomerates so as to override safe-harbor protections under the federal Bankruptcy Code or similarly spirited rules in other jurisdictions. To some degree, federal authorities may in effect be pursuing something like this approach in all but mandating that systemically important institutions accept reforms embodied in recent ISDA protocols.[27] But it remains available to government authorities to condition the determination of credibility of a firm's living will on the adoption of amended ISDA agreements that would increase the likelihood of option B resolutions.[28]

---

25. The text of the provision, with emphasis to key language added, reads:

(1) IN GENERAL.— (A) REQUIRED STANDARDS.—The Board of Governors shall establish prudential standards for nonbank financial companies supervised by the Board of Governors and bank holding companies described in subsection (a), that shall include—[capital, liquidity requirements, risk management requirements, resolution plan requirements, and concentration limits] . . .

(B) ADDITIONAL STANDARDS AUTHORIZED.—*The Board of Governors may establish additional prudential standards* for nonbank financial companies supervised by the Board of Governors and bank holding companies described in subsection (a), that include—
 (i) a contingent capital requirement;
 (ii) enhanced public disclosures;
 (iii) short-term debt limits; and
 (iv) such other prudential standards as the Board or Governors, on its own or pursuant to a recommendation made by the Council in accordance with section 115, determines are appropriate.

26. Among other things, such a regulatory requirement could address situations when an affiliated entity itself is in default on a swap agreement (something not currently covered in the ISDA reforms); see Roe and Adams 2015). In addition, it could impose restrictions on regulated entities doing business with other entities that have not already adopted the ISDA reforms. In fact, in the spring of 2016, the Board announced a proposed rule pursuant to its § 165(b) authority that would go a good deal of the way toward the goal of correcting the cross-default problem by effectively mandating adherence to the ISDA reforms or equivalent QFC contract amendments. See *Restrictions on Qualified Financial Contracts of Systemically Important U.S. Banking Organizations and the U.S. Operations of Systemically Important Foreign Banking Organizations; Revisions to the Definition of Qualifying Master Netting Agreement and Related Definitions*, 81 Fed. Reg. 29,169 (May 11, 2016) (proposing release). See also Davis Polk & Wardwell 2016. While we think this proposed rule represents a strong and important step in the right direction, there remain potential gaps in the proposal's coverage, and it does not necessarily cover all QFCs that could run in the face of financial distress.

27. See Sidley Austin LLP 2015.

28. In practice, federal authorities would likely need only to threaten such a formal requirement to lead ISDA to adopt further reforms. From the outside, it is difficult to ascertain how far federal authorities might wish to push

Clearing Potential Obstacles to Downstreaming Value and Intracorporate Loan Conversion

Federal authorities also have the capacity to address potential legal obstacles to downstreaming value or converting intracorporate loans in an SPOE-like resolution plan executed under the federal Bankruptcy Code.[29] As mentioned earlier, creditor resistance to the board's initial efforts to establish a holding-company source-of-strength doctrine back in the 1990s led Congress to amend the federal Bankruptcy Code with a new section, 365(o), which creates a priority for "any commitment [of a holding company placed in bankruptcy] to maintain the capital of an insured depository."[30] By its terms, this provision makes it possible for the FDIC to gain bankruptcy priority for a holding company's downstream commitments under an SPOE strategy with respect to insured depository institution subsidiaries. As a result, holding-company creditors in a bankruptcy proceeding should not be able to object to well-drafted holding-company obligations to FDIC-insured bank subsidiaries.

Section 365(o) can also be used to prioritize holding-company commitments to other material affiliates as well. Figure 3 illustrates a three-step process that federal authorities might use to extend section 365(o) priorities to holding-company commitments to other affiliates. First, in step A, the holding company would make a commitment to downstream value and convert intracorporate loans to other affiliates (for example, offshore securities affiliates) in accordance with the firm's SPOE resolution plan. Then, in step B, an FDIC-insured bank subsidiary would guarantee the holding company's commitment made in step A.[31] Finally, in step C, the holding company would make a 365(o) qualified commitment to maintain the capital of the FDIC-insured bank subsidiary for any losses caused as a result of that subsidiary's honoring the guarantee made in step B. With these three steps in place, holding-company commitments to all material affiliates can gain priority in bankruptcy. If holding-company creditors attempt to block the holding company's commitments to the securities affiliate in step A, the step B guarantee will kick in, and the holding company's step C prioritized commitment to its FDIC-insured subsidiary will come into play. The tactic is, admittedly, a bit artful, but hardly exceptional when compared to the sort of in-

---

ISDA reforms. Our point here is that these officials, especially if they work with foreign counterparts through the FSB, have considerable leverage to impose stay procedures that facilitate option B resolutions and they need not demur if private-party solutions are not fully satisfactory.

29. Another tactic, beyond those discussed in the text, would be to limit the range of liabilities that holding companies can incur and to make those that remain contractually subordinated to any holding-company obligations to support material subsidiaries. While unlikely to be foolproof, this preplanning could reduce the likelihood of effective challenges from bankruptcy creditors.

30. Section 365(o) of the Bankruptcy Code (emphasis to key language added) reads in full as follows:

> In a case under chapter 11 of this title, the trustee shall be deemed to have assumed (consistent with the debtor's other obligations under section 507), and shall immediately cure any deficit under, any commitment by the debtor to a Federal depository institutions regulatory agency (or predecessor to such agency) to maintain the capital of an insured depository institution, and any claim for a subsequent breach of the obligations thereunder shall be entitled to priority under section 507. This subsection shall not extend any commitment that would otherwise be terminated by any act of such an agency.

31. Section 23A of the Federal Reserve Act, which is designed to limit extensions of credit from FDIC-insured banks to affiliates, could present a technical impediment to this guarantee, and so the approach might require a waiver from regulatory authorities. See Section 608 of the Dodd-Frank Act, discussed in Barr, Jackson, and Tahyar 2016, 224–25. Although federal authorities may be disinclined to accept such proposal waivers as formal components of section 165(d) resolution plans, the capacity to provide such waivers might still remain available in times of financial stress if necessary to achieve an option B resolution.

Figure 3. Extending Section 365(o) Priorities to Holding Company Commitments to Other Affiliates

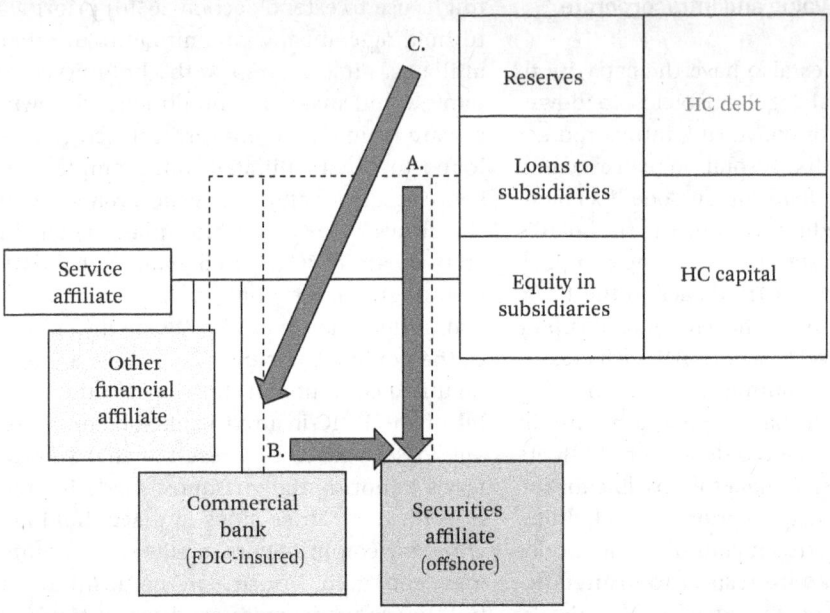

Source: Authors' compilation.

tracorporate commitments that one routinely encounters in modern finance.[32]

Providing Credible Liquidity in Bankruptcy
The final, and in some respects most challenging, technical obstacle to using bankruptcy proceedings to resolve distressed financial conglomerates is access to liquidity or DIP financing during bankruptcy proceedings. As other commentators have noted, the liquidity needs of major financial conglomerates in bankruptcy can be substantial (Skeel 2015). Although a number of revisions in ex ante liquidity regulation will likely ameliorate this problem—the imposition of an effective stay of QFCs for affiliate firms would also be helpful—federal authorities clearly need to have a credible strategy for providing liquidity for a distressed financial conglomerate before allowing that entity to seek protection under the federal bankruptcy code. In descending order of desirability, we offer four approaches.[33]

---

32. Conceptually, this three-step strategy makes the FDIC-insured affiliate the linchpin of holding-company commitments. In contrast to the traditional source-of-strength doctrine, where all commitments ran to the FDIC-insured entity, this approach creates commitments running out to other material affiliates. However, this reversal is necessary to make the SPOE strategy work. One needs a mechanism to ensure that holding-company commitments to all material subsidiaries are given priority in bankruptcy. Since section 365(o) as currently drafted only covers commitments to FDIC-insured bank subsidiaries, the bank subsidiary necessarily becomes the clearing house for holding-company support. Should federal authorities pursue this strategy, it may well be necessary for them to require nonbank SIFIs to create an FDIC-insured bank affiliate to make section 365(o) available in bankruptcy. Note that many of the proposals to amend the federal Bankruptcy Code to facilitate option B resolutions include amendments of section 365(o) to expand the scope of the priority along the lines this work around is designed to accomplish.

33. Again, several of these approaches might not be acceptable in formal section 165(d) resolution plans; nevertheless they would be available in an actual resolution under the federal Bankruptcy Code, when regulatory authorities would be shaping events.

1. Prepackaged DIP Financing

As discussed earlier, major holding company resolution in bankruptcy should look less like the chaotic Lehman Brother's filing of September 2008 and more like a routine section 363 transaction, planned well in advance. Just as the FDIC lines up bidders to take over typical bank failures in purchase-and-assumption transactions resolved over weekends, the FDIC could attempt to line up private DIP financing before a bankruptcy filing is made. Especially for distressed financial conglomerates resolved when not in an existential financial crisis, a private solution may well be viable, with sufficient advanced planning.

2. Broad-Based Lender-of-Last-Resort Programs and Facilities Available Under Section 13(3)

Under reforms of the Dodd-Frank Act, the Federal Reserve Board is precluded from using its section 13(3) powers to extend credit to insolvent borrowers, including borrowers in bankruptcy or in OLA proceedings under Title II of the Dodd-Frank Act.[34] So section 13(3) is likely not a viable source of liquidity for holding companies being resolved in the bankruptcy court. In unusual or exigent circumstances, however, the Federal Reserve Board retains its capacity to engage in lender-of-last-resort functions for appropriately collateralized credit under a "program or facility with broad-based eligibility." Such programs and facilities, to the extent they are implemented, should be open to operating subsidiaries of financial conglomerates under an SPOE approach, as these entities are supposed to remain solvent and viable.[35] Although it may be difficult to predict the availability of such broad-based programs far into the future, in the days and weeks immediately preceding an option B resolution, federal authorities will have a very good idea which broad-based programs and facilities the Federal Reserve Board is prepared to launch.[36] Thus, as the agencies finalize the terms of a prepackaged SPOE-style resolution effort to be run through bankruptcy court and approach private lenders to assemble a DIP financing consortium, they may well be able to factor in support likely to be forthcoming from the Federal Reserve Board under section 13(3). Such lending must have appropriate collateral. While any such credit will undoubtedly be subject to intensive after-the-fact review by Congress, the availability of broad-based credit facilities under section 13(3) can somewhat ameliorate the financing requirements for financial conglomerates being resolved under option B. By assuring private lenders that such Federal Reserve Board support is likely to be forthcoming, federal authorities may have an easier time lining up private DIP financing.

3. Liquidity Support Under the FDIC's Systemic Risk Exception

Another source of liquidity funding could come from the FDIC itself. Under 12 U.S.C. 1823(c)(4)(G), the FDIC has wide latitude "to take other action or provide assistance ... for the purpose of winding up the insured depository institution for which the Corporation has been appointed receiver" in the event that the action is necessary to avoid or mitigate "serious adverse effects on economic conditions or financial stability."[37] Provided certain proce-

---

34. See 12 U.S.C. §343.

35. To comply with the solvency requirement, care would need to be taken that any distressed operating subsidiary was recapitalized before the section 13(3) credit was extended. That is, the downstreaming of holding-company value and the conversion of intracorporate loans would have to occur first. Only after the recapitalization took place would section 13(3) be available to an affiliate that had been in financial distress. Healthy affiliates, in contrast, should be eligible before recapitalization.

36. For example, section 13(3) lending might be employed to support an specific asset class held by many entities including affiliates of a conglomerate in financial difficulties.

37. 12 U.S.C. 1823(c)(4)(G) reads as follows (emphasis to key language added):

(G) Systemic risk.—
 (i) Emergency determination by secretary of the treasury.— Notwithstanding subparagraphs (A) and

dural steps are taken—steps that are quite similar to the steps required to invoke OLA powers under Title II of the Dodd-Frank Act—the FDIC could use this power to extend credit to facilitate an SPOE-like transaction that transferred control to another party an FDIC-insured bank "in default" or "in danger of default." As a result of statutory amendments adopted as part of the Dodd-Frank Act, this emergency authority is only available "for the purpose of winding up the insured depository institution for which the [FDIC] has been appointed receiver." Accordingly, the FDIC would need to interpret the term "winding up" to include resolution under an SPOE-style plan executed at the holding-company level. In our view, this is a plausible reading, given the FDIC's past practices of resolving bank failures through holding-company vehicles.[38] Certainly, distress at the holding-company level will typically be thought to impair operations of a banking affiliate and, if banking affiliates had entered into the guarantee arrangement for nonbanking affiliates described earlier, the bank subsidiary would bear the risk of capital shortfalls of affiliated entities and be even more easily characterized as having to be wound up in an SPOE transaction.[39] One of the advantages of invoking the FDIC's emergency authority under section 1823(c)(4)(G) is that the provision includes an assessment mechanism to recoup any losses the FDIC suffers on such assistance through payments from other insured institutions. So, while the FDIC should only be using this power to provide liquidity support (as opposed to solvency coverage), the cost of error here would be borne by the financial services industry and not U.S. taxpayers.

4. Transfer to Title II and Access to OLF

A final solution, should other forms of liquidity prove inadequate, would be for the receivership to be transferred to an OLA proceeding under Title II of the Dodd-Frank Act, where funding under OLF would be available. Although such a transfer would represent a failure of the option B alternative, the availability of such a transfer makes option B a more viable approach. Having an OLA backup with OLF liquidity as a fallback position, federal authorities can accept some uncertainty as to whether other alternative forms of liquidity will prove adequate in a bankruptcy proceeding.

DIP financing for a major financial conglomerate in bankruptcy proceedings does pose genuine challenges for federal authorities contemplating an option B resolution, but the task is not quite as insurmountable as some analysts suggest. Especially with careful advanced planning, a number of sources of liquidity can be made available. And, of course, OLA remains available if matters do not pan out as planned.

(E), if, upon the written recommendation of the Board of Directors (upon a vote of not less than two-thirds of the members of the Board of Directors) and the Board of Governors of the Federal Reserve System (upon a vote of not less than two-thirds of the members of such Board), the Secretary of the Treasury (in consultation with the President) determines that

(I) the Corporation's compliance with subparagraphs (A) and (E) with respect to an insured depository institution for which the Corporation has been appointed receiver would have serious adverse effects on economic conditions or financial stability; and

(II) any action or assistance under this subparagraph would avoid or mitigate such adverse effects, the Corporation may take other action or provide assistance under this section for the purpose of winding up the insured depository institution for which the Corporation has been appointed receiver as necessary to avoid or mitigate such effects.

38. Federal authorities have been similarly creative in interpreting "liquidation" authority of title II of the Dodd-Frank Act to facilitate option A-style reorganizations. Again, this approach might require waivers of section 23A of the Federal Reserve Act in order to facilitate the transfer of funds from an FDIC-insured affiliate to other entities within the corporate group. See note 31.

39. If a bank subsidiary were forced into FDIC receivership in order to pursue this strategy, care would need to be taken not to extend even broad-based Federal Reserve credit under section 13(3), lest that provision's solvency requirement be violated. See note 35.

Figure 4. Anticipating Resolution Options from the Perspective of Holding Company Creditors

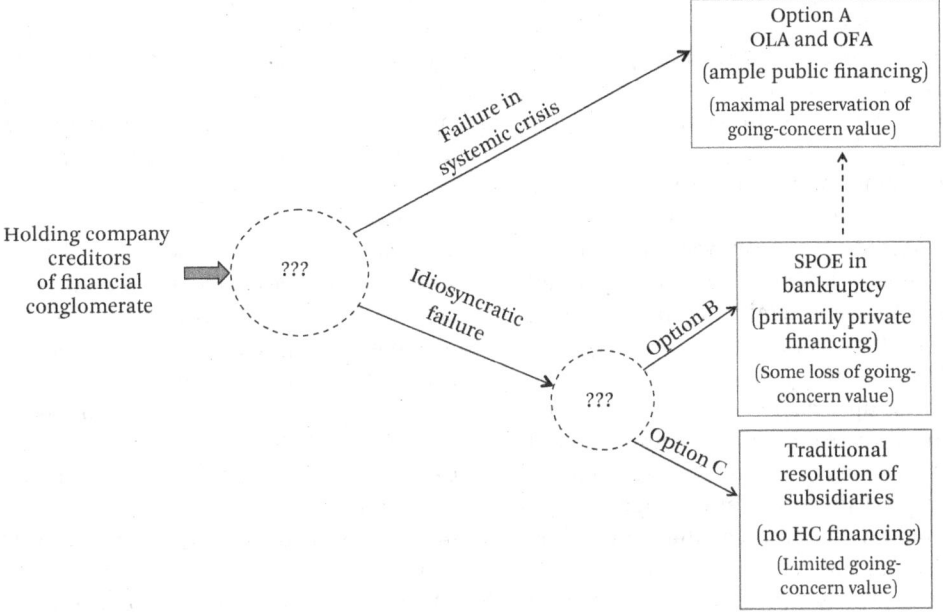

Source: Authors' compilation.

CONCLUDING THOUGHTS: PLANNING FOR TWO (OR MORE) FUTURE STATES OF THE WORLD

We conclude this essay with a few words explaining why we have made the effort to work through the major problems presented by an option B resolution strategy. The Dodd-Frank Act created with Title II and OLA an exceptional regulatory tool designed to be capable of resolving major financial conglomerates in periods of financial distress of the sort experienced in September 2008. In addition to granting federal regulatory authorities an unusual and far-ranging set of new powers, the legislation provided for Title II resolutions with a very generous line of credit from the U.S. Treasury. The existence of this line of credit makes some critics of the Dodd-Frank Act fear that Title II perpetuates "too big to fail" and exposes taxpayers to the cost of potential bailouts down the road. That is not the way Title II was intended to work, but the concerns expressed over OLA are not entirely fanciful. At a minimum, the presence of Title II and the OLF may lead some financial institutions and holding-company creditors to conclude that ample public funding will be available for distressed financial conglomerates. To the extent that market participants now assume that Title II is the only viable approach to resolving financial conglomerates, the market, including holding-company creditors, may well be assessing the riskiness of financial conglomerates under the assumption that public financing will be forthcoming in resolution and there will be a maximal preservation of going-concern value in the event of failure.

Consequently, it is highly desirable to open up some additional resolution alternatives—in the language of this essay, to make option B and perhaps even option C credible—both to address the problems of political economy and render market assessments of financial conglomerate distress a bit less sanguine. Figure 4 converts this point into a decision tree drawn from the perspective of holding-company creditors. As things currently stand, when holding-company creditors consider the likely outcome of the insolvency of a major financial conglomerate, they may well assume that the entity would be resolved under OLA and Title II of the Dodd-Frank Act. That means a resolution structure with access to ample public financing and a good chance to preserve going-concern value. To be sure, there remains some chance that the appropriate political triggers will not be pulled, but the received wisdom today in many circles is that neither option B nor option C is practical for a major financial firm, or that such a path threatens Lehman-like chaos.

If federal authorities implemented the reforms we have outlined, option B would become imaginable for even very large firms if they became insolvent in an idiosyncratic failure rather than a systemic crisis of the September 2008 variety. From the ex ante perspective of holding-company creditors, that change would open up a whole new branch of the decision tree, where the primary source of liquidity funding would come from private resources, and maximal preservation of going-concern value would not be assured. And, for creditors dealing with medium-sized financial firms that could conceivably be resolved through traditional resolution methods at the regulated subsidiary level, the potential for holding company creditor losses in the event of financial distress would be even more substantial.

The decision tree presented in figure 4 offers several insights. First, to the extent that one is concerned about the moral hazard effects of OLA and Title II, there is value in opening up other resolution alternatives that might be credible for at least idiosyncratic failures of financial firms. Devising resolution strategies that do not necessarily have access to public funding will increase the perceived ex ante risks to holding-company creditors and reduce the moral-hazard cost of OLA and Title II. This will be true even if a resolution only starts in federal bankruptcy and ultimately must be moved into a Title II proceeding (the dotted line in figure 4).

A secondary implication is that to improve the capacity and incentives of holding-company creditors to police the business strategies of financial conglomerates, regulators should err on the side of disclosing the potential costs to holding-company creditors in the event of resolution under all three options discussed in this essay. At least on an ex ante basis, authorities should attempt to increase the perceived likelihood of distressed firms' being handled under options B and C. If and when a financial crisis arises (or appears imminent), government officials may well need to pivot toward option A to forestall market volatility and destabilizing runs. But ex ante, the smart money is on making option B viable for as many financial conglomerates as possible. Presenting that case is the goal of this chapter.

REFERENCES

Baer, Gregory. 2014. "Regulation and Resolution: Towards a Unified Theory." *Banking Perspectives* 1 2014: 12–21. New York: The Clearing House.

Bank of America Corporation. 2016. Letter from Board of Governors of the Federal Reserve System and Federal Deposit Insurance Corporation in response to 2015 Resolution Plan Submission Letter (April 12). Available at: http://www.documentcloud.org/documents/2800591-Bank-of-America-Letter-20160413.html; accessed July 11, 2016.

The Bank of New York Mellon Corporation. 2016. Letter from Board of Governors of the Federal Reserve System and Federal Deposit Insurance Corporation in response to 2015 Resolution Plan Submission Letter (April 12). Available at: http://www.documentcloud.org/documents/2800590-Bank-of-New-York-Mellon-Letter-20160413.html; accessed July 11, 2016.

Barr, Michael S., Howell E. Jackson, and Margaret E. Tahyar. 2016. *Financial Regulation: Law and Policy*. St. Paul: Foundation Press.

Board of Governors of the Federal Reserve System and Federal Deposit Insurance Corporation. 2016. "Regulation Plan Assessment Framework and Firm Determinations." Washington, D.C.: Board of Governors of the Federal Reserve System and Federal Deposit Insurance Corporation.

Bovenzi, John F., Randall D. Guynn, and Thomas H. Jackson. 2013. "Too Big to Fail: The Path to a Solution." A Report of the Failure Resolution Task Force of the Financial Regulatory Reform Initiative of the Bipartisan Policy Center. Washington, D.C.: Bipartisan Policy Center.

Christiansen, Brian D., Van C. Durrer, Sven G. Mickisch, and William S. Rubenstein. 2014. "Chapter 11 Strategies Increasingly Appeal to Banks in Need of Recapitalization." *Skadden Insights*. New York: Skadden, Arps, Slate, Meagher & Flom LLP.

Citigroup Inc. 2016. Letter from Board of Governors of the Federal Reserve System and Federal Deposit Insurance Corporation in response to 2015 Resolution Plan Submission Letter (April 12). Available at: http://www.documentcloud.org/documents/2800589-Citi-Letter-20160413.html; accessed July 11, 2016.

Davis Polk & Wardwell LLP. 2016. "Federal Reserve's Proposed Rule on QFCs with U.S. G-SIBs and the U.S. Operations of Foreign G-SIBs." Visual Memorandum. New York: Davis Polk & Wardwell LLP.

Federal Deposit Insurance Corporation. 2011. "The Orderly Liquidation of Lehman Brothers Holdings Inc. under the Dodd-Frank Act." *FDIC Quarterly* 5(2): 31–49. Washington, D.C.: Federal Deposit Insurance Corporation.

Financial Stability Board. 2014. "Adequacy of Loss-Absorbing Capacity of Systemically Important Banks in Resolution." Basel: Financial Stability Board.

Geen, David, Seth Grosshandler, Katherine Hughes, Igor Kleyman, Knox L. McIlwain, Samantha Riley, and M. Benjamin Snodgrass. 2015. "A Step Closer to Ending Too-Big-To-Fail: The ISDA 2014 Resolution Stay Protocol and Contractual Recognition of Cross-border Resolution." *Futures & Derivatives Law Report* 35(3): 1–17.

The Goldman Sachs Group Inc. 2016. Letter from Board of Governors of the Federal Reserve System and Federal Deposit Insurance Corporation in response to 2015 Resolution Plan Submission Letter (April 12). Available at: http://www.documentcloud.org/documents/2800588-Goldman-Sachs-Letter-20160413.html; accessed July 11, 2016.

Gordon, Jeffrey N., and Wolf-Georg Ringe. 2015. "Bank Resolution in Europe: The Unfinished Agenda of Structural Reform." ECGI Law Working Paper No. 282/2015. Brussels: European Corporate Governance Institute.

Guynn, Randall D. 2012. "Are Bailouts Inevitable?" *Yale Journal on Regulation* 29(1): 121–54.

———. 2014. "Framing the TBTF Problem: The Path to a Solution." In *Across the Great Divide: New Perspectives on the Financial Crisis*, edited by Martin Neil Baily and John B. Taylor. Stanford, Calif.: Hoover Institution.

Huertas, Thomas C. 2015. "A Resolvable Bank. In *Building on Bankruptcy: A Revised Chapter 14 Proposal for the Recapitalization, Reorganization, or Liquidation of Large Financial Institutions.*" In *Making Failure Feasible*, edited by Kenneth E. Scott, Thomas H. Jackson and John B. Taylor. Stanford, Calif.: Hoover Institution.

Jackson, Howell E. 1994. "The Expanding Obligations of Financial Holding Companies." *Harvard Law Review* 107(3): 507–619.

Jackson, Thomas H. 2015. "Building on Bankruptcy: A Revised Chapter 14 Proposal for the Recapitalization, Reorganization, or Liquidation of Large Financial Institutions." In *Making Failure Feasible*, edited by Kenneth E. Scott, Thomas H. Jackson and John B. Taylor. Stanford, Calif.: Hoover Institution.

Jarque, Arantxa, and David A. Price. 2015. "Living Wills: A Tool for Curbing Too Big to Fail." *Federal Reserve Bank of Richmond Economic Quarterly* 101(1): 77–94. Richmond, Va.: Federal Reserve Bank of Richmond.

JPMorgan Chase & Co. 2016. Letter from Board of Governors of the Federal Reserve System and Federal Deposit Insurance Corporation in response to 2015 Resolution Plan Submission Letter (April 12). Available at: http://www.documentcloud.org/documents/2800587-Jpmorgan-Chase-Letter-20160413.html; accessed July 11, 2016.

Kupiec, Paul H. 2015. "Will TLAC Regulations Fix the G-SIB Too-Big-To-Fail Problem?" AEI Economic Working Paper 2015-08. Washington, D.C.: American Enterprise Institute.

Kupiec, Paul H., and Peter J. Wallison. 2014. "Can the 'Single Point of Entry' Strategy Be Used to Recapitalize a Failing Bank?" AEI Economic Working Paper 2014-08. Washington, D.C.: American Enterprise Institute.

Lee, Paul L. 2012a, "The Source of Strength Doctrine: Revered and Revisit—Part I." *Banking Law Journal* 129(9): 771–801.

———. 2012b, "The Source of Strength Doctrine: Revered and Revisit—Part II." *Banking Law Journal* 129: 867–906.

———. 2015. "Bankruptcy Alternatives to Title II of the Dodd-Frank Act—Part II." *Banking Law Journal* 132 (November–December): 503–52.

Massman, Stephanie P. 2015. "Developing a New Resolution Regime for Failed Systemically Important Financial Institutions: An Assessment of the Orderly Liquidation Authority." *American Bankruptcy Law Journal* 89(4): 525–71.

Merrill, Thomas W., and Margaret L. Merrill. 2014. "Dodd-Frank Orderly Liquidation Authority: Too

Big for the Constitution?" *Columbia Law Review* 163: 165–247.

Morgan Stanley. 2016. Letter from Board of Governors of the Federal Reserve System and Federal Deposit Insurance Corporation in response to 2015 Resolution Plan Submission Letter (April 12). Available at: http://www.documentcloud.org/documents/2800586-Morgan-Stanley-Letter-20160413.html; accessed July 11, 2016.

PwC. 2015. "Resolution: Single Point of Entry Strategy Ascends." Regulatory Brief. Chicago: PwC Financial Services.

Roe, Mark J., and Stephen D. Adams. 2015. "Restructuring Failed Financial Firms in Bankruptcy: Selling Lehman's Derivatives Portfolio." *Yale Journal on Regulation* 32(2): 363.

Sidley Austin LLP. 2015. "Sidley Update: New ISDA Resolution Stay Protocols: Challenges for Buy-Side and Sell-Side Firms Alike." New York: Sidley Austin LLP.

Skeel, David A. 2014. "Single Point of Entry and the Bankruptcy Alternative." In *Across the Great Divide: New Perspectives on the Financial Crisis*, edited by Martin Neil Baily and John B. Taylor. Stanford, Calif.: Hoover Institution.

———. 2015. "Financing Systemically Important Financial Institutions." In *Making Failure Feasible*, edited by Kenneth E. Scott, Thomas H. Jackson, and John B. Taylor. Stanford, Calif.: Hoover Institution.

———. 2016. "The New Synthesis of Bank Regulation and Bankruptcy in the Dodd-Frank Era." ECGI Law Working Paper No. 308-2016. Brussels: European Corporate Governance Institute.

State Street Corporation. 2016. Letter from Board of Governors of the Federal Reserve System and Federal Deposit Insurance Corporation in response to 2015 Resolution Plan Submission Letter (April 12). Available at: http://www.documentcloud.org/documents/2800585-State-Street-Corporation-Letter-20160413.html; accessed July 11, 2016.

Tucker, Paul. 2014. "Regulatory Reform, Stability and Central Banking." Hutchins Center on Fiscal and Monetary Policy at Brookings Working Paper No. 1. Washington, D.C.: Brookings Institution.

Wells Fargo & Company. 2016. Letter from Board of Governors of the Federal Reserve System and Federal Deposit Insurance Corporation in response to 2015 Resolution Plan Submission Letter (April 12). Available at: http://www.documentcloud.org/documents/2800584-Wells-Fargo-Letter-20160413.html; accessed July 11, 2016.

PART III
Consumer Protection

The Consumer Financial Protection Bureau and the Quest for Consumer Comprehension

LAUREN E. WILLIS

To ensure that consumers understand financial products' "costs, benefits, and risks," the Consumer Financial Protection Bureau has been redesigning mandated disclosures, primarily through iterative lab testing. But no matter how well these disclosures perform in experiments, firms will run circles around the disclosures when studies end and marketing begins. To meet the challenge of the dynamic twenty-first-century consumer financial marketplace, the bureau should require firms to demonstrate that a good proportion of their customers understand key pertinent facts about the financial products they buy. Comprehension rules would induce firms to inform consumers and simplify products, tasks that firms are better equipped than the bureau to perform.

Keywords: consumer finance, performance standards, disclosures, deception, Consumer Financial Protection Bureau

Title X of the Dodd-Frank Wall Street Reform and Consumer Protection Act of 2010 tasked the Consumer Financial Protection Bureau (CFPB) with ensuring that "consumers . . . understand the costs, benefits, and risks associated with" financial products and services (section 1032, 12 U.S.C. 5532). Despite this ambitious mandate, the bureau's pursuit of consumer comprehension has thus far focused on the same twentieth-century tool that has already proved ineffective at regulating consumer finance: required disclosures. No matter how well the bureau's "Know Before You Owe" disclosures perform in the lab, or even in field trials, firms will run circles around these disclosures when the experiments end, misleading consumers and defying consumers' expectations.

Even without any intent to deceive, firms not only will but *must* leverage consumer confusion to compete with other firms that deceive customers. Although firms are not always responsible for their customers' confusion, firms today take advantage of this confusion to sell products. As elucidated in a recent work by nobel laureates George Akerlof and Robert Shiller (2015), without effective regulation, markets in equilibrium will produce manipulation and deception.

To meet its mandate to ensure that consumers understand the financial transactions in which they engage, the CFPB must summon the innovative data-driven twenty-first-century spirit that otherwise characterizes the bureau's approach to consumer protection. Specifically, the bureau must induce firms themselves to promote consumer comprehension, whether by helping their customers understand financial transactions, by conforming transactions to their customers' understanding, or both. To generate this change in firm behavior, the bureau should require firms to periodically demonstrate, through third-party testing of random samples of their customers ("customer

Lauren E. Willis is professor of law and Rains Senior Research Fellow at Loyola Law School, Los Angeles.

Direct correspondence to: Lauren E. Willis at lauren.willis@lls.edu, 919 Albany St., Los Angeles, CA 94705.

confusion audits"), that a good proportion of their customers know, at the time the customers can make use of this knowledge, the key pertinent costs, benefits, and risks of the financial products they have been sold.

For example, the bureau should require firms to prove that their customers are aware of all costs at the moment when the customers are deciding whether to take an action that will trigger those costs, whether that action be taking out a mortgage, overdrawing a checking account, or calling customer service to inquire about a prepaid debit card balance. Where consumers are confused about benefits, such as the benefit of signing up for a "credit repair" service, enrolling in a credit card rewards program, or paying a debt that is beyond limitations, firms should show that their customers understand restrictions on benefits the firm is offering.

In promulgating comprehension rules, the bureau could set the proportion of a firm's customers that must pass a customer confusion audit in a variety of ways. For example, the proportion might be set with reference to existing false advertising law, on the basis of median industry performance, or at whatever proportion of consumers understand mandated disclosures in the bureau's lab-based consumer testing.

Demonstrating sufficient customer comprehension could be a precondition firms must meet before enforcing a term or charging a fee, or firms could be sanctioned (or rewarded) for low (or high) demonstrated comprehension levels. In effect, rather than prescriptively regulating the marketing and sales process with mandated disclosures or pursuing firms on an ad hoc ex post basis for unfair, deceptive, and abusive marketing and sales practices, the bureau would monitor firms and incentivize them to minimize customer confusion as the marketing and sales process unfolds over time.

Comprehension rules are a form of performance-based regulation, in that they regulate outputs not inputs. Performance-based regulation is widely used in other fields and its use has been expanding. Environmental and building code regulations have long employed it. Rather than the law dictating the scrubber a factory smokestack must use or the material a builder must use, the law sets emissions limits or imposes strength and durability requirements, and the factory owner or builder can decide how to meet those limits or requirements. In the consumer arena, the law now requires firms affirmatively to demonstrate compliance with safety standards for food and children's products through routine performance testing (Title I, sections 103–5 of the FDA Food Safety Modernization Act, 21 U.S.C. 350j, 350g, and 2201; Title I, section 102 of the Consumer Product Safety Improvement Act of 2008, 15 U.S.C. 2063).

Specifically with respect to consumer comprehension, the Food and Drug Administration requires pharmaceutical firms to show that actual customers understand the usage and dosing directions for a medication during a trial of over-the-counter sales before the firm can broadly sell the drug directly to consumers (Leonard-Segal et al. 2009). In the European Union, food sellers making front-of-package nutrition claims will soon be required to affirmatively demonstrate "scientifically valid evidence of [consumer] understanding [of the claims]" (Article 31, Regulation [EU] 1169/2011 on the Provision of Food Information to Consumers [OJL 304/18]). Customer confusion audits are also used in the United States by regulators to establish deception claims and by competitors to prove false advertising claims, although testing is currently ex post and ad hoc.

Making firms responsible for effectively informing their own customers would capitalize on firms' greater knowledge of and access to their customers and greater ability to experiment and innovate. Comprehension rules would incentivize firms to educate rather than obfuscate and to develop product designs that align with rather than defy consumer expectations.

The CFPB already has more than an inkling that mandated disclosure is a poor tool for regulating financial products. A bureau policy statement acknowledges that the effectiveness of such disclosures is only an "assumption," albeit one on which much of consumer protection law is based (Consumer Financial Protection Bureau 2013a, 64392).

The bureau's inaugural banner project was "Know Before You Owe," but recently it has turned to approaches that step beyond disclosure and even tiptoe toward comprehension rules. The bureau has moved testing of disclosures from the lab to the field. It has been trying to stimulate firms to develop creative disclosure methods. It has performed its own testing of consumer understanding of arbitration clauses and class action waivers. These steps implicitly acknowledge that (a) disclosures that do well in experimental conditions may not work in real-world conditions, (b) firms are better situated than regulators to innovate to achieve consumer comprehension, and (c) valid, reliable consumer confusion audits are possible. What is needed now is for the bureau to pull these insights together and see that they collectively suggest applying comprehension rules to any number of consumer financial transactions.

Of course, Congress may have been mistaken in thinking that understanding would protect consumers. Even knowledgeable consumers make bad decisions, whether as a result of inadequate willpower or decisionmaking biases. On the other hand, if firms were to make it easier for consumers to understand financial products, consumers likely would have more willpower available and be less likely to succumb to decision biases.

Cognitive capacity and willpower function as a single "cognitive-willpower bandwidth" resource in the brain, such that if cognition is taxed, so, too, is willpower (Baumeister et al. 2008). Similarly, cognitive load increases decision-making biases, including overconfidence (Kruger 1999), overoptimism (Tanner and Carlson 2009), and the effects of some other biases (Epley and Gilovich 2006; Drolet, Luce, and Simonson 2009). If consumers could more easily understand financial transactions, they would likely spend fewer cognitive resources on financial decisions, freeing up cognitive-willpower bandwidth to use for exercising self-control and reducing overconfidence, overoptimism, and other biases that might otherwise lead to improvident choices.

In this article I explain the feebleness of mandated disclosures, the inherent flaws in the alternatives the CFPB has been pursuing, the advantages firms have over regulators in ensuring their customers' comprehension, and the CFPB's legal authority to require customer confusion audits and enforce comprehension rules. I then elaborate on a few examples of how this form of regulation might operate in practice, including these four key elements:

1. Measuring the quality of a valued outcome (comprehension) rather than of an input that is often pointless (mandated or preapproved disclosure);

2. Assessing actual customer comprehension in the field as conditions change over time, rather than imagining what the "reasonable consumer" would understand or testing consumers in the lab or in single-shot field experiments[1];

3. Requiring firms to affirmatively and routinely demonstrate customer understanding, rather than relying on the bureau's limited resources to examine firm performance ad hoc when problems arise[2]; and

4. Giving firms the flexibility and responsibility to effectively inform their customers about key relevant costs, benefits and risks through whatever means the firms see fit, whether that be education or product simplification, rather than asking regulators to dictate how disclosures and products should be designed.

I conclude with a discussion of some further benefits of establishing comprehension rules and implementing customer confusion audits. In particular, the process might lead to the discovery of many situations in which the

---

1. This proposal thus parts from Barr, Mullainathan, and Shafir (2008), which suggests using an "objective reasonableness test" accompanied by "safe harbors for reasonable disclosure," preapproved "model disclosure forms," and "'no action' letters" issued to firms ex ante (7–8).

2. This proposal again parts from Barr, Mullainathan, and Shafir (2008), which suggests ad hoc enforcement by making unreasonableness a defense to payment in foreclosure or bankruptcy proceedings (8).

benefits of consumer understanding are low and the costs are high. Certainly comprehension is often neither necessary nor sufficient for good decisions, and it might well be more cost effective for society to engage in substantive regulation of product design or performance-based regulation of consumer welfare outcomes resulting from financial transactions.[3] Fundamentally, we cannot know the real costs and benefits of consumer comprehension until we seriously pursue it, *and Dodd-Frank requires the CFPB to do so.*

THE FLAWS IN THE BUREAU'S CURRENT APPROACH TO CONSUMER COMPREHENSION

The CFPB today is testing disclosures in the lab and in the field and is trying to stimulate firms to generate new disclosures themselves. Each of these implicitly recognizes some of the elements of a regulatory policy that seriously pursues the goal of consumer comprehension. But, tethered to the straitjacket of "disclosure," none of these can reach that goal.

DOUBLING DOWN IN THE LAB: DISCLOSURE 2.0

The fact that consumers are unable to use mandated disclosures well has prompted widespread concern. The CFPB has responded by doubling down on disclosure. Disclosures were at one time formatted according to regulators' notions about what consumers would notice, read, and understand. But the last fifteen years has seen the emergence of Disclosure 2.0: disclosures developed through multiyear lab testing of iteratively redesigned disclosures.

The bureau's redesign of mortgage disclosures epitomizes the approach. Consumers are brought into the lab and asked to read through a proposed disclosure and think aloud, explaining what they understand the information to mean and how they might hypothetically use the information. In response, the regulator makes changes to the disclosure and tests the new design. Testing and modification are repeated until the regulator can obtain no further improvement in subject comprehension of some product attributes without decreasing comprehension of more important attributes. The regulator then shows the new and old disclosure forms to a large swath of consumers, and determines whether consumers understand more about the transaction when looking at the new disclosure than at the old one. The bureau has embarked on similar disclosure redesign processes for other products, such as prepaid debit cards and student loans.

Testing actual consumers is an improvement on regulators sitting around a table deciding what disclosure format seems best to them. But there are serious limits to comprehension and effective use of disclosure that Disclosure 2.0 does not surmount: bounds that impair understanding in the lab; even more bounds that affect decisions outside the lab; and the exploitation of these bounds by firms when disclosures are deployed in the field.

Even without all of the real world's challenges, comprehension and decision quality in the lab are limited. In none of the government's Disclosure 2.0 efforts have anywhere near 100 percent of the consumers tested understood or accurately used 100 percent of the information disclosed.[4] Comprehension is inherently constrained where literacy and numeracy are below the level needed to use the disclosure. Further, many decisions require basic financial knowledge that consumers lack.

---

3. In related work, I develop a proposal for performance-based regulation of consumer transactions based on consumer welfare outcomes (Willis 2015). The CFPB has proposed regulations that also incorporate performance-based rules. For certain small dollar loans, a lender that does not follow the bureau's underwriting rules can instead demonstrate annually that no more than five percent of its loan portfolio defaulted (or face a penalty of having to refund to its customers all origination fees it collected from them over the past year) (Consumer Financial Protection Bureau 2016).

4. For example, on average, subjects in lab conditions could provide correct answers to only about three-quarters of questions asked about a hypothetical mortgage using the CFPB's new disclosure (Kleimann Communication Group 2013, 41). In mall-intercept testing, fewer than half of subjects were able to use regulators' new financial information privacy disclosures as regulators intended (Garrison et al. 2012).

For example, effective annual percentage rate for a credit card account, a figure that retrospectively incorporates interest and fees into a single number, is a concept that "defies plain language efforts" because consumers lack the background needed to make sense of the concept (Hogarth and Merry 2011, 11).

A related problem is that consumer rationality is bounded. Consumers are capable of taking only a few attributes into account when making a decision (Agnew and Szykman 2005). If the transaction has more moving parts than consumers can consider at one time, it will make no difference that all those parts are disclosed.

Less well recognized in the literature is that consumers' priors can prevent consumers from understanding disclosures. When consumers' background mental models or beliefs conflict with the information disclosed, mandated disclosure may not be able to shake these beliefs. One example is double-cycle billing in credit card contracts, a billing method whereby when a borrower pays late, the creditor in the next billing cycle retrospectively charges interest for the normally interest-free grace period between the time of purchase and the due date of the late payment. The Federal Reserve Board tried mightily to explain this to consumers using various text and disclosure formats. These efforts failed (Bernanke 2009). In the abstract, the concept is probably not beyond the ken of the average consumer. But in reality, the idea that a card issuer could retrospectively charge interest when none had been charged previously is too antithetical to consumers' mental models of how credit cards work to be believed, even in the lab.

The real world is a far more demanding decision environment. In the lab, consumers face at most a few products, presented clearly, with nothing to do but read the disclosures. In the field, consumers encounter a plethora of options positioned variously in a sea of distractions. In the lab, even adding a single distraction—casual conversation—can markedly reduce comprehension of a mortgage disclosure (Stark, Choplin, and LeBoeuff 2013). In the real world, people have many more distractions and habitually spend as little of their limited resources as possible to make many decisions.

Even for significant consumer transactions such as obtaining a home mortgage, many consumers spend less than a minute reading disclosures (Sovern 2010).

Moreover, consumers have less cognitive-willpower bandwidth in the real world than in the lab. Stress, including the stress created by the decision itself, depletes cognitive resources (Kahn and Baron 1995, 325–26). Consumers having difficulty meeting financial obligations are particularly likely to have constrained cognitive-willpower bandwidth and thus to engage in "tunneled thinking"—considering only the most immediate costs, risks, and benefits (Mullainathan and Shafir 2013).

Finally, consumers in the real world use their mental resources selectively. They attend to the pieces of information they want to hear and ignore those they find unpleasant (Loewenstein, Sunstein, and Golman 2014). They then process this limited information in a manner that supports the decision they want to make (Kunda 1990). Outside the lab they may apply more effort, but effort cannot overcome limits on knowledge and rationality.

MOVING TO THE FIELD: DISCLOSURE 2.5

Implicitly acknowledging the limited external validity of lab testing, the CFPB has launched Disclosure 2.5: designing disclosures using field experiments. The first of these is a rollout by the Pentagon Federal Credit Union (PenFed) of a new, bureau-designed credit card disclosure (Consumer Financial Protection Bureau, n.d.). Customers are randomized into one group that receives the new disclosure and another that receives the disclosure PenFed usually gives its customers. The bureau is testing whether customers who receive the new disclosure are more accurate in their answers to questions about the card's terms, such as the interest rate on purchases and the size of the fee charged for late payments. This improves on the lab-based approach because the experiment is run on consumers who have self-selected the product, in their actual decision environments, where they are distracted by life and are not directed to read the disclosure.

It remains to be seen whether Disclosure 2.5's experimental results will indicate that the new disclosure has improved these PenFed customers' understanding of the products they have bought. However, no matter what the experiment shows, it cannot capture changes that take place after the experiment. Some of these changes happen organically, as product offerings and market structure evolve. Consider, for example, the old Truth-in-Lending Act and Real Estate Settlement Procedures Act forms that were used for home mortgages. These may have been useful to consumers when mortgages were structured in only a few ways (thirty-year or fifteen-year fixed-rate mortgages) and were homogeneously priced (on any given day, each creditor lent at a single price for each type of mortgage). But these disclosures failed many consumers when the market changed to one of heterogeneously structured loans, carrying individualized "risk-based" (or vulnerability-based) prices that might not be known until the consumer was well into the application process (Willis 2006).

More problematic is that Disclosure 2.5 cannot account for the effects of firm responses to the new disclosures. The firm that cooperates with the bureau to facilitate the experiment will not work to undermine the disclosure during the study (and may even be an atypical firm, as PenFed likely is) but may well do so later, when the experiment has ended.

Indeed, firms have a bevy of means at their disposal to undermine mandated disclosures' effectiveness.

First, firms can defuse disclosures by altering the design of the transaction. If some price components must be disclosed prominently, firms stuff more of the cost of the product into less visible components (Bar-Gill and Bubb 2012). Firms build complex products not merely to satisfy diverse consumer preferences, but also to confuse consumers and raise the cost of comprehension high enough that consumers will not bother to spend the time and effort that would be required to eliminate confusion. Firms shape purchasing processes to ensure that the consumer has sunk significant costs into the effort, and has perhaps switched from a decision making to an implementation mindset, before receiving the disclosure. Firms can also use social pressure to discourage consumers from reading disclosures, as, for example, when closing agents discourage borrowers from reading mortgage documents.

Second, firms wield advertising and sales talk to frame consumers' thought processes long before consumers see a disclosure. Consumers may think they are unaffected, but advertising works (Wood and Poltrack 2015; Lewis and Reiley 2014). Individualized sales pitches can be even more powerful. A former loan broker explains how idle chitchat distracts consumers, creates positive consumer feelings, and engenders trust (Brunner 2006):

> You tell the loan salesperson you want the loan to upgrade a room. He or she will ask you why, and you innocently will say that you want your daughter to have a nice new room. "Oh really, what color?" asks the loan arranger. Purple, you say.
>
> Rest assured, as the process moves along, the salesperson . . . will continuously remind you that your goal is to "paint a nice new purple room." The salesman seems to . . . truly care that the room . . . ensure[s] your daughter's complete happiness.
>
> It's easy to forget that your goal is not a purple room, it's a loan at the best price and terms possible.

Trust in a salesperson or in a brand may lead a consumer to misinterpret a disclosure in a way that favors the outcome suggested by the salesperson or advertising. Alternatively, trust may lead a consumer to select a product without bothering to read the disclosure carefully, or at all. For example, merely adding a brand name to over-the-counter drug packaging in the lab led some subjects to read the label more quickly and to fail to notice or understand a number of contraindications (Catlin, Pechmann, and Brass 2011).

Third, firms physically divert attention from disclosures. An example comes from AT&T's addition of a mandatory arbitration clause to its contract with its customers; it designed the envelope, cover letter, and amended contract after extensive "antimarketing" market testing to ensure that most consumers would *not* open the envelope, or if they did open it, would not read beyond the cover letter (*Ting v. AT&T*, 319

F.3d 1126, 9th Cir. 2003). Another example: in an online survey, a reminder about who could see subjects' answers delivered just before subjects answered some very personal questions led subjects to behave in more privacy-protective ways. But adding just a fifteen-second delay between the privacy disclosure and the loading of the webpage where the subjects answered the questions eliminated the privacy-protective effect of the disclosure (Adjerid et al. 2013).

Fourth, firms take proactive steps to ferret out easy marks, or even to place consumers in situations where disclosure is likely to be ineffective. Locating vulnerable customers is becoming increasingly sophisticated now that consumer activity online and on cell phones can be tracked. Late-twentieth-century mortgage sellers fished for disclosure-insensitive prospects by mailing "live checks" that when cashed would result in loans at exorbitant interest rates; homeowners who cashed the checks were good prospects for a high-priced mortgage. Firms in the early twenty-first century buy lists of consumers who engage in impulse shopping or are financially stressed (Office of Oversight and Investigations Majority Staff, U.S. Senate Committee on Commerce, Science, and Transportation 2013). Marketing lists include "Rolling the Dice" and "Oldies but Goodies" segments, so as to allow marketers to pinpoint consumers who are "gullible [and] want to believe that their luck can change" (Duhigg 2007).

Firms can even engage in real-time marketing through Internet and mobile devices to reach consumers at vulnerable moments (Calo 2014). As noted earlier, cognitive load can decrease willpower and increase overconfidence, overoptimism, and other decisionmaking biases. In addition, mood (Keller, Lipkus, and Rimer 2002) and stress levels (Mather and Lighthall 2012) can affect risk perception and responses. Savvy firms might use inferred cognitive load, mood, or stress levels to sell consumers products at the very moment when mandated disclosures will be misinterpreted or ignored. Advertisers already track consumers as they play online games and differentially target advertisements to consumers experiencing success or defeat, to tailor the advertising pitch to exploit the consumer's likely mood (Carney 2013). Firms can even influence consumer mood, cognitive load, and risk-taking propensity directly (Kramer, Guillory, and Hancock 2014; Shapiro and MacInnis 2002).

Ultimately, the bureau's single-shot field experiments occur under conditions that are not realistic in crucial respects. Field testing is the right approach, but the testing should measure the effects of firms' actual activities over time, not in a single experiment.

BRINGING FIRMS INTO THE DISCLOSURE DESIGN PROCESS: PROJECT CATALYST

The CFPB recognizes that firms have information and expertise that could allow them to design disclosures better than regulators can do. Dodd-Frank authorizes the bureau to give firms the opportunity to conduct trials of disclosures designed "to improve upon any model form" (section 1032, 12 U.S.C. 5532). The bureau's program—called Project Catalyst—has used this authority to encourage firms to develop their own disclosures (Consumer Financial Protection Bureau 2013a, 64389), explaining:

> There may be significant opportunities to enhance consumer protection by facilitating innovation in financial products and services and enabling companies to research informative, cost-effective disclosures.... In-market testing, involving companies and consumers in real world situations, may offer particularly valuable information with which to improve disclosure rules and model forms.

Unfortunately, Project Catalyst takes an approach to consumer comprehension that is at odds with modern business-to-consumer communication techniques in at least three repects.

First, the approach requires language-based, minimally interactive disclosures; under the policy, a trial disclosure's content must "be in plain language, reflect a clear format and design, and be succinct" (Consumer Financial Protection Bureau 2013a, 64393n12). But modern communication techniques are not limited to words, and the best communication techniques are often interactive. A picture is worth a thousand words—and might be worth 2 percent interest per month. In one experiment, adding a photo of a pretty woman to an advertisement for a consumer loan increased men's take-up of the loan as much as lowering the monthly interest rate by 2 percent (Bertrand et al. 2010). A video can often convey far more information, more effectively, than a document or script. Turning the process into a game, called "gamification," might be the best way to help some consumers understand a product. Imagine consumers winning points for discovering a financial product's "hidden" price components. The most effective communications may well not use plain language, employ a clear format and design, or be succinct.[5]

Second, the policy assumes a relatively static approach to communication. It requires firms to submit "a copy of the trial disclosures to be tested ... and a clear statement of how they would be provided to consumers" (Consumer Financial Protection Bureau 2013a, 64393n14). Although the policy purports to permit firms to engage in the iterative testing and redesign process used by marketers, every tested disclosure must be specifically authorized by the bureau.

Such preapproval is at odds with modern marketing, which employs a quickly evolving five-step trial-and-error approach (Akerlof and Shiller 2015, 53–54):

1. Release marketing that is diverse in content, format, channel, audience, etc.
2. Measure results.
3. Tweak the marketing for each audience segment in response to the data.
4. Measure results.
5. Repeat.

The velocity of this process is only increasing with the ever-increasing capacity of data analytics. The bureau is unlikely to be able to preapprove disclosures at anything like this pace.

Third, effective modern communication techniques are often emotion-based and targeted, segmented by detailed personal characteristics, sometimes right down to the individual consumer and in real time to leverage mood, as described earlier. CFPB approval of such communications is problematic.

Public sentiment is likely to be hostile to government approval of segmentation and mood manipulation. When Illinois required some consumers in targeted zip codes hard-hit by foreclosure to receive pre-mortgage counseling, the state was accused of racism and quickly rescinded the rule. Mood manipulation by the government would almost certainly provoke outrage; recall the criticism Facebook received for intentionally manipulating user emotions. In addition, the bureau has committed to making information about each firm's disclosure testing public. Firms are unlikely to want to divulge details about how they segment consumers and manipulate mood. Like sausage-makers, marketers do not want the public to know how their product is made. It is therefore unsurprising that few firms have yet taken up Project Catalyst's invitation to engage in a trial disclosure program, and it is likely that none have put their marketing departments on the case.

Project Catalyst is on the right track in its assumption that firms are better at effectively communicating with consumers than regulators. But bureau preapproval of the communication will undermine that effectiveness.

COMPREHENSION TESTING BY THE BUREAU TO INFORM DISCLOSURE AND PRODUCT DESIGN REGULATION

The CFPB also recognizes the feasibility and utility of testing consumers to determine what they do and do not understand about financial products. Using third-party experts on consumer survey and testing techniques, the bureau has begun assessing consumer comprehension in a number of controlled trials and field experiments (Consumer Financial Protection Bureau 2014) and surveying consumers about their understanding, for example, of their legal rights (Consumer Financial Protection Bureau 2015a, 49). A completed bureau-commissioned survey of credit card account holders has revealed that consumers generally

---

5. Even if the bureau were to eliminate such language requirements, it lacks the expertise to assess and preapprove photos, videos, and highly interactive materials such as games.

do not know their dispute resolution rights and that most consumers whose card agreements prohibit suing in court and participating in class actions wrongly believe that they can do both (Consumer Financial Protection Bureau 2015b, 11).

The testing the bureau is doing is the right idea. Regulating the font size and color of arbitration clauses in credit card contracts is useless. Requiring certain words to appear in debt collectors' letters to consumers is a very long way from achieving consumer comprehension of their debt collection rights. Determining whether a firm "meaningfully conveyed the information required for a typical consumer to make a reasonable judgment" (Barr, Mullainathan, and Shafir 2008, 7) is not possible without data about what actual consumers know at the time they are making those judgments. The CFPB experience with commissioning experts to perform consumer testing can inform the bureau's oversight of third-party auditors that will perform the customer confusion audits necessary for firms to comply with a comprehension rule.

The experience can also inform the bureau's cost-benefit calculations in selecting the right policy response to consumer confusion. When the testing undertaken by the Federal Reserve Board, discussed earlier, demonstrated that consumers did not understand double-cycle billing terms in credit card contracts, the board banned issuers from using this billing method. This is the right response where the financial product term or feature provides little benefit to consumers, but it is possible that some terms will be beneficial for one group of consumers and misunderstood and harmful for another group. Comprehension rules would preserve greater space for welfare-enhancing innovation by firms, but would be more costly to enforce than a ban. The bureau's experience with testing consumers could help it estimate how much more costly, and thus to choose the right policy response.

ADVANTAGES FIRMS HAVE IN ATTAINING COMPREHENSION

Comprehension rules would align firms' goals with the CFPB's mandate to ensure consumer understanding of financial product costs, benefits, and risks. Such rules would bring to bear on the regulatory problem the firm's greater knowledge of its own processes, greater facility with experimentation, and greater ability to segment consumers and to adapt to changes in the environment and in technology. Firms know a lot about their customers, as they already collect this information for marketing and product development purposes. Firms have access to their customers through many "touch points"—marketing, sales talk, and product packaging and presentation. Firms are not constrained by political concerns that prevent the bureau from tailoring disclosures to consumer segments and leveraging consumer emotions. The bureau may even be legally prohibited from mandating particularly effective disclosures. Some courts have struck down regulations requiring firms to place on product packaging graphics intended to evoke an emotional response so as to ensure consumer retention of disclosed information (*R. J. Reynolds Tobacco Co. v. FDA*, 696 F.3d 1205, 1216, D.C. Cir. 2012). In contrast, evoking emotional responses and ensuring that consumers retain information are the bread and butter of marketing.

The very capacities that modern firms use to market products and defeat mandated disclosures enable them to attain better consumer comprehension more quickly and at a lower cost than regulators. The bureau can try to educate consumers, but nothing beats professional marketers when it comes to sending consumers a message. The bureau spent three years developing its "Know Before You Owe" mortgage disclosures. Without the constraints of notice, comment, and Office of Management and Budget approval, firms can engage in the trial and error market testing process described above and obtain results within days or weeks, adjust their approach accordingly for the next round, and do it again a few days or weeks later.

The bureau has recognized: "In-market testing of consumer behavior and reactions to new products or new ways of delivering services is a constant of modern life. Companies routinely carry out such tests using their customer base" (Consumer Financial Protection Bureau

2013a, 64391). Through this process, marketers have discovered that "even minute details such as ink color and envelope size" matter (Lewis and Reiley 2014, 237n3). Firms could use the same dynamic consumer testing approach to determine how to effectively inform their customers about key relevant costs, benefits, and risks of the financial products firms sell their customers. Firms can further leverage the approach to discover how to adapt their educational methods over time as technology, social practices, and cultural understanding change.

In addition, firms can creatively manage the comprehension problem by increasing education or eliminating complexity and counterintuitive features, and by making tradeoffs between these approaches over time. For example, if a customer confusion audit would demonstrate that the customers of a prepaid debit card issuer believe they will not be charged a fee to inquire about their account balances, the issuer can select between effectively informing its customers about this fee or changing its card pricing structure to eliminate the fee. Firms are in a better position than regulators to decide when it is worth the cost of educating consumers about complex or unintuitive features and when simplifying products is more cost-effective. Firms already know more about consumer valuation of product attributes than regulators and can learn more about these valuations at lower cost.

The bureau would need to remain mindful of firm agility at circumventing disclosure, and guard against firms' manipulation of customer confusion audit results. One can imagine poorly constructed tests that might allow a firm to teach its customers to answer the questions correctly without teaching them about the underlying substance of the transaction. Early responses to environmental emissions performance standards provide a cautionary tale. Firms built higher smokestacks so that the emissions monitors at ground level would produce lower pollution readings, allowing the firms to pass the tests without reducing their emissions. Regulators responded by changing testing methods to take both ground-level emissions readings and smokestack height into account (U.S. Government Accountability Office 2011).

Consumer testing in the context of false advertising claims presents the same issue. As per the Federal Judicial Center's *Manual on Scientific Evidence*, courts demand the use of generally accepted practices in the consumer studies field, such as proper sampling techniques; clear, precise, nonleading questions; rotating the order of questions and answers; avoiding nonresponse bias; and robust statistical analysis (Diamond 2011). The bureau would need to certify and oversee third-party auditors to ensure use of these generally accepted practices. Again, the bureau's experiences with its Disclosure 2.0, Disclosure 2.5, and Project Catalyst trial disclosure programs could inform the oversight function it would need to perform to maintain the validity of customer confusion audits under a comprehension rule.

But if firms teach their customers to pass a test that accurately gauges comprehension, this teaching is the *intended* result of comprehension rules. For example, even a firm teaching its customers not only that their contract contains an arbitration clause but also that arbitration is better for the customer than litigation, is not problematic.[6] If arbitration is better, the customer should choose it, and if it is not better yet the customer has been fooled into thinking it is, the right public policy response may be to ban these clauses. Without comprehension rules, arbitration clauses can be slipped silently into a contract with an unwitting consumer. The firm avoids market competition over dispute resolution terms in consumer contracts and avoids public engagement with the question of whether the clause should be permitted.

Comprehension rules would place an evaluation of the product features currently controlled entirely and silently by firms squarely into public discussion, facilitating market competition and democratic control.

---

6. This puts aside the potential second-order effect whereby arbitration clauses may decrease firm liability and thus undermine firm incentives not to engage in unfair, deceptive, or abusive practices.

AUTHORITY FOR IMPOSING COMPREHENSION RULES

The Dodd-Frank Act plainly gives the CFPB authority to establish comprehension rules and to require firms selling consumer financial products to obtain customer confusion audits. The bureau's very statutory purpose is to ensure that the fast-moving financial marketplace encountered by consumers is "fair, transparent, and competitive" (section 1021, 12 U.S.C. 5511). As previously noted, where firms understand products and consumers do not, poorly regulated market forces dictate that firms will take unfair advantage of consumers. Savvy consumers may benefit, but the less savvy suffer. Markets are not transparent to consumers unless consumers understand their choices within them. Substantive competition over transaction terms depends on consumers' understanding transactions well enough to drive prices down and benefits up.

More directly, section 1032 of Dodd-Frank sweepingly supports comprehension rules. Under this section, the bureau has authority to promulgate and enforce "rules to ensure that the features of any consumer financial product or service, both initially and over the term of the product or service, are fully, accurately, and effectively disclosed to consumers in a manner that permits consumers to understand the costs, benefits, and risks associated with the product or service, in light of the facts and circumstances." The statute directs that "in prescribing rules under [section 1032], the Bureau shall consider available evidence about consumer awareness, understanding of, and responses to disclosures or communications about the risks, costs, and benefits of consumer financial products" (section 1032, 12 U.S.C. 5532).

The evidence discussed previously shows both that many consumers have little awareness or understanding of mandated disclosures and that firms can and do effectively communicate with consumers through marketing. This suggests that the best way to ensure that product features are "effectively disclosed ... in a manner that permits consumers to understand costs, benefits, and risks" is to require that firms be held responsible for widespread confusion among their customers. In fact, it may be the only way to do so in today's market.

Of course, every consumer financial product presents a plethora of potential costs, benefits, and risks. Deciding which of these a consumer needs to understand, selecting which facts and circumstances consumer understanding must account for, and pinpointing when consumers need to know these things are not easy tasks. But answering these questions is not impossible, and every regulation mandating disclosure already implicitly does so by selecting what to disclose and when to disclose it.

Dodd-Frank itself suggests that the universe of what customer confusion audits would test for is a smaller set of facts than those disclosed in the bloated mandated disclosures common today. The only features that must be "effectively disclosed" are those that must be understood to comprehend the costs, benefits, and risks of the financial product. A consumer who knows she is buying a mortgage that requires identical monthly payments and leaves no balance at term does not need to understand the details of amortization.

Further, the consumer must understand the product not in an abstract sense, but "in light of the facts and circumstances." Not every consumer needs to understand every feature. A credit card account holder who carries a balance and is making domestic purchases only would need to understand the interest rate applicable to those purchases but not the cost associated with foreign transactions. A jet-setting account holder who pays off her balance each month would need to know about foreign transaction fees but not the interest rate on prepaid balances

In addition, reading section 1032 in light of Dodd-Frank's purpose, consumers do not need to possess a continuous understanding of these personally relevant product costs, benefits, and risks. Rather, consumers need to understand the pertinent information at a time and in a way that allows them to use the information well in making financial decisions, so as to help drive the market toward better outcomes.

Even knowledge of the costs the particular consumer will encounter, the benefits she can expect, and the risks she is taking on, at the time she is making the pertinent financial decision, is an ambitious goal, given current product offerings. But firms can set their own bar by managing the complexity of products and the intuitiveness of product features.[7] Consumer comprehension will be higher for a product that is easier to understand, ceteris paribus. Further, the way in which information is conveyed dramatically affects the skills needed to use that information. Consumers need minimal skills to use a well-constructed energy star rating; consumers need expertise that few possess to use a set of technical energy use specifications. Comprehension rules hold firms responsible for reaching consumers where firms find them, which is where firms sell to them.

Additional support in Dodd-Frank for comprehension rules includes explicit authorization for the bureau to promulgate rules that identify and prophylactically prevent unfair, deceptive, or abusive acts or practices (section 1031, 12 USC 5531).[8]

A practice is unfair if it is likely to cause substantial injury to consumers that is not reasonably avoidable by consumers themselves, and is not outweighed by countervailing benefits to consumers or competition (Federal Trade Commission 1980). A feature of a transaction that is not understood by most consumers is not reasonably avoidable by them, and any resultant injuries will rarely be outweighed by benefits to consumers, given that competition over the feature will not take place.

A deceptive practice is a material act or omission that is likely to mislead a reasonable member of the group of consumers to whom the firm's sales practices are directed (Federal Trade Commission 1983). A firm's failure to ensure that most of its customers comprehend all material features of a product is thus a deceptive omission, even where the firm makes no affirmatively misleading statements.

An abusive practice is one that "takes unreasonable advantage of—(A) a lack of understanding ... of the material risks, costs, or conditions of the product ... or (B) the inability of the consumer to protect the interests of the consumer in selecting or using" the product (section 1031, 12 U.S.C. 5531). Consumers who do not understand material product features cannot protect their own interests and selling a product with material terms that consumers do not comprehend can take advantage of this inability and the underlying lack of understanding.

Regulation keyed to actual consumer comprehension would be the ideal tool, and perhaps the only feasible tool, for preventing unfairness, deception, and abuse. The bureau has tiptoed toward recognition of this in its examination procedures, which contemplate that examiners might survey or interview samples of a firm's customers during the examination process (Consumer Financial Protection Bureau 2012, 5, 7, 16, 30). But examiners have insufficient resources to do the market-wide customer confusion audits that would be required to uniformly pressure firms to effectively inform their customers.

Some operations that the bureau would need to perform to deploy comprehension rules would be new, but Dodd-Frank envisioned that the bureau would engage in new activities along these lines. The bureau's primary statutory functions include supervising firms that are covered by the act, issuing rules and orders, taking enforcement actions, and "collecting, researching, monitoring, and publishing information relevant to the functioning of markets for consumer financial products and services to identify risks to consumers and the proper functioning of such markets" (section 1021, 12 U.S.C.

---

7. To the extent that heterogeneity among products and services offered and terminology used by different firms drives consumer confusion, comprehension rules might need to be complemented by increased uniformity in product designs and marketing terminology, perhaps specified by the bureau, trade associations, or national standards-setting bodies such as the American National Standards Institute.

8. One of the bureau's five statutory objectives is to protect consumers from unfair, deceptive, or abusive acts or practices (section 1021, 12 USC 5511). The bureau has broad authority to issue rules and orders to prevent evasion of federal consumer financial laws (section 1022, 12 U.S.C. 5512).

5511). The statute also requires the bureau to monitor the market for "risks to consumers," considering consumer "understanding" of those risks, and gives the bureau authority to require firms to produce reports and answers to specific questions to assist in this monitoring (section 1022, 12 U.S.C. 5512). The bureau would likely, at least initially, confine the application of comprehension rules to large firms that it examines regularly, or exempt smaller firms for which customer confusion audits might be disproportionately costly. But lessons learned from large firms could inform the bureau's approach to enforcement actions, substantive product regulation, and even disclosure rules that would affect all firms.[9]

The CFPB has authority to issue rules requiring disclosures and to produce model disclosures, the use of which gives firms a safe harbor from the disclosure rules (section 1032, 12 U.S.C. 5532). But both authorities are discretionary. Other than for home mortgages, the bureau need neither require particular disclosures nor produce model forms. There may be instances where comprehension rules and mandated disclosures would be complementary, such as when the disclosures provide standardization that assists firms in preventing customer confusion. Nothing in Dodd-Frank would prevent the bureau from using disclosure and comprehension rules as complementary tools in ensuring fair, transparent, and competitive markets.

MECHANICS

Nearly any financial transaction could be regulated using comprehension rules. The content tested for in customer confusion audits will depend on how far the CFPB wants to go in pursuit of comprehension, given the costs and benefits of this form of regulation. Testing for bare knowledge might require only a simple true-false, fill-in-the-blank, or multiple-choice test. Testing for applied understanding might be accomplished by assessing whether the reasons given by a customer for a product choice reflect an accurate or inaccurate understanding of the product.[10]

These approaches involve not insignificant per-subject testing costs, but sufficient information to make valid inferences will often be possible with small random or stratified (to capture subpopulations) samples of each firm's customers. An alternative would be to test only traditionally underserved consumers; if they comprehend a product, less vulnerable populations likely do too.

To ensure reliability, testing should be performed by independent, qualified, bureau-certified auditors assigned randomly.[11] Auditors would need to have the necessary expertise in survey research to perform the testing and interpret the results, the same qualifications required of experts in deceptive advertising litigation and consultants who currently perform consumer research for the bureau. Random assignment is necessary to ensure that the auditor is not beholden to or otherwise biased

---

9. In the specific case of predispute arbitration clauses in contracts for consumer financial products, the bureau has explicit authority to "prohibit or impose conditions or limitations on the use of" these clauses if it is "in the public interest or for the protection of consumers" (section 1028, 12 U.S.C. 5518). Particularly given that the bureau's own comprehension testing demonstrates that consumers do not understand the arbitration clauses in their own credit card contracts, meeting comprehension rules would be a natural condition to impose on firms going forward, if the clauses are not prohibited altogether.

10. In developing new mortgage disclosures, the bureau asked subjects in a simulated mortgage choice experiment to explain their reasons for preferring one mortgage over another (Kleimann Communication Group 2013, 65). Published results of that testing report only the average number of reasons given by subjects for selecting one loan over another and not the accuracy of the reasons. Customer confusion audits, in contrast, would assess whether, for example, customers who reported that they chose loan A because they preferred a fixed-rate loan were accurate in their assessment that loan A's rate was fixed.

11. Analogously, the third parties from which manufacturers and importers of children's products must obtain safety testing must be accredited by the Consumer Product Safety Commission or an independent accreditation organization designated by the commission (Consumer Product Safety Improvement Act of 2008, 15 U.S.C. 2063, Title I, section 102).

toward the firm who hires the auditor. Third-party auditors and government oversight also would protect consumer privacy, preventing firms from using individual customer test results to, for example, target marketing of unsuitable products on those who test poorly.

Firms should be free to give customers an incentive to answer the questions in confusion audits accurately. Firms might engage in their own testing and refuse to transact with potential customers who do not understand the transaction. Firms might also reward customers who perform well in confusion audits performed by third parties.[12]

The benchmarks against which firm performance in customer confusion audits ought to be judged depend on which of the bureau's statutory purposes it is pursuing: transparency, competition, or fairness. If the goal is for transactions to be transparent to most consumers engaged in them, the benchmarks would need to be high, perhaps as high as the approximately 85 percent benchmark implicitly used in false advertising cases (see Willis 2015, 154, reviewing cases). If the goal is to ameliorate the market failure caused by consumer confusion and thereby increase substantive product competition, the benchmarks might be lower, depending on the firm's ability to differentiate informed from uninformed consumers. If the goal is merely to prevent firms from undermining mandated disclosures, the benchmarks might be set at the comprehension levels the bureau can obtain in its disclosure testing, provided that the bureau's subject pool is similar to the firm's actual customers. If the goal is only to increase consumer comprehension from where consumers stand now, the benchmark might be set based on industrywide performance, perhaps penalizing firms whose customers test below the median and rewarding firms whose customers beat the market.

Sanctions (or rewards) for a firm that fails to meet (or exceeds) the benchmark would be tailored to the context. For example, if a sufficient proportion of a firm's tested customers did not understand a price component, the sanction might be to require the firm to disgorge that price component over a look-back period.[13] If a firm's tested customers failed to meet the benchmark for comprehension with respect to the true nature of a benefit the firm appeared to be offering, the sanction might be to require the firm to provide the full benefit customers expected or refund the price the consumers paid for that illusory benefit. Where the issue is customer confusion about waiver of a legal right, a nonperforming firm might be required to refrain from enforcing that term until testing demonstrated that the firm's customers' confusion was dispelled. Exceeding a benchmark might be rewarded with a longer hiatus before the firm must conduct the next round of customer confusion audits.

In the following section I sketch out how comprehension rules might operate in several contexts. This is not to advocate that comprehension rules be used in all of these contexts. Upon further study, it may become clear that substantive regulation of terms or performance-based regulation of consumer financial outcomes would be a more reliable or more cost-effective regulatory method. But before dismissing Dodd-Frank's presupposition that consumers would use their own understanding to instigate substantive product competition and promote their own welfare, we must map out how to produce this understanding and assess the costs and benefits of pursuing this path.

COMPREHENSION OF PRICE

Firms are required to disclose the price components of the financial products they sell, but consumers do not always understand these, particularly at the time when they could use the knowledge to select a product or choose whether to take an action. When buying a product, consumers consider the most salient and easily understood price components, which are typically lump sum amounts expressed in dollar terms such as the annual fee

---

12. To maintain anonymity, the third party auditors would administer the rewards.

13. Disgorgement over a look-back period would parallel the bureau's proposed small dollar loan regulation described in footnote 3.

for a checking account or credit card. But consumers often do not understand or fail to account for back-end fees, fees contingent upon future events, fees buried in fine print, and fees expressed in terms that would require consumers to perform calculations to determine the total dollar amount they will pay.[14]

One such fee is overdraft charges on checking accounts. These fees are, in effect, very small, very expensive, very short-term loans, with a typical implied APR of over 17,000 percent (Willis 2015, 171–72). The price structures banks use for calculating overdraft fees are complex, shifting, and multifarious. Banks are required to inform consumers about overdraft fees and obtain affirmative consumer consent to overdraft coverage, a process that regulators hoped would ensure comprehension. But a PEW Charitable Trusts survey found that over half of consumers who had incurred overdraft fees in the prior year did not understand that they had agreed to overdraft coverage. Most overdrew their accounts unintentionally and did not realize it until they received their account statements (Pew Charitable Trusts 2014, 5, 9).

A major contributor to consumer confusion is the invisibility of overdraft fees at the moment they are incurred. Consumers are not informed in real time that they are about to overdraw their accounts and thus to incur a fee, and therefore are not given the choice at that moment to decline the loan by not overdrawing. Consumers may not know the account balance their bank will assign them at any moment because deposits take varying amounts of time to clear, holds can be placed on account funds, banks reorder transactions within a single day, and account balance statements can be inaccurate (U.S. Government Accountability Office 2008, 21, 62). In addition, people who are already financially stressed might not realize they are about to overdraw their accounts because they have insufficient cognitive-willpower bandwidth and must focus on immediate financial demands.

The law might respond with a disclosure mandate to address this, but banks are adept at sabotaging overdraft disclosures (Willis 2013). A requirement that banks demonstrate that their customers know that they are about to incur an overdraft fee and know the size of the fee shortly before incurring it would stimulate banks to develop (and redevelop as technology and customs change) the best methods for informing their customers about these fees in a timely manner, whether it be through text messages, automated cell phone calls, ATM screen messages, or new methods that would be invented for this purpose. A comprehension rule might also encourage banks to simplify their fee structures so that their customers could understand them.

Confusion audits would be straightforward. Third parties could test a bank's customers with questions such as "Which, if any, of the following recent transactions overdrew your account?," followed by a list of recent transactions and their dates. If the customer indicated knowledge of a transaction that overdrew the account, the follow-up question could be "How many dollars did your bank charge you in fees as a result of overdrawing your account on that date?" The same basic design could be used for any financial product fee that is opaque at the time it is incurred.

A similar approach might be applied to short-term credit that is commonly used as a longer-term cash flow solution, such as payday and auto title loans. For example, the cost of payday loans seems clear, disclosed at the time the loan is disbursed in both dollar and APR terms. But these figures represent the price for a single period of borrowing. Payday lenders depend on long borrowing sequences to turn a profit (Pew Charitable Trusts 2013, 62n9) and most borrowers stay indebted for months.[15] Consumers know the periodic fee on a payday

---

14. This is why monthly payments for high-priced mortgages must include taxes and insurance for the first year. Because the monthly payment is the most salient figure for most borrowers, a payment that includes taxes and insurance will ensure that consumers take these costs into consideration in addition to the loan principal and interest payments when deciding whether to enter the transaction.

15. Long borrowing sequences are long periods over which payday loan borrowers remain indebted nearly continuously, with breaks of less than thirty days, indicating that the borrower lacks sufficient income to simultane-

loan and a recent study suggests that many consumers, if asked, can estimate the time it will take them to retire the debt fairly accurately (Mann 2013). But even those consumers who know they will take a long time to repay the loan are unlikely to estimate their total borrowing duration, multiply it by the periodic fee, and then ask themselves whether they want to pay, for example, $525 over and above the principal they will have to repay to borrow $350 for ten pay periods.[16]

A $525 fee figure at the moment of a $350 loan decision might be sufficiently dramatic to cause even a desperate consumer to change course. One experiment found that providing borrowers with information about the dollar costs of the loans over time, the number of times most loans are rolled over, and the relative prices of other sources of borrowing can collectively somewhat reduce the frequency and amount of payday borrowing (Bertrand and Morse 2011). The law might require that the disclosures used in this experiment be given to consumers, but again, mandated disclosures are easily foiled in the field.

Instead, payday lenders could be required to demonstrate that at loan origination, their customers understand how and when the customer expects to retire the debt and the total dollar cost of borrowing if the customer retires the debt on the anticipated date. In effect, lenders would need to spur consumers to consider how and when they will repay their loans and then to disclose the total price the consumer will pay if the loan is paid off on that date. This might lead lenders to redesign the product into a longer term less expensive loan or to lend only to borrowers who are likely to repay the loan on its due date.[17]

COMPREHENSION OF BENEFITS

Where confusion about benefits is common, firms could be required to demonstrate that their customers understand the true benefits the transaction provides. Add-on products and debt settlement (or "credit repair") services might fall into this category. Firms have far better information than consumers about the value of these products and services.

For example, customers of debt settlement services likely believe that the service will reduce their total debt, even when it will not (Abrams and Silver-Greenberg 2014, B1). The bureau has brought charges against firms that charge up-front fees and provide consumers little if any benefit in return. But these companies are not deterred. On its website, the bureau warns consumers that debt settlement services can be a bad deal for a long list of reasons: these services can reduce consumers' credit scores and future ability to obtain credit; fees payable to the firms, taxes payable on forgiven debt, and penalties and late fees on existing bills the firms require consumers to stop paying can collectively leave consumers deeper in debt than they were when they started, and so forth.[18] But few people read the bureau's warnings.

To ensure that consumers understand these sorts of limitations on the benefits of this product, debt settlement firms could be required to demonstrate through confusion audits that their customers knew about these limitations at the time the customers signed up. This might stimulate these firms to change their pricing structures; if consumers knew that benefits are uncertain, they might demand pricing that is contingent on benefits received.

---

ously pay other monthly expenses and pay off the payday loan. Sometimes the loans are rolled over on the dates they become due, but sometimes there is a brief break between loans.

16. In a 2013 study, the bureau found that $350 and $15 per $100 were the median payday loan size and fee. It also found that the median number of loans a borrower took in twelve months of data was ten (Consumer Financial Protection Bureau 2013b, 17 table 1, 23 table 3).

17. The CFPB's proposed regulations require payday lenders in most instances to do the latter, lending only to borrowers who are likely to repay.

18. Most debt settlement firms require their customers to suspend making regular payments on the customers' existing debt.

Add-on products present an even easier case for comprehension rules. Currently the law requires that the fact that the consumer is buying the add-on product, and in some cases the consumer's right to decline to buy it, be disclosed. But in the midst of a stack of paperwork for a car loan, for example, a consumer might not notice that she had agreed to credit life, disability, unemployment, property, and debt cancellation insurance. Even if she notices these add-ons, she might assume that she is required to buy them or that they provide her a cost-justified benefit. However, these products frequently provide few benefits. For example, some consumers think credit life insurance is life insurance, when it only pays off the remaining debt on a loan at the beneficiary's death.

Comprehension rules would require firms to draw their customers' attention to these add-on products at the time the transaction takes place and to educate their customers about limits on the benefits add-ons provide. Alternatively, firms could redesign add-on products to conform to their customers' expectations.

COMPREHENSION OF LEGAL RIGHTS

A similar approach could also be used for other terms about which consumer confusion is widespread, such as legal rights and waivers of those rights. For instance, the Fair Debt Collection Practices Act of 1978, its implementing regulations, and applicable state law give debtors a host of legal rights, many of which must be disclosed in dunning letters. But do consumers actually know that debt collectors are prohibited from threatening to sue the consumer for the debt once the statute of limitations for that debt has passed? How many consumers know that if they agree to a new repayment schedule, the debt can be revived? Sophisticated consumers and those being aided by counsel or counselors may know, but it seems likely that others do not.

Rather than requiring more disclosures of consumers' rights in debt collection, an alternative would be customer confusion audits. For example, before a collector could treat an out-of-limitations debt as revived, the collector might be required to demonstrate that its debt-ors knew their actions would revive the debt. Collectors could then choose between educating their debtors or ceasing collection efforts on out-of-limitations debt.

Comprehension rules might similarly be employed for fine print clauses that waive consumers' legal rights. These clauses include arbitration clauses, class action waivers, caps on damages consumers can recover, clauses substantially shortening limitations periods within which consumers can raise claims against the firm, and more. Except for the few transaction types where such clauses are prohibited, firms regularly use these to change the background procedural and substantive rules of the civil justice system that apply to their interactions with their customers. As noted, the bureau's testing found that consumers are confused about arbitration clauses and class action waivers. The bureau has proposed prohibiting arbitration clauses that deny consumers the right to file or join class actions, and such an approach might work well for other fine print waiving consumers' legal rights. Alternatively, the bureau might employ comprehension rules. Firms could then decide whether to teach their customers about these waivers or remove the waivers from their contracts.

BENEFITS OF COMPREHENSION RULES

The effect of successful regulation through comprehension rules would be to bring transactions into closer alignment with consumer expectations, whether because consumers become educated about the transaction or because firms simplify the transaction or eliminate unintuitive features. Clearer explanations of financial transactions and increased product simplicity and usability would reduce demands placed on consumers' attention, time, and effort in selecting products and would give consumers increased confidence in the marketplace. The quality of decisionmaking would almost certainly improve, not only because consumers would understand transactions better, but also because the reduced demands on consumer cognitive resources would likely increase consumers' willpower and decrease their overconfidence and overoptimism. The ultimate direct benefit of comprehension rules is increased consumer decisional autonomy; consumers would get what they think they are getting, not whatever hidden features firms can slip into the transaction.

Rhetorical support for decisional autonomy runs deep—the imagined "empowered consumer" a favorite of liberals and the imagined "free market" a favorite of conservatives. But empowered choices free of confusion are only possible, and the market is only driven to efficiency, when consumers comprehend the transactions in which they engage. Today we pretend that individual consumers use disclosures to drive market competition and make welfare-enhancing decisions, but we do not spend the resources needed to realize actual consumer understanding. As a result, consumers neither discipline the market nor consistently enhance their own welfare.

When some degree of demonstrated consumer comprehension becomes legally required, we may find that decisional autonomy is overrated. As discussed previously, the Dodd-Frank Act's mandate to the CFPB to ensure consumer understanding of financial transaction costs, benefits, and risks rests on the assumption that consumers will use this understanding to instigate substantive product competition and promote their own welfare. This assumption may be incorrect. For many financial transactions, comprehension is probably neither necessary nor sufficient to ensure consumer welfare.

Even where solid consumer understanding of financial products would lead to better consumer choices, it might be an inefficient means of getting there. Firms might find that educating their customers is so costly that it would be cheaper for firms to directly channel consumers to suitable products. Some confusing products, when sold only to consumers for whom they are suitable, might improve consumer welfare more than simplified, transparent versions of those products.

Moreover, consumers might rather not have to understand much about the financial transactions in which they engage. They might prefer for regulators to discipline the marketplace directly. Substantive product design regulation thus might produce more consumer welfare and be truer to deep consumer autonomy—including the autonomy to decide *not* to become financially educated and make informed choices for oneself—than comprehension rules. But unless the bureau complies with Dodd-Frank's mandate to ensure consumer understanding of financial products—a mandate that can probably only be met, if at all, through comprehension rules—we will not know when and where informed consumer decisionmaking is worth its price.

REFERENCES

Abrams, Rachel and Jessica Silver-Greenberg. 2014. "Companies That Offer Help with Student Loans Are Often Predatory, Officials Say." *New York Times*, July 13, 2014.

Adjerid, Idris, Alessandro Acquisti, Laura Brandimarte, and George Loewenstein. 2013. "Sleights of Privacy: Framing, Disclosures, and the Limits of Transparency." *Symposium on Usable Privacy and Security* (SOUPS). Newcastle, United Kingdom (July 24–26, 2013).

Agnew, Julie R., and Lisa R. Szykman. 2005. "Asset Allocation and Information Overload: The Influence of Information Display, Asset Choice, and Investor Experience." *Journal of Behavioral Finance* 6(2): 57–70.

Akerlof, George A., and Robert J. Shiller. 2015. *Phishing for Phools: The Economics of Manipulation and Deception*. Princeton, N.J.: Princeton University Press.

Bar-Gill, Oren, and Ryan Bubb. 2012. "Credit Card Pricing: The Card Act and Beyond." *Cornell Law Review* 97(5): 967, 997–99.

Barr, Michael S., Sendhil Mullainathan, and Eldar Shafir. 2008. "Behaviorally Informed Financial Services Regulation." Available at: www.newamerica.net/files/naf_behavioral_v5.pdf; accessed January 10, 2016.

Baumeister, Roy F., Erin A. Sparks, Tyler F. Stillman, and Kathleen D. Vohs. 2008. "Free Will in Consumer Behavior: Self-Control, Ego Depletion, and Choice." *Journal of Consumer Psychology* 18(1): 4–13.

Bernanke, Ben S. 2009. "Innovation and Consumer Protection, at the Federal Reserve System's Sixth Biennial Community Affairs Research Conference, Washington, D.C." Last modified April 17, 2009. Available at: www.federalreserve.gov/newsevents/speech/bernanke20090417a.htm; accessed January 10, 2016.

Bertrand, Marianne, Dean Karlan, Sendhil Mullainathan, Eldar Shafir, and Jonathan Zinman. 2010. "What's Advertising Content Worth? Evidence from a Consumer Credit Marketing Field Experiment." *Quarterly Journal of Economics* 125(1): 263–306.

Bertrand, Marianne, and Adair Morse. 2011. "Information Disclosure, Cognitive Biases, and Payday Borrowing." *Journal of Finance* 66(6): 1865–93.

Brunner, Dieter. 2006. "The Mistakes Borrowers Make, and How to Avoid Them." Last modified June 6, 2006. Available at: http://consumeraffairs.com/news04/2006/06/mortgage_geek.html; accessed January 10, 2016.

Calo, Ryan. 2014. "Digital Market Manipulation." *George Washington Law Review* 82(4): 995–1051.

Carney, Michael. 2013. "Mediabrix Enables Targeted Advertising During Moments of Positive and Negative Emotion in Social Games." Available at: http://pando.com/2013/04/18/mediabrix-enables-targeted-advertising-during-moments-of-positive-and-negative-emotion-in-social-games/; accessed January 10, 2016.

Catlin, Jesse R., Cornelia Pechmann, and Eric P. Brass. 2011. "The Influence of Need for Cognition and Principal Display Panel Factors on Over-the-Counter Drug Facts Label Comprehension." *Health Communication* 27(3): 264–73.

Consumer Financial Protection Bureau. n.d. "Information Collection Request–Supporting Statement, Credit Card Agreement Testing Survey." Available at: www.reginfo.gov/public/do/DownloadDocument?objectID=34998102; accessed January 10, 2016.

———. 2012. Supervision and Examination Manual—Version 2.0. Washington, D.C.: October. Available at: files.consumerfinance.gov/f/201210_cfpb_supervision-and-examination-manual-v2.pdf; accessed July 12, 2016.

———. 2013a. "Policy to Encourage Trial Disclosure Programs." *Federal Register* 78(209): 64389–94.

———. 2013b. "Payday Loans and Deposit Advance Products: A White Paper of Initial Data Findings." Washington, D.C.: April.

———. 2014. "Generic Information Collection Plan for Studies of Consumers Using Controlled Trials in Field and Economic Laboratory Settings." *Federal Register* 79 (71): 20865–66.

———. 2015a. *Fair Debt Collection Practices Act: CFPB Annual Report 2015*. Washington, D.C.: March.

———. 2015b. *Arbitration Study: Report to Congress Pursuant to Dodd-Frank Wall Street Reform and Consumer Protection Act § 1028(a)*. Washington, D.C.: March.

———. 2016. *Payday, Vehicle Title, and Certain High-Cost Installment Loans*. Docket No. CFPB-2016-0025, Proposed C.F.R. 91041.12, 1292.

Diamond, Shari Seidman. 2011. "Reference Guide on Survey Research." In *Reference Manual on Scientific Evidence*, edited by the Federal Judicial Center and the National Research Council. Washington, D.C.: National Academies Press.

Drolet, Aimee, Mary Frances Luce, and Itamar Simonson. 2009. "When Does Choice Reveal Preference? Moderators of Heuristic versus Goal-Based Choice." *Journal of Consumer Research* 36(June): 137–47.

Duhigg, Charles. 2007. "Bilking the Elderly, with a Corporate Assist." *New York Times*, May 20.

Epley, Nicholas, and Thomas Gilovich. 2006. "The Anchoring-and-Adjustment Heuristic: Why the Adjustments Are Insufficient." *Psychological Science* 17(4): 311–18.

Federal Trade Commission. 1980. "Policy Statement on Unfairness." Appended to International Harvester Co., 104 FTC 949, 1070 (1984).

———. 1983. "Policy Statement on Deception." Appended to *In re* Cliffdale Associates Inc., 103 FTC 110, 174 (1984).

Garrison, Loretta, Manoj Hastak, Jeanne M. Hogarth, Susan Kleimann, and Alan S. Levy. 2012. "Designing Evidence-Based Disclosures: A Case Study of Financial Privacy Notices." *Journal of Consumer Affairs* 46(2): 204–34.

Hogarth, Jeanne M., and Ellen A. Merry. 2011. "Designing Disclosures to Inform Consumer Financial Decisionmaking: Lessons Learned from Consumer Testing." *Federal Reserve Bulletin* 97(3): 1–27.

Kahn, Barbara E., and Jonathan Baron. 1995. "An Exploratory Study of Choice Rules Favored for High-Stakes Decisions." *Journal of Consumer Psychology* 4(4): 305–28.

Keller, Punam Anand, Issac M. Lipkus, and Barbara K. Rimer. 2002. "Depressive Realism and Health Risk Accuracy: The Negative Consequences of Positive Mood." *Journal of Consumer Research* 29(1): 57–69.

Kleimann Communication Group. 2013. "Know Before You Owe: Quantitative Study of the Current and Integrated TILA-RESPA Disclosures." Rockville, Md.: Kleimann Communication Group Inc.

Kramer, Adam D. I., Jamie E. Guillory, and Jeffrey T. Hancock. 2014. "Experimental Evidence of Massive-Scale Emotional Contagion Through Social Networks." *Proceedings of the National Academy of Sciences* 111(24): 8788–90.

Kruger, Justin. 1999. "Lake Wobegon Be Gone! The 'Below-Average Effect' and the Egocentric Nature of Comparative Ability Judgments." *Journal of Personality and Social Psychology* 77(2): 221–32.

Kunda, Ziva. 1990. "The Case for Motivated Reasoning." *Psychological Bulletin* 108(3): 480–98.

Leonard-Segal, Andrea, Laura E. Shay, Daiva Shetty, and Joel Schiffenbauer. 2009. "Unique Role of Consumer Studies in Nonprescription Drug Development." *Journal of the American Pharmacists Association* 49(5): 670–73.

Lewis, Randall A., and David H. Reiley. 2014. "Online Ads and Offline Sales: Measuring the Effects of Retail Advertising via a Controlled Experiment on Yahoo!" *Quantitative Marketing Economics* 12(3): 235–66.

Loewenstein, George, Cass R. Sunstein, and Russell Golman. 2014. "Disclosure: Psychology Changes Everything." *Annual Review of Economics* 6(1): 391–19.

Mann, Ronald J. 2013. "Assessing the Optimism of Payday Loan Borrowers." *Supreme Court Economic Review* 21(1): 105–32.

Mather, Mara, and Nichole R. Lighthall. 2012. "Risk and Reward Are Processed Differently in Decisions Made Under Stress." *Current Directions in Psychological Science* 21(2): 36–41.

Mullainathan, Sendhil, and Eldar Shafir. 2013. *Scarcity: Why Having Too Little Means So Much.* New York: Times Books.

Office of Oversight and Investigations Majority Staff, U.S. Senate Committee on Commerce, Science, and Transportation. 2013. "A Review of the Data Broker Industry: Collection, Use, and Sale of Consumer Data for Marketing Purposes." Available at: www.commerce.senate.gov/public/?a=Files.Serve&File_id=0d2b3642-6221-4888-a631-08f2f255b577; accessed January 10, 2016.

Pew Charitable Trusts. 2013. "Payday Lending in America: How Borrowers Choose and Repay Payday Loans." Washington, D.C.: Pew Charitable Trusts.

———. 2014. "Overdrawn: Persistent Confusion and Concern About Bank Overdraft Practices." Washington, D.C.: Pew Charitable Trusts.

Shapiro, Stewart, and Deborah J. MacInnis. 2002. "Understanding Program-Induced Mood Effects." *Journal of Advertising* 31(4): 15–26.

Sovern, Jeff. 2010. "Preventing Future Economic Crises through Consumer Protection Law or How the Truth in Lending Act Failed Subprime Borrowers." *Ohio State Law Journal* 71(4): 761–844.

Stark, Debra Pogrund, Jessica M. Choplin, and Mark A. LeBoeuff. 2013. "Ineffective in Any Form: How Confirmation Bias and Distractions Undermine Improved Home-Loan Disclosures." *Yale Law Journal Online* 122(1): 377–400.

Tanner, Robin J., and Kurt A. Carlson. 2009. "Unrealistically Optimistic Consumers: A Selective Hypothesis Testing Account for Optimism in Predictions of Future Behavior." *Journal of Consumer Research* 35(5): 810–22.

U.S. Government Accountability Office. 2008. *Bank Fees: Federal Banking Regulators Could Better Ensure That Consumers Have Required Disclosure Documents Prior to Opening Checking or Savings Accounts.* Washington: U.S. Government Printing Office.

———. 2011. *Information on Tall Smokestacks and Their Contribution to Interstate Transportation of Air Pollution.* Washington: U.S. Government Printing Office.

Willis, Lauren E. 2006. "Decisionmaking and the Limits of Disclosure: The Problem of Predatory Lending: Price." *Maryland Law Review* 65(3): 707–840.

———. 2013. "When Nudges Fail: Slippery Defaults." *University of Chicago Law Review* 80(3): 1155–1229.

———. 2015. "Performance-Based Consumer Law." *University of Chicago Law Review* 82(3): 1309–1409.

Wood, Leslie A., and David F. Poltrack. 2015. "Measuring the Long-Term Effects of Television Advertising." *Journal of Advertising Research* 55(2): 123–31.

A Public Choice Approach to the Unequal Treatment of Securities Market Participants and Home Borrowers

JONATHAN MACEY

This article contrasts the protections provided to participants in U.S. securities markets with the protections provided to participants in the U.S. mortgage markets. Participants in securities markets purchase and sell equity and debt securities. Participants in the mortgage markets borrow money to buy homes, using those homes as collateral for the mortgage loans they receive. Even after Dodd-Frank, participants in securities markets are afforded significantly higher levels of protection than participants in mortgage markets. The doctrine of suitability is a prime example of this inequity. Exploring possible explanations for this odd asymmetry of treatment, I conclude that interest group politics is to blame for the anomaly.

Keywords: securities, mortgages, regulation, consumer protections, interest groups

Reckless and predatory mortgage lending practices were among the key drivers of the financial meltdown of 2008.[1] I, along with my coauthors Geoff Miller, Maureen O'Hara, Gabe Rosenberg, have argued that changes in the nature of the mortgage contract make it both legally plausible and normatively desirable that subprime mortgage brokers be treated as securities broker-dealers for the purposes of the Securities Act of 1933 and the Securities and Exchange Act of 1934 (Macey et al. 2009). Given the recent revival in mortgage lending in general and higher-priced lending with interest rates greater than 1.5 points above the prime offer rate in particular—which made up 7.1 percent of home purchase loans in 2013, as compared to 2.2 percent in 2010 and 23.2 percent in 2006 (Board of Governors of the Federal Reserve System 2014)—this regulatory issue is in need of timely address.

As a technical matter, subprime mortgages are in large part derivative securities that contain embedded options (Quercia and Stegman 1992), but they are not subject to the significant anti-fraud and consumer protection provisions of the securities laws. Nor are mortgages subject to any alternative comprehensive regulatory regime. Unlike other financial contracts that are individualized and not fungible such as insurance contracts and annuities and certificates of deposit (CDs), mortgages are bundled together to formulate mortgage-backed securities. This differentiates mortgages from other types of private contracts, creating a unique need for securities-type regulation.

Writing from the perspective of legal theory

Jonathan Macey is the Sam Harris Professor of Corporate Law, Corporate Finance and Securities Regulation at Yale Law School.

I gratefully acknowledge helpful suggestions from Michael Barr and two excellent anonymous reviewers. I received outstanding research assistance from Kayla DeLeon, Yale Law School class of 2017. Direct correspondence to: Jonathan Macey at jonathan.macey@yale.edu, Yale Law School, P.O. Box 208215, New Haven, CT 06520.

1. "The Bubble Keeps Deflating," editorial, *New York Times*, October 19, 2008.

predicated on normative arguments about basic fairness and the desirability of logical symmetry between the protections for people trafficking in securities and people trafficking in home mortgage loans, in previous works I have argued that subprime mortgages should be regulated like securities, especially given their complicated, unusual lending terms and their thorny relationship with the mortgage-backed securities industry (Macey et al. 2009). From this analysis, it inevitably follows that home buyers who take out subprime mortgage loans should have the same protections as people who buy and sell securities such as options and common stock.

In this article I take a positive rather than a normative perspective. Here, I ponder the issue of why, as a descriptive matter, home buyers are afforded such paltry legal protections when compared to the robust panoply of legal protections enjoyed by buyers and sellers of securities subject to the Securities Act of 1933 and the Securities Exchange Act of 1934. Why, in other words, is it the case that a large investment bank that buys a security backed by home mortgages is entitled to so much more legal protection than an individual who incurred massive indebtedness by taking out one of the subprime mortgage loans bundled into that mortgage-backed security?

Simply put, as Kathleen C. Engel and Patricia A. McCoy (2002, 1319) argue, "If the duty of suitability is appropriate for financial instruments that have been the traditional province of the affluent, certainly it is appropriate for financial instruments that are peddled to the poorest rung of society." As I previously have pointed out (Macey et al. 2009, 790):

> Kafka would have loved this story: According to our current understanding of U.S. law there is far better consumer protection for people who play the stock market than for people who are duped into buying a house with an exotically structured subprime mortgage, even when the mortgage instrument is immediately packaged and sold as part of a security. We live on a peculiar legal landscape in which homeowners have almost no recourse under consumer protection laws against people who peddled unsuitable mortgages to them, unless the funds generated by the mortgage financing happened to have been used by the homeowner to purchase securities rather than a house.

Subprime mortgages incorporate abnormal, and arguably predatory, terms that are "present either because of the risk profile of subprime borrowers or the need of lenders to counteract the lower expected repayment rate of this group" (Macey et al. 2009). Examples of these terms include prepayment penalties for paying off a mortgage before it comes due, and a payment of a certain number of percentage "points" of the mortgage upfront (Macey et al. 2009). One acutely troubling facet of subprime lending is that foreclosure scars subprime borrowers' already low credit scores, leaving them with even less access to credit than they had at the origination of their defaulted mortgages.

Subprime mortgage loans are not garden-variety loans, and neither are the circumstances of their origination. Subprime mortgages, bundled together, constitute the base material of exotic securities such as CDOs and RMBSs. The issuance of these securities should be regulated as such to protect those borrowers suckered into entering them against their best interest. With subprime mortgage–backed securities "gearing up for a comeback," this pressing regulatory issue requires immediate attention (Shenn 2015).

SUITABILITY

A number of protections are afforded to securities transactions from which mortgage financings do not benefit. For the purpose of brevity, this article will focus on the protection most readily applicable to subprime mortgages: suitability.

> The doctrine of suitability requires that broker-dealers only recommend to their clients those financial transactions that are suitable given the customer's level of financial sophistication, current investments, financial status, personal circumstances, and anything else that might bear on the clients' ability to accept the risk associated with a particular investment. The suitability doc-

trine requires broker-dealers to tailor the securities sold to a customer with that customer's specific financial needs and objectives, and forbids agents from simply pushing those products that offer the greatest profit margins for the seller. (Macey et al. 2009, 815)

The suitability doctrine arose from "fears about unsophisticated investors taken advantage of by financially savvy (and unscrupulous) professionals" and is administered federally by "overlapping, though not identical, rules" (Macey et al. 2009, 816).[2]

The first of these rules is the descendent of National Association of Securities Dealers (NASD) Conduct Rule 2310, Financial Industry Regulatory Authority (FINRA) (2015). Rule 2111(a):

> A member or an associated person must have a reasonable basis to believe that a recommended transaction or investment strategy involving a security or securities is suitable for the customer, based on the information obtained through the reasonable diligence of the member or associated person to ascertain the customer's investment profile. A customer's investment profile includes, but is not limited to, the customer's age, other investments, financial situation and needs, tax status, investment objectives, investment experience, investment time horizon, liquidity needs, risk tolerance, and any other information the customer may disclose to the member or associated person in connection with such recommendation.[3]

The second rule is the descendent of the New York Stock Exchange suitability requirement or "Know Thy Customer rule," FINRA Rule 2090. This rule requires that members "use reasonable diligence, in regard to the opening and maintenance of every account, to know (and retain) the essential facts concerning every customer and concerning the authority of each person acting on behalf of such customer." "Essential Facts" include those required to (a) effectively service the customer's account; (b) act in accordance with any special handling instructions for the account; (c) understand the authority of each person acting on behalf of the customer; and (d) comply with applicable laws, regulations and rules.[4]

Finally, broker-dealers are liable for suitability violations under section 10(b) of the Securities Exchange Act and Securities and Exchange Commission (SEC) Rule 10b-5. Section 10(b) of the Securities Exchange Act states:

> It shall be unlawful for any person directly or indirectly, by the use of any means or instrumentality of interstate commerce or of the mails, or of any facility of any national securities exchange . . . to use or employ, in connection with the purchase or sale of any security registered on a national securities exchange or any security not so registered, or any securities-based swap agreement any manipulative or deceptive device or contrivance in contravention of such rules and regulations as the Commission may prescribe as necessary or appropriate in the public interest or for the protection of investors).[5]

And SEC Rule 10b-5 states:

> It shall be unlawful for any person, directly or indirectly, by the use of any means or instrumentality of interstate commerce, or of the mails or of any facility of any national securities exchange,
> (a) to employ any device, scheme, or artifice to defraud;
> (b) to make any untrue statement of a material fact or to omit to state a material

---

2. There are additional requirements under state laws that this article does not discuss.

3. For FINRA Rule 2111 see http://finra.complinet.com/en/display/display_viewall.html?rbid=2403&element_id=9859&print=1; accessed June 8, 2016.

4. For FINRA Rule 2090 see http://finra.complinet.com/en/display/display_viewall.html?rbid=2403&element_id=9858

5. See SEC Rule 10b-5, 17 C.F.R. 240.10b-5, "Employment of Manipulative and Deceptive Devices," www.law.cornell.edu/cfr/text/17/240.10b-5.

fact necessary in order to make the statements made, in light of the circumstances under which they were made, not misleading; or

(c) to engage in any act, practice, or course of business which operates or would operate as a fraud or deceit upon any person, in connection with the purchase or sale of a security.[6]

Basic product-suitability claims are not the only conflict-of-interest, broker-buyer issues that implicate the suitability doctrine. Regulators also rein in churning, or "encouraging customers to engage in more trades than are in the customers' best interests," as well as flawed commission structures such as recommending that customers "pay a flat fee to the broker-dealer for a number of services rather than paying for each transaction individually" through the suitability doctrine (Macey et al. 2009, 830).

Given that in the subprime mortgage context brokers sometimes encourage "borrowers to engage in an excessive number of costly refinancing transactions in order to generate [more] fees" and that brokers receive yield spread premium incentives to "steer their customers towards higher cost loans," the suitability doctrine appears particularly apt to address issues of conflicting interests in the subprime mortgage industry (Macey et al. 2009, 830).

The purpose of these suitability rules is clear. They serve as an "ex ante protection against improper investment, not a way for investors to recoup losses from investing insecurities with full knowledge of, and ability to handle, the attendant risks" (Macey et al. 2009, 819). Providing a regulatory framework for suitability claims on behalf of subprime mortgage borrowers would allow an opportunity for regulatory agencies, and the mortgage borrowers themselves, to curb predatory lending executed through unsuitable financial products, excessive refinancings, and problematic broker compensation structures. If given the regulatory green light, suitability claims in the subprime mortgage context could theoretically be brought in the same ways as their sister claims in the securities context: (1) via individual suits, (2) via class actions, and (3) via interventions of regulators on behalf of mortgage holders.

Some might argue that the suitability doctrine as it applies to securities is relatively toothless, and thus the lack of its application for individual mortgage holders is irrelevant. In regard to the first avenue just discussed, although individual suitability claims may not always involve large financial penalties, studies show that securities buyers embrace them as a mechanism for policing the investment recommendations they receive. In fact, in a random sample of 422 arbitrators' cases from 1992 to 2006, 49.76 percent of customer arbitrations against broker-dealers involved a suitability claim (Choi, Fisch, and Pritchard 2010). Given that "virtually all brokerage customer agreements contain a clause requiring disputes between the customer and the broker to be submitted to arbitration," this finding is highly salient (Choi, Fisch and Pritchard 2010, 110). Moreover, a separate study found that 48.9 percent of arbitrations involving a suitability claim were victorious, and in 9.9 percent of those successful arbitrations, punitive damages were awarded (Choi and Eisenberg 2010). Sure, this figure is underwhelming, but keep in mind: 0 percent of subprime mortgage borrowers are awarded punitive damages on the basis of suitability claims. They currently have no right to bring them.

In regard to the second avenue for suitability claims discussed, admittedly, "Class actions are not necessarily easy to certify in predatory-lending cases. In damages class actions under Federal Rule of Civil Procedure 23(b)(3), plaintiffs must show that the common issues predominate over the individual ones in order to achieve class certification. Loan-underwriting decisions often turn on facts that are unique to the borrowers, making commonality difficult to prove" (Engel and McCoy 2002, 1362). That said, it is unlikely that class actions would play a large role, if any at all, in suitability claims against subprime lenders.

Nevertheless, supervision of the subprime mortgage industry via the suitability doctrine

---

6. Ibid.

would allow for increased regulatory oversight of subprime lenders that could be exceptionally effective, given the concentrated nature of the subprime lending industry.[7] Regulators have brought about nontrivial suitability penalties in the securities industry,[8] and could do the same in the subprime mortgage industry.

Alternatively, critics of a suitability requirement for subprime mortgages sometimes focus on the threat of the suitability requirement constraining the subprime mortgage market too much. Yet arguments about regulation in this arena causing a credit gap fall flat. Studies show that many subprime borrowers (somewhere between 10 and 35 percent) could have qualified for prime loans (Mahoney and Zorn 1996). In addition, the predatory lending that the suitability requirement seeks to isolate and eliminate creates undesirable and financially fatal loan options without which mortgage borrowers would be better off.

THE POSSIBILITIES

One mechanism for protecting home borrowers would be to classify subprime mortgages as securities, and give them the same antifraud protections that are given to swap agreements. The more likely regulatory apparatus, however, would be to regulate the fraudulent actions of subprime mortgage brokers on the grounds that securitized mortgages are made "in connection with the purchase and sale of" mortgage-backed securities. Doing so would give the SEC as much jurisdiction over subprime mortgage brokers as it has over securities broker-dealers. As I have previously argued (Macey et al. 2009, 814):

> It seems clear that maneuvering an unsophisticated client into taking on an unsuitable mortgage on which the borrower is bound to default unless interest rates stay low and housing prices stay high is done in connection with the purchase and sale of a security, where all parties understand that the payments being made on the mortgage are an integral part of a securitization. Thus, even if a mortgage itself is not a security, where the mortgage is used as part of a securitization, that transaction is done in connection with the purchase or sale of a security and the protections of Rule 10b-5 should protect the mortgagee. Similarly, there appears to be little distinction between cases in which a mortgage broker convinces a person to refinance in order to purchase securities (where 10b-5 clearly applies), and cases in which a mortgage broker convinces a person to refinance so that the mortgage broker himself can participate in the creation of a new security.

RECOGNIZING THE PROBLEM

The government's primary response to the problem of struggling, unsophisticated home buyers saddled with expensive subprime mortgages was the creation of a new bureaucracy, the Consumer Financial Protection Bureau, an organization that has yet to fully address this problem. The CFPB recognizes that subprime mortgages contain high rates of interest that "can rise significantly over time." But they also recognize that lenders and brokers are not obligated to offer consumers the best deal available in the market for them. Additionally, the CFPB recognizes that consumers shunted into high-interest subprime loans may be eligible for a prime mortgage or the Federal Housing Administration (FHA) program of loan insurance that can reduce interest payments dramatically, but neither of these facts need be disclosed to subprime borrowers (Consumer Financial Protection Bureau 2016).

Although the "ability to pay" requirement of Regulation Z of the Truth in Lending Act of 1968 is a step in the right direction, it does not go so far as to implicate the full-fledged suitability requirement for which I advocate here. Regulation Z forbids lenders from making "a

---

7. Seventy-two percent of the loans made between the boom of subprime mortgages in 2005 and the Financial Crisis were made by twenty-five leading subprime lenders (Dunbar 2009). Moreover, there were only 213 subprime lenders in 2005 identified by the U.S. Department of Housing and Urban Development (2006).

8. For example, FINRA recently fined Barclays Capital $13.75 million and Royal Bank of Canada (RBC) $1.4 million for suitability violations (Financial Industry Regulatory Authority 2015a, 2015b).

loan that is a covered transaction unless the creditor makes a reasonable and good faith determination at or before consummation that the consumer will have a reasonable ability to repay the loan according to its terms."[9]

This inquiry into a prospective mortgage holder's ability to pay is necessary, but not sufficient, for determining the suitability of a particular mortgage for an individual's unique investment situation. For example, when a candidate is presented with several alternative mortgage options, he or she may be "able to pay" at least initially what is required on a monthly basis for all of them, and thus a simple ability-to-pay analysis would fail to distinguish among these. If one option in particular is starkly better suited for the candidate's situation, however, a suitability analysis would forbid a broker to recommend any alternative that is inferior from the borrower's point of view.

ANALYSIS: WHY CHANGE DOESN'T HAPPEN

If mortgage financings had qualified for the protections of rules such as SEC Rule 10b-5, which forbid the sale of financial instruments to any person unless investing in those instruments is appropriate (suitable) to the investment needs and risk tolerance of that investor, it is likely that the financial crisis of 2008 never would have occurred.[10] As I have argued before (Macey et al. 2009, 804):

> The inability of subprime borrowers to pay the interest on their mortgages, and the foreclosures that resulted, percolated through financial markets via mortgage-backed securities, collateral debt obligations, and other esoteric financial contracts. The resulting "credit crunch" stopped business lending in its tracks, ended Wall Street's ability to employ leverage, and shut down a multi-billion dollar industry, leaving investment banks scrambling to find buyers for illiquid, suddenly worthless securities.

The mortgage industry of today generates an entirely different set of incentives than the historical mortgage industry that status quo mortgage regulations were intended to tame. As I previously acknowledged (Macey et al. 2009, 838):

> The current legal landscape is informed by the view that the agents selling the mortgages did not securitize them, but instead kept them as assets on their books until the principal and interest had been repaid, or until there was default and foreclosure. This, of course, closely aligned the interests of the mortgagee and the mortgagor, since, in sharp contrast with today, in bygone times, the person originating the mortgage was as interested in making sure that the principal and interest on that mortgage could be repaid as the person receiving the financing from the mortgage transaction. This is no longer the case, of course, as mortgage originators today are brokers who do not plan to hold the mortgage note, but rather to sell it immediately so that it can be bundled into a security and sold to investors.

Meaningful reform addressing the underlying cause of the financial crisis has not occurred because lawmakers and bureaucrats lack the incentives to effectuate change. As I will discuss further, consumers are not sufficiently resourced and the plaintiff's bar—the portion of the legal profession that specializes in representing consumers and other prototypical plaintiffs—is not sufficiently motivated to advocate for this necessary suitability update to the current regulation structures governing subprime mortgages. Mortgage lenders and the banks that structure mortgage-backed securities, in complete contrast, have both the resources and incentives to push to retain the status quo.

Consumers seeking subprime mortgage loans (and consumers on whom such loans are foisted) are not sophisticated and are not able

---

9. Truth in Lending Act (Regulation Z), 12 C.F.R. Part 226, www.law.cornell.edu/cfr/text/12/part-226; accessed June 8, 2016.

10. References to "the crisis" or the "financial crisis" refer to the global financial crisis of 2008.

to transform themselves into the sort of well-organized, well-financed interest group that is able to lobby successfully for protection. Moreover, sophisticated borrowers are insulated from problems in the subprime mortgage market by their ability to shop for desirable terms when they are in the market for a mortgage.

Some may look to the plaintiff's bar as a powerhouse to provoke reform through litigation. Unfortunately, however, pursuing individual suitability claims is uneconomical for plaintiffs' lawyers, and class actions, as discussed earlier, are not a plausible vehicle for these highly individualized claims.

It could even be argued that lawmakers are dis-incentivized to bring about this reform. The commercial and investment banks and the mortgage brokers who benefit by gaining access to a large pool of high-interest assets are well organized and capable of resisting reform. We saw subprime lobbying play a central role in the lead-up to the financial crisis, with subprime lenders such as Ameriquest "maneuver[ing] to defeat legislation that might have contained some of the damage" (Simpson 2007). This influence has not disappeared.

Lobbying expenditures for the real estate sector rank fourteenth among the 121 industries that the Center for Responsive Politics monitors. In fact, lobbying in the real estate industry, including by the Mortgage Bankers Association, the Federal Home Loan Bank, and the Association of Mortgage Investors, reached a ten-year high in 2014: $95,293,540. The Mortgage Bankers Association—which argued that Congress "should resist pressure to enact a suitability standard which would harm consumers" via decreased access to credit (Mortgage Bankers Association 2007)—spent approximately $2.7 million lobbying in 2015. That same organization has lobbied against bills such as the Mortgage Choice Act of 2013, and the Housing Finance Reform and Taxpayer Protection Act of 2014 (Center for Responsive Politics 2015a, 2015b).

On the other hand, it appears likely that the Securities and Exchange Commission (SEC) would benefit from expanding its regulatory turf to include home mortgages. However, the SEC appears to be captured by the very financial firms—investment banks—that profit most from the status quo (Macey 2010).

The current incentive landscape, dominated by well-funded interest groups that drown out subprime borrowers' needs regardless of how hard they try to voice them, is the reason no suitability requirement has surfaced for subprime mortgages. Nevertheless, there is hope for the reform.

Should the SEC affirmatively create a rule that subjects subprime mortgage lending to a suitability requirement, it is likely that it would benefit from *Chevron* deference, or "the deference that federal courts give to the interpretations of statues made by administrative agencies where those interpretations fall within the agencies' delegated zone of expertise" (Macey et al. 2009, 841).[11] Section 10(b) of the Securities Exchange Act of 1934 increases the likelihood of this deference, as it conveys upon the SEC the ability to create "such rules and regulations as the Commission may prescribe as necessary or appropriate in the public interest or for the protection of investors" in order to prevent fraud, manipulation and deception in connection with the sale of securities (Securities and Exchange Act of 1934 Section 10[b]).[12]

IT'S TIME

"Residential mortgage-backed securities tendered on the private market jumped to 78 percent of all new offerings last year from 46 percent in 2013 and just 10 percent in 2007" (Levinson 2015). If subprime mortgage-backed securities make a comeback in the markets, mortgage brokers will be incentivized to origi-

---

11. The term *"Chevron* deference" refers to a rule of administrative law that requires courts to defer to the interpretations of statutes that previously have been articulated by the government agency charged with enforcing that statute unless such interpretations are unreasonable. The term *"Chevron* deference" is derived from the landmark case that first articulated the principle. See *Chevron U.S.A. Inc. v. Natural Resources Defense Council Inc.*, 467 U.S. 837 (1984).

12. Securities Exchange Act of 1934, Section 10(b), "15 U.S. Code § 8j(b), Manipulative and Deceptive Devices," www.law.cornell.edu/uscode/text/15/78j.

nate increasing amounts of subprime loans to serve as raw material for those securities. Without regulatory reform discouraging mortgage brokers from saddling mortgage borrowers with unsuitable loans, brokers blinded by profits could build a new generation of mortgage-backed securities on the backs of unsuspecting Americans, herded into subprime mortgages sometimes for the sole reason of creating subprime securities.

REFERENCES

Board of Governors of the Federal Reserve System. 2014. "The 2013 Home Mortgage Disclosure Act Data." *Federal Reserve Bulletin* 100(6). Available at: hwww.federalreserve.gov/pubs/bulletin/2014/articles/hmda/2013-HMDA-Data.htm; accessed June 8, 2016.

Center for Responsive Politics. 2015a. "Mortgage Bankers Assn." Available at: www.opensecrets.org/orgs/lobby.php?id=D000000309; accessed January 18, 2016.

Center for Responsive Politics. 2015b. "Real Estate, Industry Profile: Summary, 2015." Available at: www.opensecrets.org/lobby/indusclient.php?id=F10&year=2015; accessed January 18, 2016.

Choi, Stephen J., Jill E. Fisch, and A. C. Pritchard. 2010. "Attorneys as Arbitrators." *Journal of Legal Studies* 39(1): 109–57.

Choi, Stephen, and Theodore Eisenberg. 2010. "Punitive Damages in Securities Arbitration: An Empirical Study." Cornell Law Faculty Publications, Paper 391. Available at: http://scholarship.law.cornell.edu/cgi/viewcontent.cgi?article=1315&context=facpub; accessed June 8, 2016.

Consumer Financial Protection Bureau. 2016. "What Is a Subprime Mortgage." Ask CFPB, Mortgages." Available at: www.consumerfinance.gov/askcfpb/110/what-is-a-subprime-mortgage.html; accessed June 8, 2016.

Dunbar, John. 2009. "The Roots of the Financial Crisis: Who Is to Blame?" Center for Public Integrity, May 6. Available at: www.publicintegrity.org/2009/05/06/5449/roots-financial-crisis-who-blame; accessed June 6, 2016.

Engel, Kathleen C., and Patricia A. McCoy. 2002. "A Tale of Three Markets: The Law and Economics of Predatory Lending." *Texas Law Review* 80(6): 1255-1368.

Financial Industry Regulatory Authority. 2015a. "FINRA Orders RBC to Pay Fine and Restitution Totaling More Than $1.4 Million for Unsuitable Sales of Reverse Convertibles." News release, April 23. Available at: www.finra.org/newsroom/2015/finra-orders-rbc-pay-fine-and-restitution-totaling-more-14-million; accessed June 8, 2016.

———. 2015b. "FINRA Sanctions Barclays Capital Inc. $13.75 Million for Unsuitable Mutual Fund Transactions and Related Supervisory Failures." News release, December 29. Available at: www.finra.org/newsroom/2015/finra-sanctions-barclays-capital-inc-1375-million-unsuitable-mutual-fund-transactions; accessed June 8, 2016.

Levinson, Charles. 2015. "How Wall Street Captured Washington's Effort to Rein in Banks." *Reuters*, April 9, 2015.

Macey, Jonathan. 2010. "The Distorting Incentives Facing the U.S. Securities and Exchange Commission." *Harvard Journal of Law and Public Policy* 33(2): 639-70.

Macey, Jonathan, Geoffrey Miller, Maureen O'Hara, and Gabriel Rosenberg. 2009. "Helping Law Catch up to Markets: Applying Broker-Dealer Law to Subprime Mortgages." *Journal of Corporation Law* 34(3): 789-842.

Mahoney, Peter E., and Peter M. Zorn. 1996. "The Promise of Automated Underwriting," *Mortgage Market Trends* 1996: 18-24. Available at: http://www.freddiemac.com/finance/smm/nov96/pdfs/mhnyzorn.pdf; accessed July 11, 2016.

Mortgage Bankers Association. 2007. "Suitability—Don't Turn Back the Clock on Fair Lending and Homeownership Gains." MBA Policy Paper Series, Paper 2007-1. Available at: www.pdffiller.com/en/project/50523286.htm?form_id=5734291; accessed June 8, 2016.

Quercia, Roberto G., and Michael A. Stegman. 1992. "Residential Mortgage Default, A Review of the Literature." *Journal of Housing Research* 3(2): 341-79.

Shenn, Jody. 2015. "Subprime Bonds Are Back with a Different Name Seven Years After U.S. Crisis." *Bloomberg*, January 27.

Simpson, Glenn R. 2007. "Lender Lobbying Blitz Abetted Mortgage Mess." *Wall Street Journal*, December, 31, 2007.

U.S. Department of Housing and Urban Development. 2006. "Data Sets: HUD Subprime and Manufactured Home Lender List." Available at: www.huduser.gov/portal/datasets/manu.html; accessed June 8, 2016.

PART IV
Market Structure

Strategic Agent-Based Modeling of Financial Markets

MICHAEL P. WELLMAN AND ELAINE WAH

Understanding the implications of algorithmic trading calls for modeling financial markets at a level of fidelity that often precludes analytic solution. We describe how agent-based simulation modeling can be combined with game-theoretic reasoning to examine the effects of market variables on outcomes of interest. The approach is illustrated in a basic model where investors trade a single security through a continuous double auction mechanism. Our results demonstrate the feasibility of the approach, and raise questions about the use of spreads as a proxy for trading cost and welfare.

Keywords: algorithmic trading, agent-based modeling

Program trading has been a reality for many years now, and the pervasiveness, speed, and autonomy of trading algorithms continue to reach new heights. Algorithmic strategies designed to respond to information within a few milliseconds or less are now widely deployed. The blink of a human eye, normally lasting over 0.3 seconds, may span hundreds of rounds of high-frequency trading (HFT). Although precise definitions or prevalence measurements of HFT are hard to come by, typical estimates agree that HFT accounts for over half of trading volume on U.S. equities and futures markets, and is increasingly common on currency exchange and fixed-income markets (Cardella et al. 2014).

With the ascent of algorithmic trading and HFT has come no small amount of public controversy, for example, about whether this practice contributed to the "flash crash" of May 6, 2010. Despite an abundance of available market data, understanding this episode is challenging because of the multiplicity of actors and complexity of interactions. This is reflected in necessarily complicated and nuanced characterizations of the role of HFT, as in the conclusion by Andrei A. Kirilenko et al. (2014) that HFT was not the proximate cause, yet HFT presence shaped the environmental conditions for the crash and accelerated price movements in response to the triggering event.

One way that prevalent algorithmic trading can shape the trading environment is through strategies that quickly withdraw liquidity when observations indicate a situation outside the normal operating conditions. This response is quite rational, given that underlying algorithms were derived and vetted on the basis of data from historical experience. When evidence presents that the current situation deviates qualitatively from historical conditions, the safe move is to turn off the algorithm. Of course, this is precisely the situation when the

Michael P. Wellman is Lynn A. Conway Collegiate Professor of Computer Science and Engineering at the University of Michigan. **Elaine Wah** works at IEX Group Inc. This work was completed while she was a research assistant at the University of Michigan.

Direct correspondence to: Michael P. Wellman at wellman@umich.edu, 2260 Hayward St., Ann Arbor, MI 48109; and Elaine Wah at elaine.wah@iextrading.com.

market is most in need of liquidity, so if such algorithms control the main liquidity sources this poses a clear stability risk.

Because the markets recovered minutes after they plunged, the May 2010 flash crash caused no general economic damage beyond harm to specific investors and traders caught in the wave—save perhaps the intangible erosion of confidence in the markets. The quick recovery is as mysterious as the precipitous drop, and there is no assurance that we will fare as well in the next flash-crash event. This next event is seemingly inevitable, as mechanisms in place to act as circuit breakers have limited ability to prevent or ameliorate them (Subrahmanyam 2013), and no other measures have qualitatively changed the general conditions of our financial markets. Subsequent smaller flash crashes in other financial assets (U.S. Treasury bonds in October 2014, U.S. dollars in March 2015) remind us that the prospect looms, and with it potential contagion across exchanges and asset classes, possibly triggering generalized panic impinging on the real economy.

The spotlight on HFT grew particularly intense in 2014 with the publication of *Flash Boys*, an engaging account by Michael Lewis (2014) of strategies employed by HFT firms to obtain and exploit speed advantages. Billions of dollars have been invested in new fiber-optic, microwave, and even laser-based communication networks, in the effort to shave milliseconds or microseconds off the information latency: the time it takes to transmit information across exchanges. To compete in this latency arms race firms spend additional billions on specialized hardware, co-location with exchanges, and development of streamlined software—possibly omitting error checks and other safety-enhancing features in the quest for ultimate speed.

Much of the debate about HFT revolves around the ramifications for real and perceived transparency and fairness of market operations; see, for example, criticisms by Haim Bodek (2013) about the proliferation of special order types catering to HFT strategies. This specific issue drew the attention of regulators at the U.S. Securities and Exchange Commission, who in January 2015 fined the exchange operator Direct Edge \$14M for insufficient transparency about the availability and operation of special order types (Beeson 2015).

Some observers conclude that the state of U.S. equity trading markets is fundamentally broken (Arnuk and Saluzzi 2012) and call for sweeping reform. Others suggest that the apparent downsides of HFT are tolerable relative to the claimed beneficial effects of modern electronic trading. Some of the disconnects in this debate can be attributed to confounding qualitatively distinct forms of HFT, conflicting assumptions about market organization, or information hiding and obfuscation to protect proprietary interests.

Such issues can be addressed by careful research conducted in the public domain. Much of the finance literature on high-frequency trading (HFT) takes an empirical approach, and has come to mixed conclusions on the effects of HFT on overall market quality. For example, in a survey discussing the strategies, benefits, and costs of HFT, Charles M. Jones (2013) points to the positive role of HFT firms in market making and providing liquidity (Hendershott, Jones, and Menkveld 2011). The liquidity provided by algorithmic market makers, however, may be more erratic at high frequencies, and may be accompanied by increased adverse selection (Menkveld 2014). The effects of algorithmic trading operate along multiple pathways, with conflicting implications for market performance. As a result, most detached and deliberate commentators agree that uncertainty and concern about the ramifications of HFT, both potential and realized, are justified.

These uncertainties are difficult to resolve, in part because the factors at play in modern high-frequency trading are unprecedented. The most important new features in our view are the two following factors:

1. The very speed of operation renders details of internal market operations—especially the structure of communication channels and information—systematically relevant to market performance. In particular, the latencies (time lags) between market events (transactions, price updates, order submissions) and the point in time when various

actors find out about these events become pivotal, and even the smallest differential latency can significantly affect trading outcomes.

2. The autonomy and adaptivity of algorithmic trading strategies takes them out of the scope of direct human control, and makes it challenging to understand how they will perform in unanticipated circumstances. The challenges are exacerbated by the increasing use of sophisticated machine learning techniques to derive trading strategies, and the fundamental multi-agent nature of the execution environment.

These two factors are closely interrelated, as autonomy is necessary for operation at superhuman speed. Some issues, such as interactions among adaptive and data-driven strategies, apply to algorithmic trading even when it is not conducted at high frequency (Easley, López de Prado, and O'Hara 2012).

In this article we outline a computational approach to analysis of financial markets that offers the fidelity needed to capture complex algorithmic trading environments yet is amenable to strategic reasoning based on game-theoretic principles. Following background on simulation modeling of financial markets, we present a simple yet realistic model environment and illustrate the approach for game-theoretic selection of trading strategies and reasoning about the effects of market conditions through equilibrium comparisons. Our results provide evidence for several propositions relevant to market performance and how it is assessed. Key findings include:

- Modeling trader patience in terms of the time horizon they are willing to monitor and reenter markets, we find robustly that patient traders are able to achieve greater gains from trade, up to essentially full efficiency with sufficient horizon.

- All else equal, more frequent market reentry and reduced fundamental volatility increase welfare.

- The common use of quoted or effective spreads as a proxy for welfare is not a reliable guide for comparing market performance.

SIMULATION MODELING OF FINANCIAL MARKETS

Most of the finance community's prior research on HFT takes an empirical approach, employing available order, quote, and transaction data streams to measure market activity and relate relevant variables. This has often yielded great insight and represents an essential form of inquiry. Analysis of available data is ultimately limited, however, with respect to counterfactual questions, such as the response of financial markets to rarely occurring shocks or the effects of alternative market rules and regulations. Answering such questions inherently requires models that incorporate causal premises, specifically, assumptions as to how trading behavior is shaped by environmental conditions.

Theoretical models can support such inference, and these also represent an important resource from the finance research literature. Trading in markets can be formulated as a game, and game-theoretic equilibrium concepts can be employed to characterize behavior in markets by rational agents. However, modeling algorithmic trading entails accommodating complex information and fine-grained dynamics, which often renders game-theoretic reasoning analytically intractable.

An alternative, computational, approach is to model financial markets in simulation. Simulation can faithfully capture complex market microstructure and trading interactions at arbitrarily fine degrees of temporal granularity. Algorithmic and other traders are cast as agents, with various objectives and information sources, and available actions as dictated by market rules. This approach, generally known as agent-based modeling (ABM), analyzes a complex social system through simulation of fine-grained interactions among the constituent decisionmakers (the agents), described and implemented as (usually simple) computer programs. ABM researchers in the social sciences typically justify adopting the agent-based approach on the basis of tractability, or avoiding restrictive assumptions about rationality or other characteristics (Tesfatsion

2006). Richard Bookstaber (2012) invokes these arguments and others in expressly advocating the development of agent-based models for investigating threats to financial stability.

ABM applications to financial trading date back to the 1990s, notable early models including those by Moshe Levy, Haim Levy, and Sorin Solomon (1994) and the Santa Fe Artificial Stock Market (Arthur et al. 1997). Agent-based financial models facilitate consideration of heterogeneous agent types (Boswijk et al. 2007), and multiple forms of learning (LeBaron 2011). Researchers have employed ABMs to shed light on central issues in today's financial markets, such as the impact of a transaction tax (Fricke and Lux 2015), and conditions that can produce instabilities reminiscent of the 2010 flash crash (Lee, Cheng, and Koh 2011; Paddrik et al. 2012).

In our own previous work we have used agent-based simulation of financial markets to model a variety of trading scenarios. We focus on the impact of algorithmic trading on allocative efficiency (social welfare), which is a measure of how well markets distribute resources (in this context, financial securities) to market participants. Greater efficiency means improvements (in aggregate) in investors' gains from trading.

In one study, we investigated the effect of latency arbitrage, an HFT strategy that exploits speed advantages in identifying price disparities across fragmented markets (Wah and Wellman 2013). We found that latency arbitrage harms market efficiency, not even counting the costs of the latency arms race. We proposed that this arms race can be eliminated by replacing continuous-time trading with frequent-call markets, a mechanism whereby orders accumulate and are matched periodically, for example, once per second. Frequent-call markets neutralize tiny speed advantages (Budish, Cramton, and Shim 2015) and can improve market efficiency in many circumstances.

One of our recent studies examines the welfare effects of market making, finding that market makers generally improve efficiency, but provide benefits to investors only when the investors are sufficiently impatient (Wah and Wellman 2015). The model we present here follows the configuration of this study and reports an extended analysis of trading strategies (without the market makers) explored there.

SECURITY TRADING MODEL

Our analysis focuses on a single security traded in a two-sided market. Though the model is simple, it captures key characteristics of real-world market mechanisms and trading behavior. Here we present a basic description of market operation, and the objectives and strategies of traders. The appendix provides a more detailed mathematical description.

The market operates over a finite time horizon, which we call T. Agents enter and reenter the market at random intervals to trade. On each arrival these traders submit a *limit order* to the market (replacing their previous order, if any), indicating the price at which they are willing to buy or sell a single unit of the security.

The market mechanism is a continuous double auction (CDA) (Friedman 1993), which means that a new buy or sell order transacts immediately whenever it matches an existing order in the market. The trade executes at the price of the incumbent order. If an order does not match, it is added to the CDA's order book. The CDA maintains price quotes reflecting the best outstanding orders. These quotes comprise two parts: a bid quote BID reflects the highest current buy offer, and ask quote ASK the lowest current offer to sell.

The market environment is populated by a set of traders, representing investors. Each investor has an individual valuation for the security made up of private and common components. The common component is represented by a fundamental value, which can be viewed as the intrinsic value of the security. This fundamental value varies over time according to a stochastic process.

The private component of value is a specific agent's reason for trading. For example, an agent may have positive value for a security that complements its portfolio (for example, it hedges other risk), and negative value for undiversified risk. Similarly, the need for savings or liquidity is reflected in the private value.

The common and private components are effectively added together to determine the agent's valuation of the security. Agents accrue private value on each transaction, and at the end of the trading horizon evaluate their accumulated inventory on the basis of the end-time fundamental.

Given a market mechanism and valuation model, investors pursue their trading objectives by executing a trading strategy in that environment. As noted, we assume that traders arrive stochastically at the market over a time horizon, and at each arrival have the opportunity to submit a limit order to buy or sell a single unit of the security. The strategy defines how this order is generated, on the basis of price quotes and current holdings.

Though the CDA market mechanism and environment as described here are relatively simple, the associated bidding game is quite complex, owing to the incompleteness of information (private valuations) and the dynamics of arrivals and repeated trading. No analytic solution—nor any constructive theoretical characterization—is known for this or similar CDA games, and so the literature has generally relied on simulation studies. Many previous works have explored CDA bidding strategies (Das et al. 2001; Friedman 1993; Wellman 2011), so there is a body of ideas to work with. Many of the proposed solutions are variations of the so-called zero intelligence (ZI) family of bidding strategies (Gode and Sunder 1993), and that is the class of approaches we consider here.

In the ZI bidding strategy, agents determine an amount of surplus to ask for, and submit a corresponding limit order. The strategy parameters R_{min} and R_{max} ($0 \leq R_{min} \leq R_{max}$) govern the range of surplus requests. Our extended version of ZI employs a third parameter, $\eta \in [0,1]$, which is a threshold determining whether to just take the currently available surplus based on the price quotes. The details of our strategy implementation are provided in the appendix.

Although ZI is quite simplistic as a trading strategy, it does reflect cognizance of common and private value components, and through setting of the strategic parameters (R_{min}, R_{max}, η) it accommodates a spectrum of surplus-demanding behavior. The most effective settings of these parameters vary depending on the environment (such as number of other traders, valuation distributions, time horizon, arrival rate) and the strategies employed by other traders. Any conclusions for market performance, therefore, are sensitive to choice of these ZI parameters. We have developed a game-theoretic process for choosing strategic parameters in simulation models, described in detail in the next section.

EMPIRICAL GAME-THEORETIC ANALYSIS

A financial market simulation model provides a way for an experimenter to directly answer questions of the form "What happens when the trading strategies <*fill in strategy set*> interact in environment <*fill in environment specification*>?" Choice of environment specification is driven by the target subject of study, and may be informed by existing models and data. The choice of strategies, however, is up to the market participants, and since strategies are not generally observable in market data, the experimenter must consider how traders would be likely to act in a given market situation. The conventional economic assumption is that traders rationally pursue their objectives, and the standard economic approach to strategy choice relies on reasoning based on rationality criteria.

The empirical game-theoretic analysis (EGTA) approach incorporates such reasoning in a simulation-based framework. Figure 1 illustrates how EGTA generates a game model from financial-market simulations. First, we configure the financial-market simulator on the basis of the market mechanisms (number of markets, continuous versus periodic clearing, quoting policies), environmental conditions (numbers and types of traders, communication latencies), and agent valuations (fundamental process and private component distributions) we wish to study. These configurations may have both structural and parametric elements. For example, we used this simulator to investigate latency arbitrage, an HFT tactic that exploits speed advantage to profit in fragmented markets. Our study of latency arbitrage (Wah and Wellman, 2013) was based on a two-market model, with individual-market and global public price quotes (the national best bid and offer, or NBBO) available to regular and high-frequency traders at differential

Figure 1. Empirical Game-Theoretic Analysis

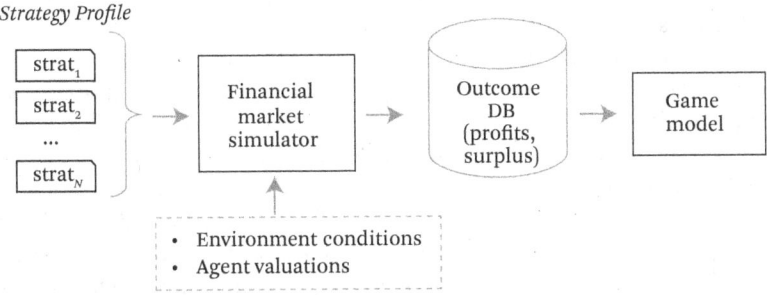

Source: Authors' compilation.
Note: Simulating a large number of strategy profiles produces data used to induce a game-theoretic model.

latency. Given this structure, we then varied the latency parameter to evaluate its effect on market outcomes. That study also compared to single-market models, employing CDA or call-market clearing mechanisms.

The simulator configuration includes a specification of the numbers of players in various roles. Each role is associated with a set of available strategies. Within each role, players are treated as ex ante symmetric. (This is without loss of generality, as we can always associate a unique role with each player.) In our study of market making, for example, there were two roles: background investor and market maker. In the current study, we consider only the investor role. The strategy set is the family of ZI bidders defined earlier.

Once configured, we can feed into the market simulator a strategy profile, defined as an assignment of strategies to each player. In our case, assigning a strategy means assigning the ZI parameters ($R_{\min}$, $R_{\max}$, η) for each trader. Each simulation run produces an outcome (set of trades), which in turn defines a net surplus for each trader (value of final holdings minus cash flow). This can be interpreted as the agent's payoff for that run of the market game. In general, given the stochastic nature of the market simulation (random draws of valuations, fundamental time series, agent arrival patterns), we require many runs to yield accurate estimates of payoffs for any given strategy profile.

To perform EGTA of a particular scenario, we evaluate a large number of strategy profiles in this manner, collecting the estimated payoffs in an outcome database. From this data we then induce a game model. This game model may generalize to nonsimulated profiles through regression (Vorobeychik, Wellman, and Singh 2007); however, in many cases (such as this study) we generate an incomplete game model that includes payoff estimates only for simulated profiles.

Given a game model, we can perform any of the usual game-theoretic analysis operations, for example, computing Nash equilibrium (NE). In our study, we focus on identifying symmetric mixed-strategy NE. Given a set of evaluated profiles, our algorithm starts by finding the maximal complete subgames (henceforth referred to as subgames): sets of strategies such that all profiles are evaluated. For each subgame, we compute subgame equilibria by the replicator dynamics algorithm (Gintis 2000), which starts from a particular probability distribution over strategies, then increases the probability of those strategies that perform better than average. We run this replicator dynamics method initialized at a diverse set of points in the simplex, then test whether these subgame equilibria are equilibria in the full game by evaluating all deviations outside the subgame.

In principle, the EGTA approach could apply to a game of any size. In practice, we are limited by the computation available for simulation, which is proportional to the number of profiles evaluated. Financial markets often involve a large number of traders, and there is a large space of possible strategies. Even if we restrict attention to ZI strategies, there is a three-dimensional parametric space of strategy settings. Let N denote the number of traders, and S the number of strategies. In this study, we investigate markets with N = 25 and N = 66, and consider S = 9 distinct settings for the ZI strategy. A symmetric game has

$$\binom{N-S+1}{N}$$

distinct strategy profiles (that is, the number of different ways of drawing N items from N – S + 1 candidates), and so even games of this modest size cannot be explored exhaustively. For example, with N = 25 and S = 9, the number of profiles is 13.9 million.

To enable analysis of games at this scale, we employ an approximation technique called deviation-preserving reduction (DPR) (Wiedenbeck and Wellman 2012). DPR approximates an N-player game by a smaller k-player game with the same strategy set. The method estimates payoffs in the reduced game based on a mapping from select profiles in the full game. For example, with N = 25 and k = 5, the payoff to the player playing strategy a in the reduced-game profile (a, b, c, d, d) would be obtained by simulating a 25-player profile where one agent plays a and the other 24 are divided across the remaining strategies as follows: 6 each play b and c, and 12 play d. This reduction is termed "deviation-preserving" because it accurately reflects the first player's relative payoffs for playing alternative strategies in this context. It is still an approximation, however, because the other players are treated as aggregates. This technique has been shown to produce good approximations for purposes of equilibrium identification in a variety of large games. In this study, we employ 5-player reductions for the N = 25 cases, and 6-player reductions for N = 66.

EXPERIMENTAL SETUP

The experiments reported here elaborate the analysis of trading environments investigated in our prior work (Wah and Wellman 2015), focusing on the games with no market maker present. Traders follow the ZI strategy described, with settings (R_{min}, R_{max}, η) selected from the following set of thirteen triples:

{ (0,65,0.8), (0,125,0.8), (0,125,1), (0,250,0.8), (0,250,1), (0,500,1), (250,500,1), (0,1000,0.8), (0,1000,1), (500,1000,0.4), (0,1500,0.6), (1000,2000,0.4), (0,2500,1) }

This set was determined in a fairly ad hoc manner. We seeded it with all of the $\eta = 1$ strategies above, then extended it to include some $\eta = 1$ cases based on finding improvements from initial equilibrium candidates. We also tried some strategies with $R_{min} \in \{2500, 5000\}$ and $R_{max} \in \{10000, 15000\}$, but these never appeared in equilibrium so were discarded.

We consider three instances of the market environment, labeled A, B, and C. All three assign traders a private valuation generated with variance parameter $\sigma_{PV}^2 = 5 \times 10^6$ and $q_{max} = 10$. (See the appendix for definitions of these and other parameters.) The global fundamental has a mean value $\bar{r} = 100000$ and evolves with mean reversion $\kappa = 0.05$. The environment differences are focused on two parameters:

- Agent reentry rate: $\lambda = 0.0005$ (environment A) or $\lambda = 0.005$ (environments B and C)
- Fundamental shock variance: $\sigma_s^2 = 10^6$ (environments A and B) or $\sigma_s^2 = 5 \times 10^5$ (environment C)

For each environment, we consider three different time horizons T (in 1,000s) and two settings for number of traders N. For N = 25 we considered an additional horizon T = 24. Thus we explored a total of 21 games using the EGTA approach. We label each game according to the environment (A, B, C) and time horizon T, where $T \in \{1, 4, 12, 24\}$; for example, B12 is environment B with time horizon 12.

RESULTS

To analyze a particular game configuration we perform a systematic search, evaluating strategy profiles through simulation with the goal of identifying equilibria. Our search process starts by considering each ZI strategy in self-play—the nine pure symmetric profiles where every agent plays the given strategy. We then

Figure 2. Median R_{mid} (the Midpoint of the ZI Range [R_{min}, R_{max}]) Value for Equilibria in the Three Environments A, B, and C, for N = 66 and N = 25

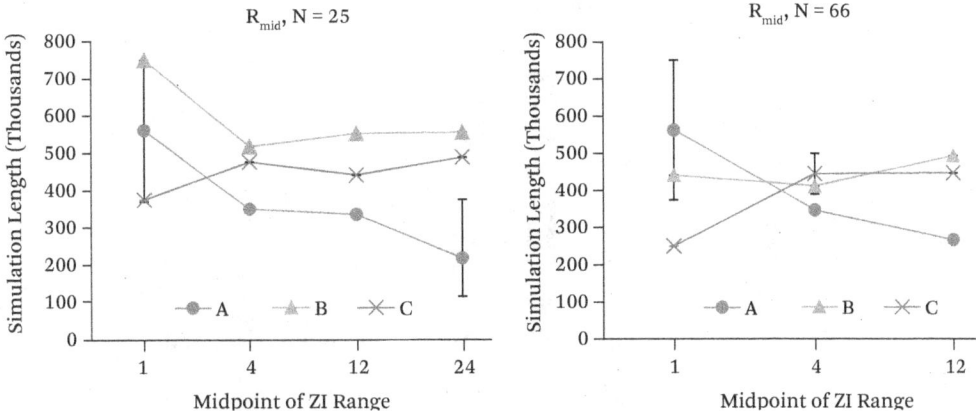

Source: Authors' simulation results.
Note: The X-axis is the simulation length T (in 1000s). The error bars for each point indicate the minimum and maximum R_{mid} values for equilibria in a market configuration.

iteratively generate additional profiles to simulate according to the following criteria:

- For any subgame equilibrium that is not refuted in the full game, evaluate all deviations outside the subgame.
- Extend a refuted subgame equilibrium by adding the best response strategy to the set of strategies in that equilibrium profile's support.

Note that deviations and subgame profiles are selected on the basis of the reduced 5- or 6-player games defined by our DPR approximation. The payoffs for these reduced games are estimated based on simulation results from corresponding full-game profiles.

For each of the 21 games analyzed, this process succeeded in identifying at least one and up to three distinct symmetric equilibria. This typically required evaluating 1,000 or 2,000 full-game profiles, with an actual range of 553 to 4,167. Each profile evaluated was simulated at least 20,000 times. Overall, the computation deployed for this study occupied dozens of cores on a large-scale computing cluster for much of the time over a period of several months.

A summary of the equilibria across environments is presented in figure 2. For each market size (25, 66) and each environment (A, B, C) we plot a series of points corresponding to the five time horizons T considered. Each point summarizes the equilibrium ZI parameters using the average of surplus-request midpoints, $R_{mid} = (R_{min} + R_{max})/2$, with the average weighted by probability in the equilibrium profile. For games with multiple equilibria, we display the range of R_{mid} values using error bars.

The R_{mid} statistic for a profile represents the average surplus requested in a trader limit order, but only approximately, as it ignores the effect of the quote threshold parameter η. Figure 2 suggests some general trends in this statistic, but we are reluctant to draw strong conclusions, given the roughness of this measure and the inconsistency in the observed trends. Nevertheless, we do generally see that the thinner markets (N = 25) have higher surplus requests, and that there is some tendency for these requests to decrease with time horizon, particularly for environment A.

Perhaps the most salient outcome variable is market efficiency, which we measure by total surplus. For each equilibrium we evaluated total surplus from 10,000 sample runs over the full-game mixed profile. Figure 3 displays the market efficiency exhibited in equilibrium across our 21 games. For this variable, the re-

Figure 3. Comparison of Welfare (Total Surplus) Across Thirty Game Environments

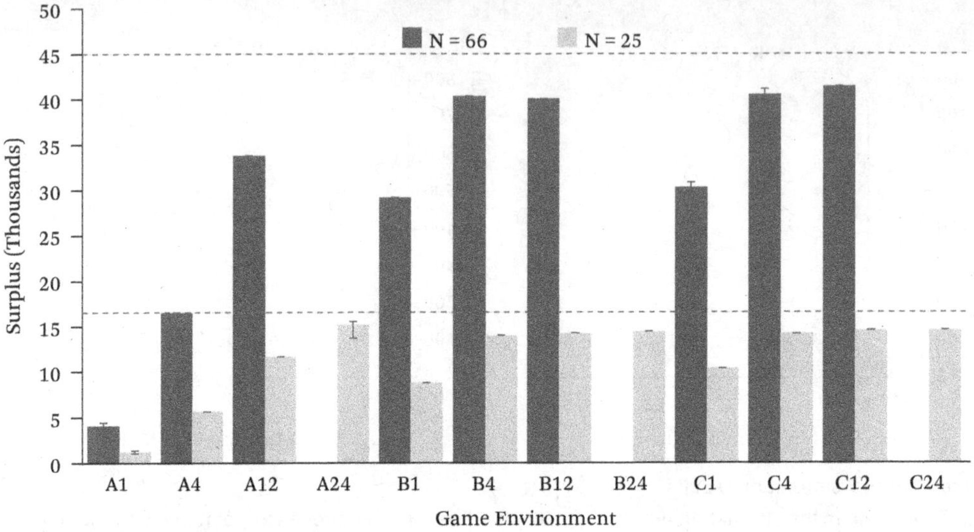

Source: Authors' simulation results.
Note: The top dotted line is the optimal social welfare available with sixty-six traders (44,155); the bottom dotted line is the optimal welfare available with twenty-five traders (16,306). Error bars indicate the minimum and maximum values for equilibria in a game.

lationships are quite apparent. Welfare generally increases with time horizon. The reason is that with longer horizons, traders have more reentries and thus greater opportunity to find mutually beneficial trades. With enough time, the ZI traders are able to achieve a high fraction of full efficiency in equilibrium.

It is also apparent from figure 3 that environments with more frequent trader entries (B and C compared to A) have higher surplus, for any given horizon. This holds for the same reason that extending horizon improves efficiency. Closer inspection of the figure reveals that when holding arrival rate and horizon fixed, for N = 66, reducing fundamental volatility (moving from environment B to C) increases efficiency to a small but consistent degree. It seems that with thick markets, high variance on the fundamental often leads to extramarginal trades, which then require additional entries to correct.

Inspection of the number of trades produced in equilibrium (figure 4) is also illuminating. A few equilibrium instances generate high efficiency but produce more trades than optimal, indicating that these runs involve agents who make trades and reverse them on subsequent entries.

SPREADS AND MARKET EFFICIENCY

The final question we examine with data from our EGTA study concerns the reliability of spreads as a proxy for market efficiency or welfare. True transaction cost, or the difference between the price of execution and the true value of the security, is a measure of the net change in welfare of market participants. When welfare is not directly observable, as is generally the case for real-world data, proxy measures for transaction costs can be employed to estimate changes in welfare (Goettler et al. 2005). Estimation of the cost of trading relies on the intuition that in the absence of execution costs, transactions would occur at the underlying value of the security. As such, the difference between trade price and any proxy for the value of the security gives an estimate of the cost of execution (Bessembinder and Venkataraman 2010). There are multiple ways to estimate these execution costs. The simplest of these is the quoted

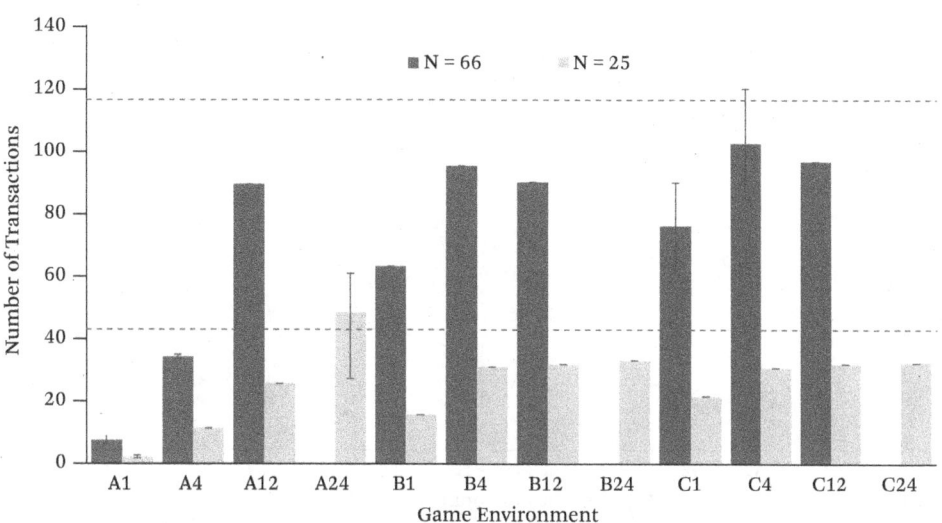

Figure 4. Average Number of Trades Generated in Equilibrium, Across Twenty-One Game Environments

Source: Authors' simulation results.
Note: The dotted lines represent the average number of trades required for socially optimal allocations, with N = 66 (115 trades, top dotted line) and N = 25 (43, bottom dotted line). Error bars indicate the minimum and maximum values for equilibria in a game.

spread, which is defined at a particular time point as the difference between the *BID* and *ASK* quotes. We summarize quoted spread for a scenario run as the median spread over all time points. Figure 5 presents statistics on quoted spreads for equilibrium trading in our 21 game configurations. As one would expect, spreads are always greater in thinner markets, all else equal. We also tend to find smaller spreads in the scenarios exhibiting greatest surplus (compare figure 3), although this correspondence is rough and inconsistent at best.

If quotes vary significantly over time, aggregating quoted spreads over all time points may not accurately reflect trading costs. An alternative is the effective spread, which focuses on spreads in effect at the time of actual trades (Bessembinder 2003; Madhavan et al. 2002).[1]

Specifically, our aggregate measure of effective spread takes the mean *BID-ASK* difference over all times when a trade occurs. These effective spread values for the equilibria found in each environment are shown in figure 6.

We see that effective spreads are sometimes substantially lower than the quoted spreads and never vice versa (figure 5), reflecting the fact that a new limit order is more likely to match at times when the spread is tight. Nevertheless, quoted and effective spreads are highly correlated, suggesting that quoted spreads can serve as a predictor for effective spreads. As for quoted spreads, tighter effective spreads often correspond to increased welfare in the corresponding environment, but this is not consistently the case.

Such inconsistency may not be surprising, given that other factors also vary systematically

---

1. Another spread metric is the realized spread, which samples the spread *n* periods after a trade, as a proxy for the post-trade value of the security, to capture the price impact of the trade or to capture how the market has incorporated the private information conveyed by the trade (Bessembinder and Venkataraman 2010). It is unclear, however, what time period *n* is appropriate in our market model. Exploratory measurements revealed that in our environments, realized spreads differ widely depending on the value of *n* selected; hence, we omit realized spreads from further discussion.

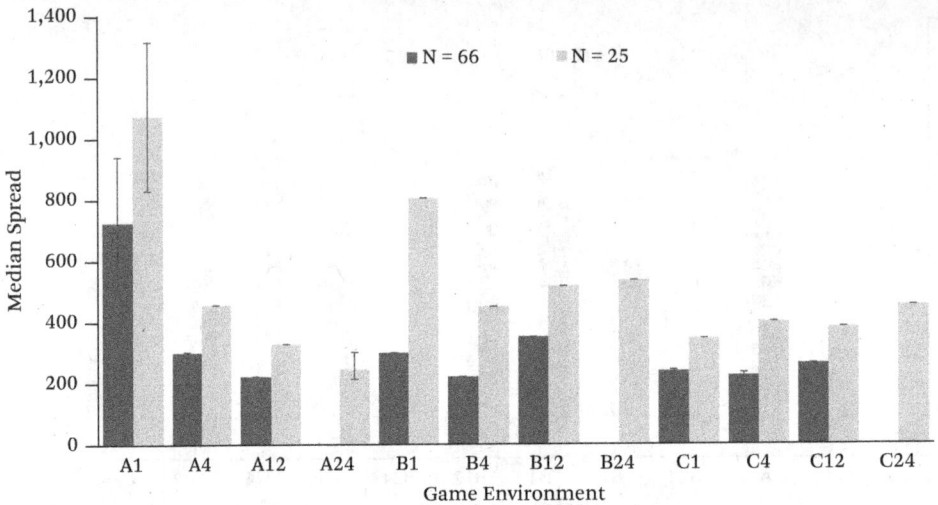

Figure 5. Quoted Spread (Measured as the Median *BID-ASK* Difference over the Duration of the Simulation) for Twenty-One Game Environments

Source: Authors' simulation results.
Note: Error bars indicate the minimum and maximum values for equilibria in a game.

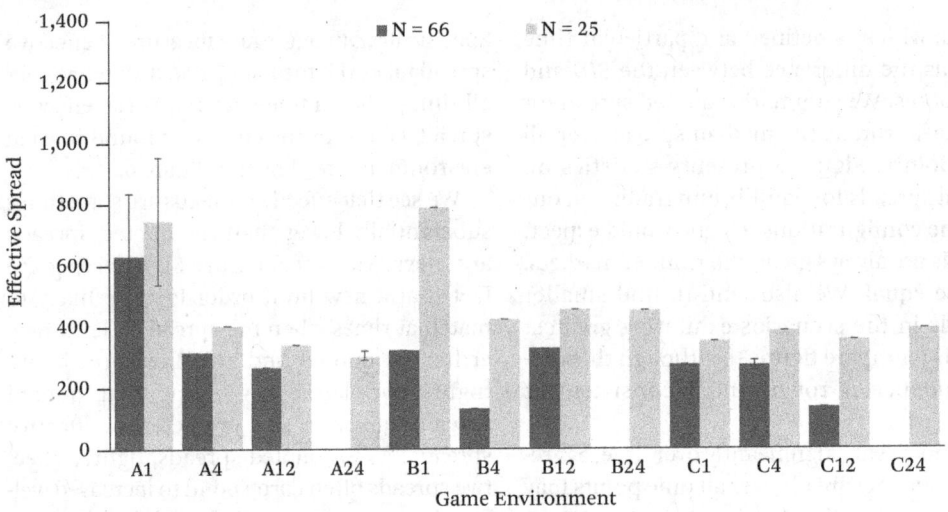

Figure 6. Effective Spread (Measured as the Mean *BID-ASK* Difference over the Transaction Time Points) for Twenty-One Game Environments

Source: Authors' simulation results.
Note: Error bars indicate the minimum and maximum values for equilibria in a game.

across game instances. We tested the correspondence of spreads and welfare within games by examining cases of multiple equilibria. Six of our games have multiple equilibria, and in only two (that is, one-third) does the ordering of quoted spread accord with the ordering of welfare. For effective spread, the correspondence also holds in only two of six cases.

To further examine the efficacy of spread measures as a proxy for welfare, we simulate 10,000 samples of five pure-strategy profiles for

Figure 7. Overall Surplus in Five Pure-Strategy Profiles for N = 66 and N = 25 in Game B12

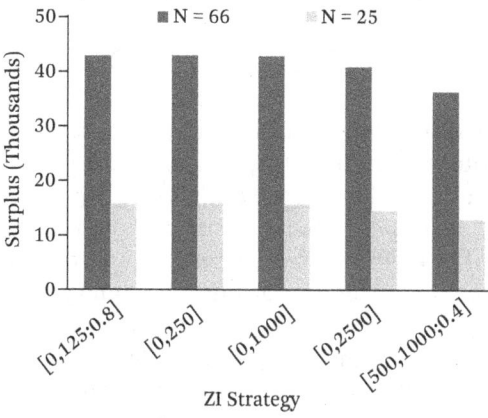

Source: Authors' simulation results.
Note: The ZI strategies are written in the form $[R_{min}, R_{max}; \eta]$.

N = 66 and N = 25 under fixed market configuration (game B12). The strategies of these profiles all belong to the ZI family, with the following ranges ($\eta = 1$ unless otherwise stated):

- B12a: ZI[0, 125] with $\eta = 0.8$
- B12b: ZI[0, 250]
- B12c: ZI[0, 1000]
- B12d: ZI[0, 2500].
- B12e: ZI[500, 1000] with $\eta = 0.4$

In each of these profiles, all N traders play the specified strategy. The surplus of each profile is shown in figure 7, and the corresponding spread measures are in figure 8. We measure quoted spread as a time series across the duration of the simulation and report the median spread, and we report effective spread as the mean over all transactions.

We find that for both populations, the surplus is the lowest for profile B12e and is relatively constant for profiles B12a to B12c. Both spread measures, in contrast, widen over the a-to-e range, which properly reflect the increase in welfare from c to e, but fail to accurately mirror the flat welfare rankings in profiles B12a to B12c. This is particularly true for quoted spread. Effective spread comes closer to matching the flat area overall surplus for N = 66, but its correspondence breaks down in the thinner market with 25 traders, for example in the increased spread from B12b to B12c.

As true value of the security is unobservable in real data, proxies such as quoted and effective spread may often be the best available predictors of transaction costs. However, accurately computing effective spreads from real data is often difficult, as it is not always readily apparent from historical trade prices and quotes which price quote corresponds to a given transaction, especially when order-level data are not available. In addition, effective spread measures can be particularly sensitive

Figure 8. Quoted Spread and Effective Spread in Five Pure-Strategy Profiles for N = 66 and N = 25 in Game B12

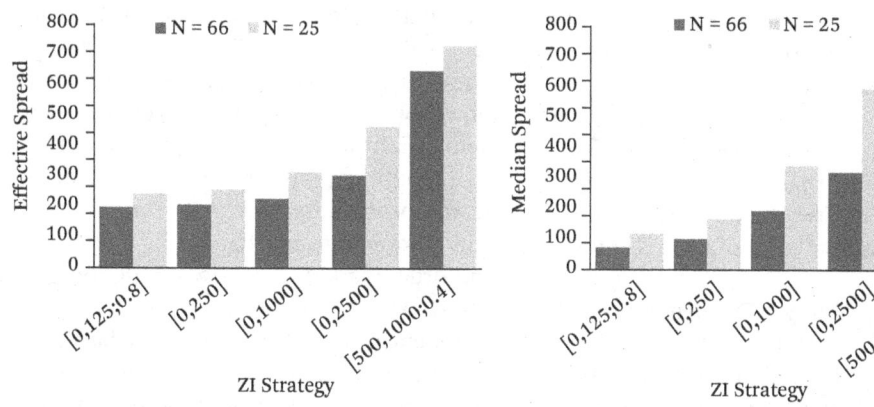

Source: Authors' simulation results.
Note: The ZI strategies are written in the form $[R_{min}, R_{max}; \eta]$.

in electronic markets, with frequent quote updates and more active trading (Piwowar and Wei 2006).

A more fundamental problem with effective spread, however, is that it was developed for intermediated markets, where prices are set by a middleman, such as a dealer. In a pure limit-order market, prices are determined by arriving traders and thus are not necessarily equal to the expected value of the security. Ronald L. Goettler, Christine A. Parlour, and Uday Rajan (2005) demonstrate that the midpoint of the BID-ASK spread is not a good proxy for a security's true underlying value. Given that it emphasizes the surplus of the trade-initiating order submitter and omits the surplus of the incumbent order submitter, effective spread is not a generally representative estimate of welfare.

CONCLUSIONS

We have presented an approach to strategic reasoning, using agent-based simulation models, for application to understanding trading behavior in financial markets. Contrary to views often expressed by advocates (and respectively, critics) of agent-based modeling and game-theoretic analysis, the two methods are actually quite complementary, together supporting principled strategic analysis of complex dynamic scenarios. We illustrated the approach by deriving and analyzing equilibrium trading strategies for a variety of continuous double auction scenarios, differing in number of traders, trading horizon, arrival rate, and fundamental volatility.

Our study confirms several expected relationships among market outcomes, and particularly underscores the importance of trader reentry in achieving efficient outcomes in continuous double auctions. Data from simulations were also instrumental in demonstrating the limitations of relying on proxies such as price quotes for statistics of central interest, such as welfare.

The unobservability of key elements (strategies, welfare) in empirical data provides a strong impetus behind the simulation approach to modeling financial markets. Our simulation studies of latency arbitrage and market making have shed light on the costs and benefits of such strategies, in terms of their effects on the welfare of investors. These works highlight the importance of distinguishing among different roles of algorithmic trading, separating the deleterious practices (latency arbitrage) from those that improve market performance (liquidity provision to impatient investors). This argues against broad-brush regulatory policies that raise the costs of algorithmic trading across the board, in favor of more targeted interventions that deter the harmful forms of algorithmic trading without unduly burdening beneficial practices.

Our ongoing research is applying the approach illustrated here to further key questions in the behavior of financial markets, for example: comparing continuous and periodic trading rules, effects of competition among market makers, and adoption of alternative market mechanisms (Wah, Hurd, and Wellman 2015). Models combining rich simulation with game-theoretic reasoning can play a constructive role in evaluating alternative market mechanisms and enhancing our understanding of the effects of algorithmic trading in a wide range of scenarios.

APPENDIX

Mathematical Model Formulation

In the Appendix we provide further technical details of our models of the market environment and agent trading strategies.

Market Operation and Agent Valuations

We model a single security traded in a two-sided market. Prices are integers, which means they are discretized at a tick size of any desired granularity. Time is also defined on a discrete domain, with finite horizon T. Agents arrive to submit their limit orders according to a Poisson distribution, with a rate parameter λ defining the probability of arriving in each unit time. The market mechanism is a standard limit-order market, or continuous double auction (CDA).

Traders value the security on the basis of a common fundamental value, in combination with an individual-specific private value. We denote by r_t the fundamental value for the security at time t. The fundamental time series is generated by a mean-reverting stochastic process:

$$r_t = \max[0, \kappa \bar{r} + (1-\kappa)r_{t-1} + u_t].$$

Parameter $\kappa \in [1,0]$ specifies the degree to which the fundamental reverts back to the mean $\bar{r}$, and parameter $u_t \sim N(0, \sigma_s^2)$ is a random shock at time t.

The private valuation component for agent i is a vector

$$\Theta_i = (\theta_i^{-q_{max}+1}, \ldots, \theta_i^{+1}, \ldots, \theta_i^{q_{max}}),$$

where $q_{max} > 0$ is the maximum number of units an agent can hold (either long or short). Θ_i specifies the marginal private benefits to agent i of trading single units, according to i's current net position. Element θ_i^q is the incremental private benefit obtained from selling one unit of the security, given current position q, where positive (negative) q indicates a long (short) position. Similarly, θ_i^{q+1} is the marginal private gain from buying an additional unit given current net position q. This representation is similar to the model of Goettler, Christine A. Parlour, and Uday Rajan (2009).

Agent i's private valuation vector is generated by drawing $2 q_{max}$ values independently from a Gaussian distribution, $N(0, \sigma_{PV}^2)$. To ensure that the valuation reflects diminishing marginal utility, that is, $\theta^{q'} \geq \theta^q$ for all $q' \leq q$, we sort the drawn values before assigning the vector Θ_i.

At the end of the trading horizon, an agent's total value is the sum of private values accrued on each transaction, plus the worth of its final holdings evaluated at r_T, the end-time fundamental value. Agent i's valuation $v_i(t)$ for the security at time t therefore depends on its current position q_t and the value of the common fundamental at the end of the trading horizon:

$$v_i(t) = r_T + \begin{cases} \theta_i^{q_t+1} & \text{if buying one unit} \\ \theta_i^{q_t} & \text{if selling one unit} \end{cases}$$

The surplus of a trade is the difference between valuation (including both common and private components) and transaction price. For a single-quantity limit order transacting at time t and price p, a buyer B obtains surplus $v_B(t) - p$, whereas seller S obtains surplus $p - v_S(t)$. Since the price and fundamental terms cancel out in exchange, the total surplus achieved when B buys from S is $\theta_B^{q(B)+1} - \theta_S^{q(S)+1}$, where $q(i)$ denotes the pre-trade position of agent i.

Trading Strategies

An agent's trading strategy governs how it generates a limit order each time it arrives to the market, as a function of its state and information. To simplify the strategy structure, we assume that the trader flips a coin on each arrival to decide whether its order on that round will be to buy or to sell. As a result, agent i's decision boils down a price for its new limit order, as a function of its valuation vector Θ_i, current holdings $q(i)$, and its history of market observations (transactions and price quotes).

In the zero intelligence bidding strategy, agents bid for a randomly determined amount of surplus. Our extended version of ZI employs three parameters: R_{min} and R_{max} ($0 \leq R_{min} \leq R_{max}$) define the range of surplus requests, and $\eta \in [1,0]$ is a threshold for taking the currently available surplus. Specifically, a ZI trader i constructs its bid as follows:

1. Assess its valuation $v_i(t)$ at the time of market entry t, using an estimate $\hat{r}_t$ of the end-time fundamental r_T. The estimate is simply an adjustment of the current fundamental r_t, accounting for mean reversion:

$$\hat{r}_t = (1 - (1-\kappa)^{T-t})\bar{r} + (1-\kappa)^{T-t} r_t$$

2. Determine its requested surplus s, by drawing uniformly from the interval $[R_{min}, R_{max}]$.

3. If the surplus available at the current price quote is at least ηs, then submit an offer at the quoted price. Otherwise submit a limit order requesting surplus s. For instance, if the agent is buying, its bid price is given by:

$$\begin{cases} ASK_t & \text{if } ASK_t \leq v_i(t) - \eta s \\ v_i(t) - s & \text{otherwise} \end{cases}$$

Note that a trader with $\eta = 0$ accepts any profitable quote, and one with $\eta = 1$ bids the same, regardless of the current quote.

For example, consider a trader with valuation v applying a ZI strategy with parameters $R_{min} = 0$, $R_{max} = 1000$, and $\eta = 0.6$. On entering the market, it first flips a coin to decide whether to buy or sell. Supposing the coin flip dictates BUY, it then draws a random surplus request $s \sim U[0,1000]$, which for example yields $s = 700$. It therefore aims to buy at a price 700 below its valuation. If it can buy right now at a price of $700\eta = 420$ less than v (that is, if $ASK \leq v - 420$), however, it submits a price at the current market value. Otherwise, it submits a buy order with price $v - 700$.

REFERENCES

Arnuk, Sal, and Joseph Saluzzi. 2012. *Broken Markets: How High Frequency Trading and Predatory Practices on Wall Street Are Destroying Investor Confidence and Your Portfolio.* Upper Saddle River, N.J.: FT Press.

Arthur, Brian, John H. Holland, Blake LeBaron, Richard Palmer, and Paul Tayler. 1997. "Asset Pricing Under Endogenous Expectations in an Artificial Stock Market." In *The Economy as an Evolving Complex System II*, edited by Brian W. Arthur, Steven N. Durlauf, and David A. Lane. Boulder: Westview Press.

Beeson, Ed. 2015. "SEC Fines Direct Edge $14M over Misleading Order Types." *Law360* (online journal), January 12, 2015. Available at: http://www.law360.com/articles/610484/sec-fines-direct-edge-14m-over-misleading-order-types; accessed June 12, 2016.

Bessembinder, Hendrik. 2003. "Issues in Assessing Trade Execution Costs." *Journal of Financial Markets* 6(1): 233–57.

Bessembinder, Hendrik, and Kumar Venkataraman. 2010. "Bid-Ask Spreads: Measuring Trade Execution Costs in Financial Markets." In *Encyclopedia of Quantitative Finance*, edited by Rama Cont. New York: John Wiley.

Bodek, Haim. 2013. *The Problem of HFT: Collected Writings on High Frequency Trading and Stock Market Structure Reform.* Electronic edition. CreateSpace Independent Publishing Platform.

Bookstaber, Richard. 2012. "Using Agent-Based Models for Analyzing Threats to Financial Stability." Office of Financial Research Working Paper 3. Washington: U.S. Department of the Treasury.

Boswijk, H. Peter, Cars H. Hommes, and Sebastiano Manzan. 2007. "Behavioral Heterogeneity in Stock Prices." *Journal of Economic Dynamics and Control* 31(6): 1938–70.

Budish, Eric B., Peter Cramton, and John J. Shim. 2015. "The High-Frequency Trading Arms Race: Frequent Batch Auctions as a Market Design Response." *Quarterly Journal of Economics* 130(4): 1547–621.

Cardella, Laura, Jia Hao, Ivalina Kalcheva, and Yung-Yu Ma. 2014. "Computerization of the Equity, Foreign Exchange, Derivatives and Fixed-Income Markets." *Financial Review* 49(2): 231–43.

Das, Rajarshi, James E. Hanson, Jeffrey O. Kephart, and Gerald Tesauro. 2001. "Agent-Human Interactions in the Continuous Double Auction." *Proceedings of the Seventeenth International Joint Conference on Artificial Intelligence*. San Francisco: Morgan Kaufmann and American Association for Artificial Intelligence.

Easley, David, Marcos M. López de Prado, and Maureen O'Hara. 2012. "The Volume Clock: Insights into the High Frequency Paradigm." *Journal of Portfolio Management* 39(1): 19–29.

Fricke, Daniel, and Thomas Lux. 2015. "The Effects of a Financial Transaction Tax in an Artificial Financial Market." *Journal of Economic Interaction and Coordination* 10(1): 119–50.

Friedman, Daniel. 1993. "The Double Auction Market Institution: A Survey." In *The Double Auction Market: Institutions, Theories, and Evidence*, edited by Daniel Friedman and John Rust. Reading, Mass.: Addison-Wesley.

Gintis, Herbert. 2000. *Game Theory Evolving*. Princeton, N.J.: Princeton University Press.

Gode, Dhananjay K., and Shyam Sunder. 1993. "Allocative Efficiency of Markets with Zero-Intelligence Traders: Market as a Partial Substitute for Individual Rationality." *Journal of Political Economy* 101(1): 119–37.

Goettler, Ronald L., Christine A. Parlour, and Uday Rajan. 2005. "Equilibrium in a Dynamic Limit Order Market." *Journal of Finance* 60(5): 2149–92.

———. 2009. "Informed Traders and Limit Order Markets." *Journal of Financial Economics* 93(1): 67–87.

Hendershott, Terrence, Charles M. Jones, and Albert J. Menkveld. 2011. "Does Algorithmic Trading Improve Liquidity?" *Journal of Finance* 66(1): 1–33.

Jones, Charles M. 2013. "What Do We Know About High Frequency Trading?" Available at SSRN (link for download): http://ssrn.com/abstract=2236201; accessed June 12, 2016.

Kirilenko, Andrei A., Albert S. Kyle, Mehrdad Samadi, and Tugkan Tuzun. 2014. "The Flash Crash: The Impact of High Frequency Trading on an Electronic Market." Available at SSRN (link for download): http://ssrn.com/abstract=1686004; accessed June 12, 2016.

LeBaron, Blake. 2011. "Active and Passive Learning in Agent-Based Financial Markets." *Eastern Economic Journal* 37(1): 35–43.

Lee, Bernard, Shih-fen Cheng, and Annie Koh. 2011. "Would Price Limits Have Made Any Difference to the 'Flash Crash' on May 6, 2010?" *Review of Futures Markets* 19 (Special IFM Issue): 55–93.

Levy, Moshe, Haim Levy, and Sorin Solomon. 1994. "A Microscopic Model of the Stock Market: Cycles, Booms, and Crashes." *Economics Letters* 45(1): 103–11.

Lewis, Michael. 2014. *Flash Boys: A Wall Street Revolt*. New York: W. W. Norton.

Madhavan, Ananth, Kewei Ming, Vesna Straser, and Yingchuan Wang. 2002. "How Effective Are Effective Spreads? An Evaluation of Trade Side Classification Algorithms." Working paper. ITG Analytic Incubator, November 20. Available at: http://analyticsincubator.itginc.com/library/papers/how-effective-are-effective-spreads-an-evaluation-of-trade-side-classification-algorithms/; accessed June 12, 2016.

Menkveld, Albert J. 2014. "High-Frequency Traders and Market Structure." *Financial Review* 49(2): 333–44.

Paddrik, Mark, Roy Hayes, Jr., Andrew Todd, Steve Yang, Peter Beling, and William Scherer. 2012. "An Agent-Based Model of the E-Mini S&P 500 Applied to Flash Crash Analysis." Conference on Computational Intelligence for Financial Engineering and Economics, New York (March 29).

Piwowar, Michael S., and Li Wei. 2006. "The Sensitivity of Effective Spread Estimates to Trade-Quote Matching Algorithms." *Electronic Markets* 16(2): 112–29.

Subrahmanyam, Avanidhar. 2013. "Algorithmic Trading, the Flash Crash, and Coordinated Circuit Breakers." *Borsa Istanbul Review* 13(3): 4–9.

Tesfatsion, Leigh. 2006. "Agent-Based Computational Economics: A Constructive Approach to Economic Theory." In *Handbook of Agent-Based Computational Economics*, edited by Leigh Tesfatsion and Kenneth L. Judd. Amsterdam: Elsevier.

Vorobeychik, Yevgeniy, Michael P. Wellman, and Satinder Singh. 2007. "Learning Payoff Functions in Infinite Games." *Machine Learning* 67(1): 145–68.

Wah, Elaine, Dylan R. Hurd, and Michael P. Wellman. 2015. "Strategic Market Choice: Frequent Call Markets vs. Continuous Double Auctions for Fast and Slow Traders." Paper presented at Third EAI Conference on Auctions, Market Mechanisms, and Their Applications, Chicago (August 8 to 9). Available at: http://web.eecs.umich.edu/srg/?page_id=1666; accessed July 11, 2016.

Wah, Elaine, and Michael P. Wellman. 2013. "Latency Arbitrage, Market Fragmentation, and Efficiency: A Two-Market Model." *Proceedings of the Fourteenth ACM Conference on Electronic Commerce*. Available at: http://dl.acm.org/citation.cfm?id=2482577, pp. 855–72; accessed July 11, 2016.

———. 2015. "Welfare Effects of Market Making in Continuous Double Auctions." *Proceedings of the Fourteenth International Conference on Autonomous Agents and Multiagent Systems*. Available at: http://aamas2015.com/en/AAMAS_2015_USB/aamas/p57.pdf, pp. 57–66; accessed July 11, 2016

Wellman, Michael P. 2011. *Trading Agents*. Electronic edition. San Rafael, Calif.: Morgan & Claypool.

Wiedenbeck, Bryce, and Michael P. Wellman. 2012. "Scaling Simulation-Based Game Analysis Through Deviation-Preserving Reduction." *Proceedings of the Eleventh International Conference on Autonomous Agents and Multiagent Systems*. Available at http://www.aamas-conference.org/Proceedings/aamas2012/papers/5E_1.pdf, pp. 931–38; accessed July 11, 2016.

PART V
International Perspectives

Financial Sector Health Since 2007: A Comparative Analysis of the United States, Europe, and Asia

VIRAL V. ACHARYA

This essay uses recent methodology for estimating capital shortfalls of financial institutions during aggregate stress to assess the evolution of financial sector health since 2007 in the United States, Europe, and Asia. Financial sector capital shortfalls reached a peak in the end of 2008 and early 2009 for United States and Europe; however, they declined thereafter steadily only for the United States, with Europe reaching a similar peak in the fall of 2011 during the sovereign crises in the southern periphery. In contrast, the financial sector in Asia had little capital shortfall in 2008–2009 but the shortfall has increased steadily since 2010, notably for China and Japan. These relative patterns can be explained on the basis of the regulatory responses in the United States, the lack thereof in Europe, stagnation in Japan, and the bank-leverage-based fiscal stimulus in China.

Keywords: systemic risk, capital shortfall, financial crises, *SRISK*, deleveraging

How should we assess global financial sector health? Can we provide a comparative analysis of such health across different countries and regions? Where do the future sources of vulnerability in the global financial sector lie?

This article employs recent advances in measurement of the systemic risk of financial firms to answer these questions. In particular, it exploits a theoretically well-founded notion of systemic risk contribution of financial firms—their expected capital shortfall in a crisis—and measures it using publicly available market and balance-sheet data. Using this measure provides a comparative analysis of the health of the global financial sector since early 2007, focusing on similarities and differences between the United States, Europe, and Asia.

The reason for focusing on capital adequacy as a measure of systemic risk is simply that undercapitalized financial sectors lead to significant loss of economic output due to withdrawal of efficient intermediation services and possibly misallocation of resources. In particular, when a large part of the financial sector is funded with fragile, short-term debt (or, conversely, is not funded with adequate equity capital) and is hit by a common shock to its long-term assets, there can be en masse failures of financial firms. In such a scenario, it is not possible for any individual firm to reduce its leverage or risk without significant costs, since other financial firms are attempting to achieve the same outcome. Since deleveraging and risk reduction are privately costly to owners of the financial firms, firms delay such actions, operating as undercapitalized firms that are averse

Viral V. Acharya is C. V. Starr Professor of Economics in the Department of Finance at New York University Stern School of Business.

I am grateful to Michael Robles of New York University Stern School of Business Volatility Institute for help with the computations and to Michael Barr and two anonymous referees for detailed comments on the first draft. Direct correspondence to: Viral V. Acharya at vacharya@stern.nyu.edu, NYU Stern School of Business, 44 West 4th St., New York, NY, 10016.

to expanding efficiently the provision of intermediation to households and corporations and keen to pursue risky strategies (gambling for resurrection) that offer them some chance of recovering, but at the cost of a greater chance of further stress. If further stress develops, there can be a complete disruption of payments and settlement services, which can cause trade and growth to collapse, as witnessed for several years during the Great Depression as well as in the fall of 2008 during the Great Recession.

The adverse impact of undercapitalized financial sectors on allocation of economic resources has been the focus of an important body of empirical research. Joe Peek and Eric S. Rosengren (2005), Ricardo J. Caballero, Takeo Hoshi, and Anil K. Kashyap (2008), and Hoshi and Kashyap (2010) show for the Japanese banking crisis of the 1990s that banks in the undercapitalized banking sector continued to operate as "zombie banks" that directed credit to nonperforming existing borrowers rather than directing this credit to efficient newer sectors of the economy. This theme has been confirmed again in the European countries following the financial crisis of 2007–2009. The lack of adequate recapitalization and cleaning-up of European banks' balance sheets has prevented an efficient allocation of credit for an extended period of time. Alexander Popov and Neeltje van Horen (2014) report that it has taken European banks much longer to recover in terms of their global syndicated lending than other banks. Viral A. Acharya and Sascha Steffen (2015) demonstrate that undercapitalized European banks put on "carry trades" by using short-term funding to purchase risky government bonds of southern periphery countries of Europe (Greece, Italy, Portugal, and Spain), a bet that did not pay off and resulted in a combined sovereign and banking crisis for Europe in the fall of 2011.

Given these adverse consequences of undercapitalized financial sectors, it is natural to focus on expected capital shortfall of the financial sector as a way of measuring its systemic risk or vulnerability to a future crisis. This article has four sections. In the first, I introduce the measure we employ, SRISK, based on the work of Acharya et al. (2010a, 2010b, 2010c) and Acharya, Robert Engle, and Matthew P. Richardson (2012). Next I assess global financial sector health since 2007 using SRISK as the measure of systemic risk. In the third section I discuss the divergence observed between the United States, Europe, and Asia, in terms of the evolution of financial sector health since 2007. The last section presents some conclusions.

SRISK: A MEASURE OF FINANCIAL SECTOR HEALTH

Acharya (2009) and Acharya et al. (2010a, 2010b, 2010c) argue that systemic risk should not be described in terms of a financial firm's failure per se but in the context of a firm's overall contribution to systemwide failure. The intuition is that when only an individual financial firm gets distressed—its equity capital becomes low relative to its promised debt or debtlike liabilities—there are minimal economic consequences because healthier financial firms can fill in for the void in intermediation services caused by the failed firm. When capital is low in the aggregate, however, it is not possible for other financial firms to step into the breach. This breakdown in aggregate financial intermediation is the reason there are severe consequences for the broader economy such as a credit crunch and fire sales of assets.

Acharya, Engle, and Richardson (2012) implement this intuition by proposing a measure, called *SRISK*, of the systemic risk contribution of a financial firm; *SRISK* is measured as the expected capital shortfall of a firm in a crisis. In particular, *SRISK* of firm i at time t is defined as the capital that the firm is expected to need (conditional on available information up to time $t - 1$) to operate "normally," that is, not face a run by its creditors, if we have another financial crisis. Symbolically it can be defined as

$$SRISK_{i,t} = E_{t-1}(Capital\ Shortfall_i | Crisis) \qquad (1)$$

Christian Brownlees and Engle (2011; see also Engle 2011) provide the econometrics of estimating *SRISK* by modeling the bivariate daily time series model of equity returns on firm i and on a broad market index using publicly available data. (The results of this analysis are updated weekly and are posted at the New York

University Stern School of Business Volatility Institute website: http://vlab.stern.nyu.edu/welcome/risk. Results are posted both for approximately one hundred U.S. financial firms and for twelve hundred global financial firms.)

To calculate SRISK, we first need to evaluate the losses that an equity holder will face if there is a future crisis. To do this, volatilities and correlations of an individual financial firm's equity return and the global marketwide return are allowed to change over time and simulated for six months into the future many times. Whenever the broad index falls by 40 percent over the next six months, a rather pessimistic scenario that captures the kind of market collapse witnessed during the Great Depression of the 1930s and the Great Recession in 2007–2009, this is viewed as a crisis. For these scenarios, the expected loss of equity value of firm i is called the long-run marginal expected shortfall, or *LRMES*. This is just the average of the fractional returns of the firm's equity in the crisis scenarios.[1]

The capital shortfall can be directly calculated by recognizing that the book value of debt will be relatively unchanged during this six-month period while equity values fall by *LRMES*. We assume a prudential capital ratio, denoted by k, of 8 percent (5.5 percent for Europe, to adjust for the differences between accounting standards—the European International Financial Reporting Standards and U.S. Generally Accepted Accounting Principles—in the treatment of netting of derivatives). Then we can define *SRISK*, of firm i at time t as:

$$SRISK_{i,t} = E_{t-1}((k(Debt + Equity) - Equity)|Crisis)$$
$$= k(Debt_{i,t}) - (1-k)(1-LRMES_{i,t})Equity_{i,t} \quad (2)$$

where $Equity_{i,t}$ is the market value of equity today, $Debt_{i,t}$ is the notional value of nonequity liabilities today, and $LRMES_{i,t}$ is the long-run marginal expected shortfall of equity return estimated using available information today. This measure of the expected capital shortfall captures many of the characteristics considered important for systemic risk such as size and leverage. These characteristics tend to increase a firm's capital shortfall when there are widespread losses in the financial sector. But a firm's expected capital shortfall also provides an important addition, most notably the co-movement of the financial firm's assets with the aggregate market in a crisis.[2]

Before we employ estimates of *SRISK* to provide a comparative analysis of the global financial sector health, a few points are in order.

First, *SRISK* can be considered the capital shortfall for a financial firm estimated using a market-data based "stress test." Stress tests have now become a standard device used by regulators to determine the capital that an institution will need to raise if there is a macroeconomic shock.[3] Regulatory stress tests employ book value of equity capital, estimate

---

1. In versions of the model where the simulation is not yet implemented on VLAB, *LRMES* is approximated as $1-exp(-18*MES)$ where *MES* is the one-day loss expected if market returns are less than −2 percent.

2. In this sense, *SRISK* is based on a notion of systemic risk in which a "tsunami"-type shock hits the global economy rather than a "contagion"-type shock in which an individual financial firm's interconnectedness causes losses elsewhere in the financial system. The latter would, however, also be statistically picked up in a co-movement of a financial firm's assets with the aggregate market providing that the contagion does have marketwide impact.

3. Acharya, Engle, and Pierret (2014) summarize the adoption of stress tests by regulators in the United States and the Europe: "An annual supervisory stress test of the financial sector in the United States has become a requirement with the implementation of Dodd-Frank Wall Street Reform and Consumer Protection Act (Pub.L. 111–203, H.R. 4173) of 2010. Macro-prudential stress tests have also been used by U.S. and European regulators to restore market confidence in financial sectors during an economic crisis. As a response to the recent financial crisis, the 2009 U.S. stress test led to a substantial recapitalization of the financial sector in the U.S. In Europe, the 2011 stress test also served as a crisis management tool during the European sovereign debt crisis. The European exercise lacked credibility in this role, however, due largely to the absence of a clear recapitalization plan for banks failing the stress test."

losses using models that map macroeconomic stress into asset losses, and require book values of capital to be sufficiently high based on regulatory risk-weighted assets.[4] In contrast to regulatory stress tests, SRISK is based on the market value of equity capital, estimates losses using market-data-based estimate of downside risk of market equity or its vulnerability to a crisis, and requires market values of capital to be sufficiently high relative to the quasi-market value of assets (measured as market value of equity plus the book value of nonequity liabilities). As a result, whereas the regulatory notion of leverage corresponds to risk-weighted assets divided by a measure of book value of equity of a financial firm, the notion of leverage captured in SRISK is quasi-market leverage, which is quasi-market value of assets divided by the market value of equity.

Second, as argued by Charles Calomiris and Richard Herring (2013, figures 3 and 4 in particular), an important advantage of using the market value of equity and its exposure to a crisis or aggregate downturn is that market-based signals of financial sector distress have been found to be much better as early-warning signals than regulatory measures of financial sector risk (risk-weighted assets to total assets) and book values of equity. There are several reasons why this might be the case. Book values of equity are readily gamed by management as recognition of nonperforming assets and provisioning against future losses is discretionary; to the extent such practices are anticipated by the market, market values of equity should reflect true equity values more precisely than book values. For this reason, as well as by the very nature of accounting of assets that are not marked to market, market values of equity tend to be more forward looking than book values. Finally, market values of equity may be the relevant metric for prudential purposes as financiers of a financial institution such as wholesale creditors and interbank counterparties should care about the ability of the institution to increase buffers and guard against losses on the financing; an institution whose market value of equity is collapsing to zero is unlikely to be able to raise such buffers, even if its book value is high.

Third, and related to the second point, regulatory risk weights for asset classes are inherently static in nature, whereas the true economic risk of asset classes fluctuates over time. Indeed, combined with shifts in financial leverage, the "risk that risk will change" can be considered an essential cause of financial crises. Acharya, Engle and Pierret (2014) demonstrate that market-based risk assessments of financial firms' balance sheets, in particular using the SRISK measure and its components, better captured the actual stress of financial firms in Europe during 2011, relative to the regulatory risk assessments, which relied on static risk weights, notably zero risk weights for risky sovereign bonds of countries in the southern European periphery.

Fourth, since it is based on market data, one limitation of SRISK is that it can be computed only for financial firms whose equity is publicly traded. It cannot be computed readily for privately held financial firms. Hence, all assessment of global financial sector health and comparative analysis across countries that follows is subject to this important caveat.

Finally, given the simple formulaic structure for SRISK, we can also understand changes in SRISK over time as coming from changes in its components, the book value of nonequity liabilities, the market value of equity, and the market value of equity times the LRMES, as follows:

$$SRISK_i = SRISK_{i,t} - SRISK_{i,t-1}$$
$$= Debt_i + Equity_i + Risk_i, \text{ where}$$
$$Debt_i = k(Debt_{i,t} - Debt_{i,t-1}),$$
$$Equity_i = (1-k)(Equity_{i,t} - Equity_{i,t-1}), \text{ and}$$
$$Risk_i = (1-k)(LRMES_{i,t}Equity_{i,t} - LRMES_{i,t-1}Equity_{i,t-1}) \quad (3)$$

where the changes in Debt, Equity, and Risk are measured over the period from $t-1$ to t, and

---

4. Ibid: "The current approach to assessing capital requirements is strongly dependent on the regulatory capital ratios defined under Basel Accords. The capital ratio of a bank is usually defined as the ratio of a measure of its equity to a measure of its assets. A regulatory capital ratio usually employs book value of equity and risk-weighted assets, where individual asset holdings are multiplied by corresponding regulatory 'risk weights.' The

Figure 1. International Comparisons of Aggregate *SRISK*, 2007–2014

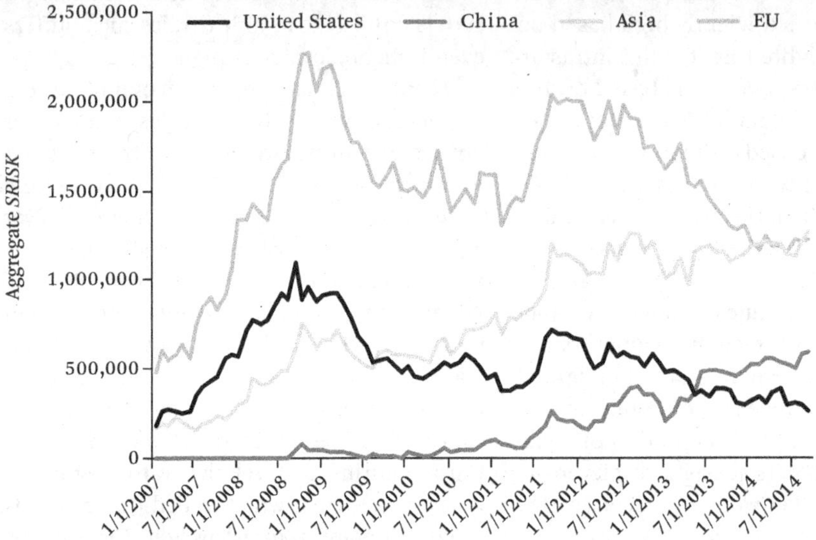

Source: Author's compilation based on data at NYU Stern Volatility Lab (website), "Documentation, Analysis List" (http://vlab.stern.nyu.edu/welcome/risk/).
Note: This figure plots the sum of *SRISK* in U.S.$ million for publicly traded financial firms (for inclusion criteria see table A1) in the United States, China, Asia (including China), and Europe. The data are from the period January 1, 2007, to September 30, 2014.

together with the appropriate weights from the *SRISK* formula in equation (2), these changes combine to explain the change in *SRISK* over the period from $t-1$ to t.

This decomposition highlights that increases in nonequity liabilities and expected losses in a crisis increase *SRISK* over time whereas increases in market value of equity decrease *SRISK* over time.

ASSESSING GLOBAL FINANCIAL SECTOR HEALTH USING *SRISK*

In order to operationalize *SRISK* and compare it across countries and regions, NYU Stern VLAB includes all publicly listed financial firms in a country with active trading in common equity that are in the top 10 percent of firms in a year by size (see table A1 for sample size distribution by year). In order to identify firms with capital shortfall, firms with positive *SRISK* are identified. All positive values of *SRISK* for a country or region in a given year are aggregated to obtain the overall *SRISK* for that country or region. In what follows, all references to the current or the present moment refer to October 10, 2014.[5]

Figures 1 to 8 and table 1 summarize our overall findings for aggregate *SRISK* across the three regions: United States, Europe, and Asia, with emphasis on China.

---

regulatory capital ratios in stress tests help regulators determine which banks fail the test under the stress scenario and what supervisory or recapitalization actions should be undertaken to address this failure."

5. Although this article focuses entirely on *SRISK* that is aggregated at the level of a country or region, prior research has shown that *SRISK* also has the right cross-sectional properties in capturing the systemic risk of individual financial firms. Acharya, Pedersen, Philippon and Richardson (2010a, 2010c) provide such firm-level evidence for 2007–2008 for the United States' financial sector, and Acharya, Engle, and Pierret (2014) provide such evidence for Europe during the period of the sovereign debt crisis in 2011.

Figure 1 plots the aggregate *SRISK* for the three regions and China and is the central figure of this essay.

In the case of the United States, systemic risk appears to have peaked in Fall 2008 and early 2009, with the estimated capital shortfall of the financial sector at over $1 trillion. This is of the order of magnitude of the capital injections and other forms of federal support for the financial sector that were deployed following the collapse of Lehman Brothers, in the form of the Troubled Asset Relief Program (TARP), Federal Deposit Insurance Corporation (FDIC) guarantees, and the Federal Reserve liquidity provision. Since then, the systemic risk appears to have steadily come down since spring 2009, with current levels being as low as in January 2007. The one exception was August 2011, when the systemic risk in the United States rose again around the debt-ceiling political crisis in the United States and the Eurozone sovereign debt and financial sector crisis.

Similar to the United States, the systemic risk of the European financial sector also reaches its peak in the fall of 2008 and early 2009—about $2.25 trillion—but reveals an important difference: it reaches another peak of $2 trillion in August 2011, coincident with the Eurozone sovereign debt crisis. In other words, Europe appears to have witnessed serial episodes of dramatic capital shortfalls in the financial sector. Although systemic risk has come down since this second peak, its current levels remain at more than twice those in January 2007, another striking difference from the United States.

The picture of Asia's systemic risk estimate is, however, quite different than that for the United States and Europe. The estimated capital shortfalls for the Asian financial sector show a steady trend upward all the way from January 2007 to September 2014 with some local peaks but overall having risen by close to $1 trillion, from a quarter trillion to currently around $1.25 trillion. China, which with Japan is the largest financial sector in Asia, mirrors this trend, as shown in the figure. The Chinese financial sector shows little estimated capital shortfall until the middle of 2010, but since then the size of the shortfall has risen meteorically, estimated as of September 2014 at over a half trillion dollars.

One limitation of comparing the absolute values of estimated capital shortfalls is that larger countries generally have larger financial sectors, and all else equal, therefore will have greater absolute values of estimated capital shortfalls in a future crisis. To confirm that inference from figure 1 is not driven by such size differences, figure 2 plots the aggregate *SRISK* for each region that is divided by the region's Gross Domestic Product (GDP). The patterns are essentially the same as in figure 1. In case of the United States, estimated capital shortfalls reach a peak of close to 8 percent of GDP in the fall of 2008 and early 2009, reaching another local peak, 4 percent of GDP, in August 2011, but are currently at less than 2 percent of GDP, as in January 2007. For Europe, the crises of 2008–2009 and fall 2011 appear to have been much worse, with estimated capital needs being close to 12 percent and 10 percent of GDP, respectively, and even as of September 2014, being high, at 6 percent of GDP, relative to the January 2007 level of 2 percent of GDP (as in the case of the United States). This illustrates well that the European financial sector is far less healthy at present than that of the United States, and also relative to itself prior to the global financial crisis of 2007–2008. Finally, for Asia the estimated capital shortfalls have trended steadily upward, from under 2 percent of GDP in January 2007 to close to 6 percent of GDP as of September 2014, and in the case of China, going from zero to over 6 percent of GDP.

Figure 3 helps us understand the diverging patterns of systemic risk for the United States, Europe, and Asia in terms of leveraging or deleveraging of the financial sector, by plotting the aggregate quasi-leverage of the respective financial sectors. It illustrates succinctly that the leverage time series for these financial sectors tracks closely the evolution of the estimated systemic risk of these financial sectors. In other words, the United States financial sector experienced a significant leverage increase until spring 2009, and since then it has been deleveraging at a rapid pace. The European financial sector experienced leverage rises until

Figure 2. *SRISK* Normalized by Comparison with GDPs of the United States, China, Asia, and the European Union

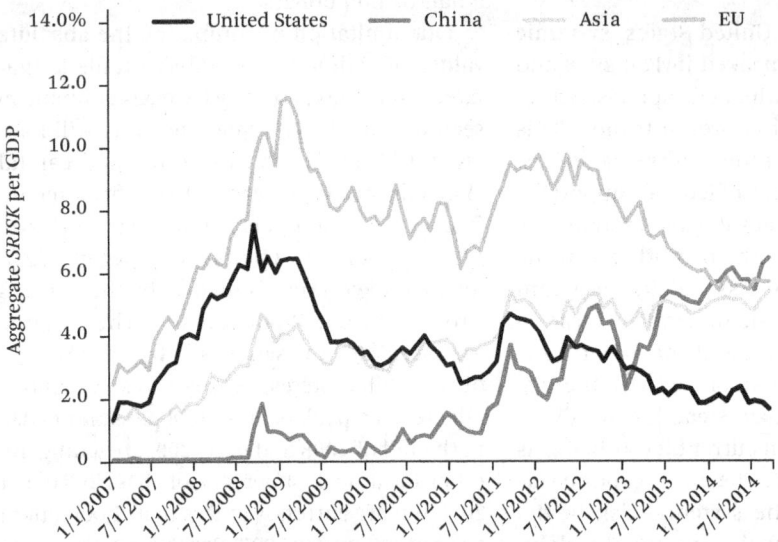

Source: Author's compilation based on NYU Stern Volatility Lab, "Documentation, Analysis List" (http://vlab.stern.nyu.edu/welcome/risk/), and Bloomberg.
Note: This figure plots the sum of *SRISK* for publicly traded financial firms (for inclusion criteria see table A1) in a given week, scaled by the country's or area's latest GDP figure available that week. Asia includes China. *SRISK* data are from January 1, 2007, to September 30, 2014.

summer 2009 and also in the period close to and leading up to fall 2011, and deleveraging to some extent since then but not to January 2007 levels. In contrast, the Asian and Chinese financial sectors have been ramping up leverage at a steady pace all along from 2007 to September 2014. It is interesting that as of 2016 the leverage in the United States financial sector is down to 5 (that is, five units of assets for one unit of market value of equity), lower than 10 for Asia, and around 15 for China and Europe. Equally interesting, the leverage of the financial sector in Europe has been pervasively greater than that of the financial sectors in the United States and Asia.

Figure 4 illustrates that in the case of the United States, the top three banks account for over half of the total capital shortfall of $250 billion, reflecting the increasing concentration in the financial sector owing in part to the acquisitions structured during 2007–2008 to resolve distressed financial firms. Interestingly, the top ten contributors include five insurance firms, whose systemic risk is increasingly coming under scrutiny, notably at the Financial Stability Oversight Council (FSOC) put in place by the Dodd-Frank Act in the United States to identify and prevent the emergence of systemic risk. Even though the insurance sector has a relatively stable liability structure compared to the banking sector, recent empirical evidence has suggested that life insurance firms in the United States have been "reaching for yield" (Becker and Ivashina 2015) by looking for highest-risk (and therefore, highest-yield) assets within a regulatory risk bucket; have been reducing statutory capital requirements by engaging in "shadow insurance," which transfers liability risks to captive reinsurance firms economically linked to the parent insurance firms (Koijen and Yogo 2016); and have been expanding their asset base of sub-investment-grade structured products in residential real estate mortgages while simultaneously shrinking their pool of investment-grade products in this asset class (Becker and Opp 2014). These changes appear to have been priced in by the market in terms of the greater

Figure 3. International Comparison of Aggregate Leverage (United States, China, Asia, European Union)

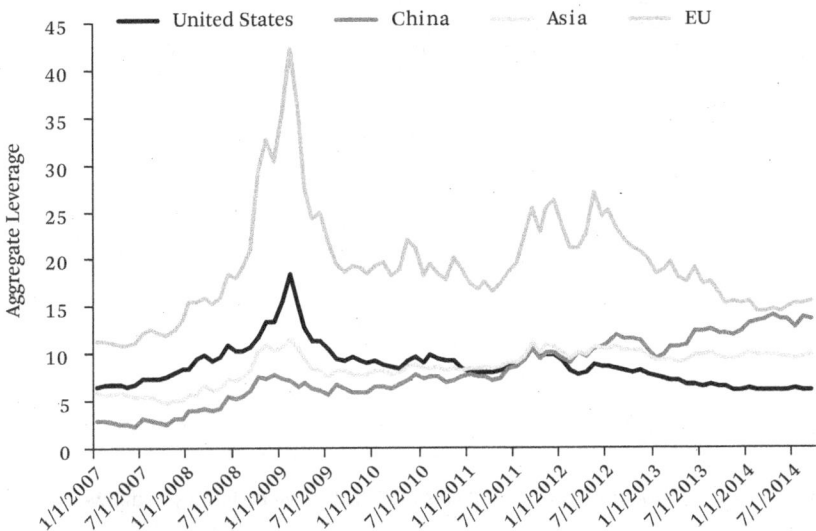

Source: Author's compilation based on NYU Stern Volatility Lab, "Documentation, Analysis List" (http://vlab.stern.nyu.edu/welcome/risk/).
Note: This figure plots the aggregate (quasi-) leverage for publicly traded financial firms (for inclusion criteria see table A1). Quasi-leverage of a financial firm is its quasi-market assets (market value of equity plus book value of nonequity liabilities) divided by the market value of equity. Quasi-leverage of financial firms in a region is weighted by the market value of equity of financial firms to obtain the aggregate quasi-leverage. The leverage data are from January 1, 2007, to September 30, 2014.

Figure 4. SRISK for Top Nineteen Publicly Traded U.S. Financial Firms (U.S.$ Million) as of October 10, 2014

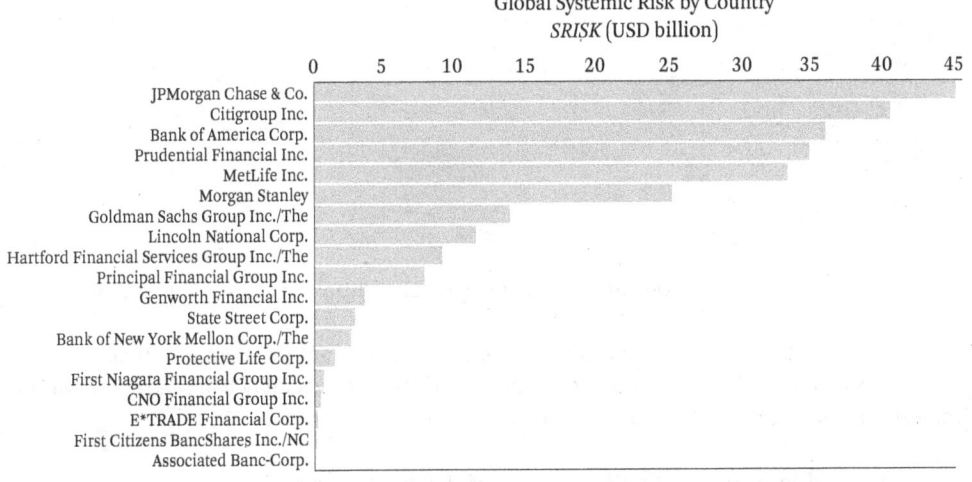

Source: NYU Stern Volatility Lab, "Documentation, Analysis List" (http://vlab.stern.nyu.edu/welcome/risk/).
Note: For inclusion criteria of firms, see table A1. The SRISK data are from NYU Stern Volatility Lab (vlab.stern.nyu.edu/welcome/risk).

Figure 5. *SRISK* Calculated for Top Twenty European Countries (U.S.$ Billions), as of October 10, 2014

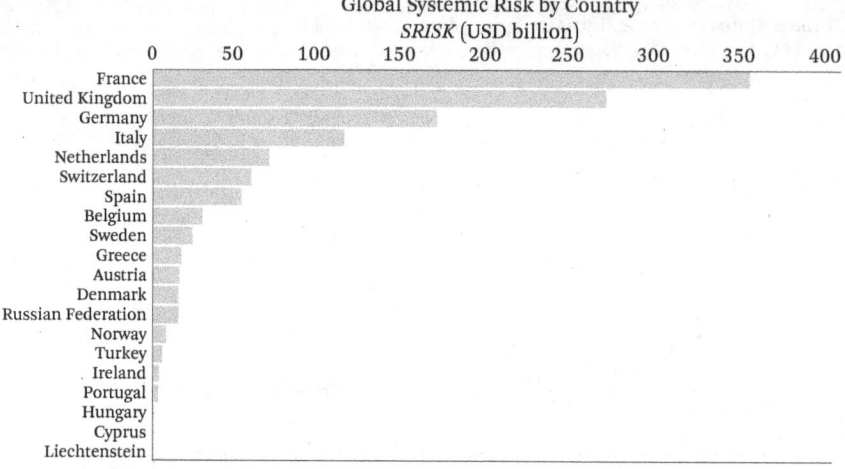

Source: NYU Stern Volatility Lab, "Documentation, Analysis List" (http://vlab.stern.nyu.edu/welcome/risk/).
Note: For inclusion criteria see table A1.

Figure 6. Sum of *SRISK* for Publicly Traded Financial Firms Normalized by GDP for Top Twenty Country-Level Values in Europe, as of October 10, 2014

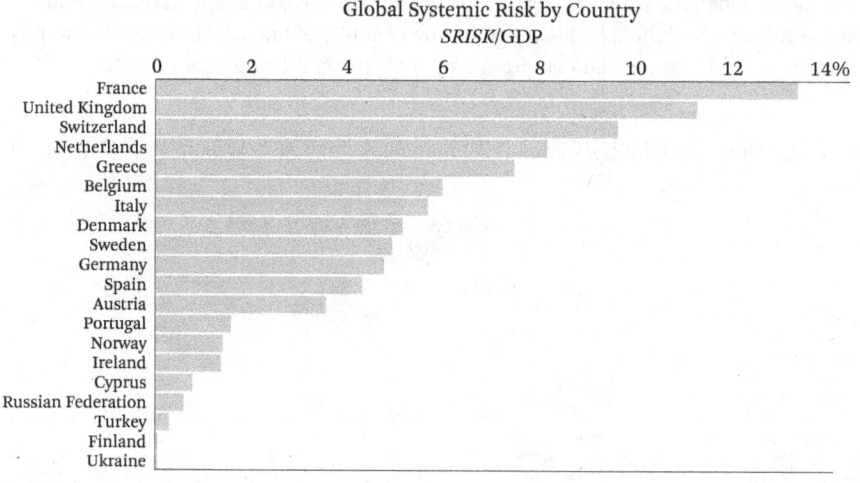

Source: NYU Stern Volatility Lab, "Documentation, Analysis List" (http://vlab.stern.nyu.edu/welcome/risk/).
Note: For inclusion criteria see table A1) in a country, scaled by the country's latest GDP figure available as of October 10, 2014. The *SRISK* data are from NYU Stern Volatility Lab (vlab.stern.nyu.edu/welcome/risk). The country GDP data are from Bloomberg.

economic risk and leverage of the life insurance sector.

Similarly, figures 5 and 6 help us understand the country-level contributors to current systemic risk assessment in Europe. In terms of absolute contributions to the estimated capital shortfalls (figure 5), France leads the way at $350 billion, over a fourth of the current shortfall estimate for Europe. Even on a percentage-of-GDP basis (figure 6), France

Figure 7. SRISK in Asia

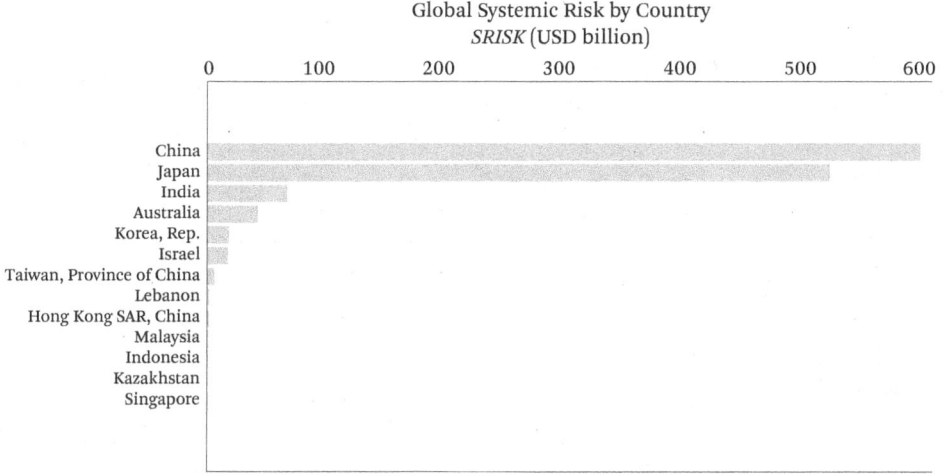

Source: NYU Stern Volatility Lab, "Documentation, Analysis List" (http://vlab.stern.nyu.edu/welcome/risk/).
Note: This figure plots the top thirteen country-level values in Asia, including Australia and New Zealand, of the sum of SRISK in U.S.$ billion for publicly traded financial firms (for inclusion criteria see table A1) in a country as of October 10, 2014.

leads the way with its estimated capital shortfall being around 13 percent of its GDP, a rather sizable fraction of GDP to put aside to recapitalize the banking sector, should future stress require public injections of capital. Whereas Switzerland and United Kingdom are expected to rank high on a percentage-of-GDP basis, given the relatively large balance sheets of their financial sectors compared to the national balance sheets, France's topping this list is somewhat surprising and highlights the relative undercapitalization of its banking sector in terms of its quasi-market leverage. Notably, although Germany ranks high in terms of absolute size of estimated capital shortfalls, on a percentage-of-GDP basis it looks much healthier than France.

Figures 7 and 8 help us understand countries that contribute to the systemic risk in Asia at the present date, 2016. China and Japan together constitute most of the estimated capital shortfall in Asia (figure 7). On a percentage-of-GDP basis, however, Japan is substantially higher, with an over 11 percent shortfall relative to GDP, whereas China is somewhat smaller, at over 6 percent.

Finally, notwithstanding that China's systemic risk relative to its GDP appears to be manageable, particularly given its vast reserves, it is intriguing to speculate what explains its dramatic rise seen in figures 1 and 2, from being practically zero to now being half a trillion dollars, or 6 percent of GDP. Table 1 provides an intuitive understanding of this rise by breaking down change in SRISK between the end of 2009 and October 10, 2014, for the highest SRISK contributors in the Chinese financial sector, into its three components—$\Delta Debt$, $\Delta Equity$, $\Delta Risk$—as explained in the concluding remarks of the first section of this article.

The top four banks in the list in table 1 are the largest state-owned commercial banks in China. Together they account for over half of the estimated capital shortfall for China. However, all these banks had negative SRISK at the end of 2009, that is, they in fact had a capital surplus. What is remarkable in table 1 is that almost all of the change in SRISK can be attributed to the increase in debt liabilities ($\Delta Debt$) for these banks. Indeed, while their debt liabilities have increased, equity valuations have suffered so that the increase in SRISK is also due to declines in equity (positive $\Delta Equity$). Interestingly, their downside risk on per dollar of

Figure 8. *SRISK* in Asia Normalized by GDP

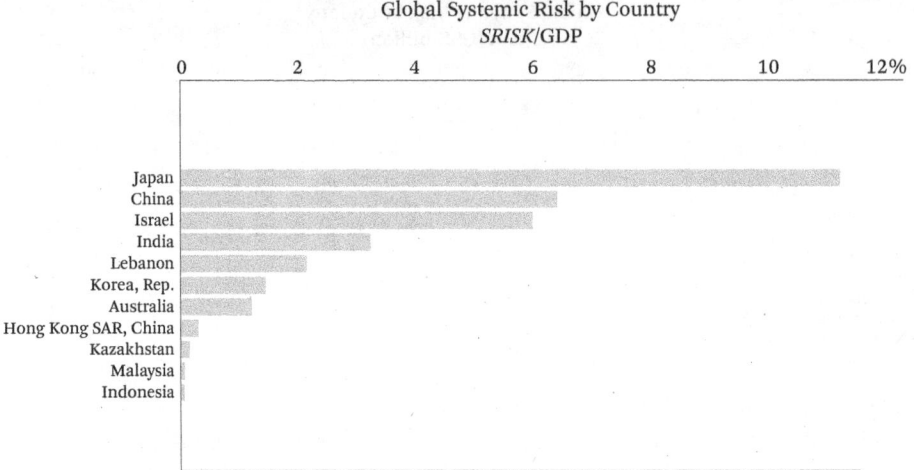

Source: NYU Stern Volatility Lab, "Documentation, Analysis List" (http://vlab.stern.nyu.edu/welcome/risk/).
Note: This figure plots for the top eleven country-level values in Asia, including Australia and New Zealand, the sum of *SRISK* for publicly traded financial firms (for inclusion criteria see table A1) in a country, scaled by the country's latest GDP figure available (from Bloomberg) as of October 10, 2014. The *SRISK* data are from NYU Stern Volatility Lab (vlab.stern.nyu.edu/welcome/risk).

equity basis has improved, so that the risk contribution ($\Delta Risk$) is negative. Together, this suggests massive financial leveraging of the largest banks in China from 2010 to September 2014, which has increased the systemic risk of the financial sector to nontrivial levels—way beyond that of the United States on percentage-of-GDP basis.

WHAT EXPLAINS THE DIVERGENCE IN EVOLUTION OF GLOBAL FINANCIAL SECTOR HEALTH SINCE 2007?

In summary, the financial sector capital shortfalls reached a peak in the end of 2008 and early 2009 for the United States and Europe; however, they declined thereafter steadily only for the United States, with Europe reaching a similar peak again in the fall of 2011 during the sovereign debt crises in the southern periphery of Europe. In contrast, the financial sector in Asia had little capital shortfall in 2008–2009, but the shortfall has increased steadily since 2010, notably for China and Japan. What explains these relative patterns? I shall argue briefly that these patterns can be explained on the basis of the regulatory responses in the United States, the lack thereof in Europe, economic stagnation in Japan, and the bank-leverage-based fiscal stimulus in China.

Following the collapse of Lehman Brothers, the United States put in place first a substantial rescue package in the form of TARP recapitalization of the financial sector up to $750 billion, FDIC deposit and loan guarantee programs, and the Federal Reserve's liquidity support of the financial sector as well as markets at large, in addition to the government conservatorship of the mortgage agencies, Fannie Mae and Freddie Mac. While these measures were not adequate to calm the volatility in markets, which remained substantially high even in early 2009, the stress-test-based recapitalization in spring 2009 (the Supervisory Capital Assessment Program, SCAP) ensured that banks injected $200 billion more capital into the balance sheets (required capital raising by regulators was $75 billion). These measures calmed fears about the health of the financial sector in the United States. Following this, the Dodd-Frank Act was enacted in 2010 and various measures were put in place to rein in systemic risk, again notably an annual stress

Table 1. Decomposition of Change in SRISK

Institution	SRISK (t)	SRISK (t − 1)	ΔSRISK	ΔDebt	ΔEquity	ΔRisk
Bank of China Ltd.	105,580.9	−4,396.9	109,977.8	90,325.2	20,038.1	−385.5
China Construction Bank Corp.	84,956.1	−12,500.5	97,456.6	90,456.5	15,262.1	−8,261.9
Industrial and Commercial Bank of China Ltd.	77,991.2	−71,501.9	149,493.1	114,137.7	48,781.9	−13,426.4
Bank of Communications Co. Ltd.	44,484.7	−678.7	45,163.4	38,475.8	6,314.8	372.7
China CITIC Bank Corp. Ltd.	33,828.5	−3,342.2	37,170.7	32,863.6	5,290.3	−983.2
China Merchants Bank Co. Ltd.	29,608.3	−14,607.5	44,215.8	38,062.1	5,430.3	723.4
Shanghai Pudong Development Bank	25,899.8	−4,037.5	29,937.3	29,607.2	−1,414.7	1,744.8
Industrial Bank Co. Ltd.	24,856.8	−8,643.1	33,499.9	33,119.3	−1,822.7	2,203.2
China Minsheng Banking Corp. Ltd.	17,584.8	−4,891.7	22,476.5	27,422.5	−6,765.6	1,819.6
Huaxia Bank Co. Ltd.	11,742.1	2,068.4	9,673.7	12,193.5	−2,690.4	170.6

Source: Author's compilation, based on the SRISK data and its component changes from NYU Stern Volatility Lab (vlab.stern.nyu.edu/welcome/risk).

Note: Table 1 shows the change in SRISK between the beginning of 2010 (t − 1) and October 10, 2014 (t) in U.S.$ billion for publicly traded financial firms (for inclusion criteria see table A1) in China with the top ten values of SRISK as of October 10, 2014. The change in SRISK is broken down further into change due to changes in book value of nonequity liabilities ("Debt"), in market value of equity ("Equity"), and in market value of equity times LRMES, the measure of downside beta of the firm's equity to a global market correction of −40 percent ("Risk").

test of the systemically important financial institutions (SIFIs) identified by the newly created Financial Stability Oversight Council (FSOC). All of these measures have ensured substantial deleveraging of the United States financial sector balance sheets, as seen in figures 1 to 3, to the point that they appear to be among the healthiest in the global economy at present.

In contrast to the United States, the regulatory response in Europe to the financial sector meltdown of 2007–2008 was half-baked. While the governments and central banks were quick to assist the ailing financial sector with asset and liability guarantees as well as liquidity injection, there was no substantial recapitalization of the financial sector, on a scale similar to the TARP was for the United States financial sector. This lack of recapitalization, in presence of massive guarantees, meant that the financial sector had poor incentives during the recovery phase. Many undercapitalized banks invested in risky assets to rebuild equity capital, in the process transferring risks to the government, by undertaking "carry trades" on southern periphery sovereign debt funded with retail and wholesale deposits (Acharya and Steffen 2015). This created a rather unfortunate nexus between financial and sovereign credit risks in the Eurozone, bringing about twin crises in the fall of 2011, the deteriorating macroeconomic and financial health of Spain and Italy (Acharya 2014). This nexus of sovereign and financial sector credit risks—first, the undercapitalized financial sector taking leveraged exposures to risky sovereigns, and second, further distress of risky sovereigns inflicting collateral damage on the financial sector—appears to have had significant real consequences. Acharya et al. (2014) show that even relatively large borrowers in Europe whose lead banks have been from the southern periphery countries have been hoarding cash and cutting back investment and employment, behaving as though they are financially constrained. This effect is not seen for borrowers whose lead banks are from the core European countries, where the banks are relatively better capitalized.

Regulators did not put a stop to the carry-trade strategies and the undercapitalization of banks that had led to them. In fact the strategies were encouraged by regulators who conducted stress tests that had little bite when compared to the SCAP exercise of the United States. As Acharya, Robert Engle, and Diane Pierret (2014) document, the European stress tests granted zero risk weights to risky southern periphery sovereign debt so that effectively not much capital was raised by banks in response; in fact, the worst banks in terms of risks were found to require the least capital in the stress tests. Furthermore, Acharya, Engle and Pierret show that assumptions regarding the net losses, that is, gross losses minus future profits, were primarily driven by future profits by the end of the stress scenario (typically in eight to nine quarters), rather than by losses up to the worst point in the stress scenario (typically the first few quarters of the stress test horizon). This discretionary choice by the regulators also implied that banks that were making the most losses by the worst point in the stress scenario were designated as well capitalized.

Acharya and Steffen (2014) document that the pattern was hardly different with the Asset Quality Review and Comprehensive Assessment of the European Central Bank in 2014. Indeed, the underlying issue here is likely political: revising sovereign risk weights to non-zero levels might require support of national governments, revisions that might be partly seen as lacking in credibility in a future economic convergence within the Eurozone. Without a Eurozone-level arrangement to inject capital and provide deposit insurance to banks, designating large banks as undercapitalized may require national taxpayer injections that would only add to their countries' sovereign debts.

Nevertheless, there is some overall improvement in the health of the financial sector relative to condition in the fall of 2011, as a result of the extraordinary liquidity injection and promises to purchase securities from the market provided by the European Central Bank, starting in December 2011.

Finally, the case of Asia can be explained by the continuing economic malaise in Japan since the regulatory failure in the 1990s to recapitalize the banking sector, and in China by the debt-based stimulus to ensure high growth rates in the short run even as the global economy suffered in the wake of the crisis of 2007–2008. In the case of Japan, leverage of the financial sector remains high or is increasing in spite of continued macroeconomic weakness. This explains the continuing rise of systemic risk in Japan since 2007.

In contrast to Japan, the Chinese case is relatively straightforward. Since the global financial and economic crisis of 2007–2008, Chinese state-owned banks have leveraged massively, including off-balance-sheet liabilities (not captured in *SRISK* analysis), to fund real estate and infrastructure projects, many of which are at unsustainable price levels and have resulted in high nonperforming rates. From 2008 to 2013, total credit outstanding in the Chinese economy grew from 125 percent to 240 percent of GDP. Much of this increase came about from stimulus expenditures undertaken since 2008 by local municipal governments. These local governments, being prohibited from raising debt directly, set up special-purpose financing vehicles that raised debt from shadow banks ("trusts") in China to invest in infrastructure and real estate development. The local government debt is backed mainly by revenues from land sales, but with house prices inevitably slowing down in the past few years from their astronomical previous growth, the shadow banks—many of which are implicitly supported by parent state-owned banks—are exposed to significant losses. This situation has created the possibility of runs as well as under-capitalized banks.

China appears to have time and resources—large quantity of reserves and a high domestic savings rate—and it exercises tight control of its banks and housing markets. Still, the question is whether—like the United States in post-Lehman era—China will take tough recapitalization decisions for its banks before its own crisis comes to fruition, or whether, like Japan in the 1990s and Europe since the Great Recession, it will let undercapitalized banks continue to operate as zombie banks engaged in the misallocation of economic resources.

CONCLUSION

In this essay I used recently developed methodology to estimate capital shortfalls of financial institutions during aggregate stress to assess the evolution of financial sector health since 2007 in the United States, Europe, and Asia. Financial sector capital shortfalls reached a peak at the end of 2008 and in early 2009 for the United States and Europe. After that, however, they decline steadily only in the United States. Europe reached a similar peak again in the fall of 2011 during the southern periphery sovereign crises. In contrast, the financial sector in Asia had little capital shortfall in 2008–2009, but the shortfall has increased steadily since 2010, notably for China and Japan. The regulatory responses in these regions explain these differing patterns: Were distressed banking sectors recapitalized or were they allowed to remain under-capitalized? The United States did not waste its crisis, and its banking sector appears to be the best-capitalized of the lot. Europe has already wasted two opportunities—two crises—to strengthen its banking sector. Japan has not yet fully recovered from consequences of its zombie-banking policy of the 1990s. And China is potentially heading into a debt-fueled banking crisis, largely from its fiscal stimulus policies since 2008. Economic outcomes in these regions appear to be mirroring the health of their financial sectors as measured by capital adequacy against future stress.

APPENDIX

Table A1. Number of Total Firms per Region

Year	United States	China	Asia	European Union
2007	155	30	336	353
2008	159	39	373	389
2009	148	52	409	395
2010	148	58	429	397
2011	156	66	453	405
2012	157	70	458	404
2013	156	70	457	394
2014	153	70	451	385

Source: Author's compilation.
Note: Publicly listed financial firms in each country with active trading in common equity that are also in the top 10 percent of financial firms by size (market equity).

REFERENCES

Acharya, Viral V. 2009. "A Theory of Systemic Risk and Design of Prudential Bank Regulation." *Journal of Financial Stability* 5(3): 224–55.

———. 2014. "The Nexus Between Financial Sector and Sovereign Credit Risks." Presentation at Copenhagen Business School (August). Available at: rn.nyu.edu/~sternfin/vacharya/public_html/pdfs/Toulouse Lectures.pdf; accessed June 9, 2016.

Acharya, Viral V., Tim Eisert, Christian Eufinger, and Christian Hirsch. 2014. "Real Effects of the Sovereign Debt Crisis in Europe: Evidence from Syndicated Loans." Unpublished working paper. New York: NYU Stern School of Business.

Acharya, Viral V., Robert Engle, and Diane Pierret. 2014. "Testing Macro-Prudential Stress Tests: The Risk of Regulatory Risk Weights." *Journal of Monetary Economics* 65: 36–53.

Acharya, Viral V., Robert Engle, and Matthew P. Richardson. 2012. "Capital Shortfall: A New Approach to Ranking and Regulating Systemic Risks." *American Economic Review Papers and Proceedings* 102(3): 59–64.

Acharya, Viral V., Lasse H. Pedersen, Thomas Philippon, and Matthew P. Richardson. 2010a. "Measuring Systemic Risk." In *Regulating Wall Street: The Dodd-Frank Act and the New Architecture of Global Finance*, edited by Viral V. Acharya, Thomas F. Cooley, Matthew Richardson, and Ingo Walter. New York: John Wiley.

———. 2010b. "Taxing Systemic Risk." in *Regulating Wall Street: The Dodd-Frank Act and the New Architecture of Global Finance*, edited by Viral V. Acharya, Thomas F. Cooley, Matthew Richardson, and Ingo Walter. New York: John Wiley.

———. 2010c. "Measuring Systemic Risk." Technical report. New York: NYU Stern School of Business, Department of Finance.

Acharya, Viral V., and Sascha Steffen. 2014. "Benchmarking the European Central Bank's Asset Quality Review and Stress Test—A Tale of Two Leverage Ratios." Brussels: Center for European Policy Studies.

———. 2015. "The Greatest Carry Trade Ever? Understanding Eurozone Bank Risks." *Journal of Financial Economics* 115(2): 215–36.

Becker, Bo, and Victoria Ivashina. 2015. "Reaching for Yield in the Bond Market." *Journal of Finance* 70(5): 1863–902.

Becker, Bo, and Marcus Opp. 2014. "Regulatory Reform and Risk-Taking: Replacing Ratings." Working Paper. Berkeley: University of California, Haas School of Business.

Brownlees, Christian, and Robert Engle. 2011. "Volatility, Correlation and Tails for Systemic Risk Measurement." Working Paper. New York: New York University.

Caballero, Ricardo J., Takeo Hoshi, and Anil K. Kashyap. 2008. "Zombie Lending and Depressed Restructuring in Japan." *American Economic Review* 98(5): 1943–77.

Calomiris, Charles, and Richard Herring. 2013. "How to Design a Contingent Convertible Debt

Requirement That Helps Solve Our Too-Big-To-Fail Problem." *Journal of Applied Corporate Finance* 25(2): 66–89.

Engle, Robert. 2011. "Dynamic Conditional Beta." New York: NYU Sterns School of Business, Volatility Institute. Available at: www.frbsf.org/economic-research/files/Thu_1340_Engle.pdf; accessed June 9, 2016.

Hoshi, Takeo, and Anil K. Kashyap. 2010. Will the U.S. Bank Recapitalization Succeed? Eight Lessons from Japan." *Journal of Financial Economics* 97(3): 398–417.

Koijen, Ralph, and Motohiro Yogo. 2016. "Shadow Insurance." *Econometrica* 84(3): 1–50.

Peek, Joe, and Eric S. Rosengren. 2005. "Unnatural Selection: Perverse Incentives and the Misallocation of Credit in Japan." *American Economic Review* 95(4): 1144–66.

Popov, Alexander, and Neeltje van Horen. 2014. "Exporting Sovereign Stress: Evidence from Syndicated Bank Lending During the Euro Area Sovereign Debt Crisis." *Review of Finance* 19(5). Available at: www.researchgate.net/publication/274310421_Exporting_Sovereign_Stress_Evidence_from_Syndicated_Bank_Lending_during_the_Euro_Area_Sovereign_Debt_Crisis; accessed June 9, 2016

The European Union in International Financial Governance

NIAMH MOLONEY

This article considers the role of the European Union in international financial governance after the institutional reforms it undertook in connection with the global financial crisis. It suggests that the new administrative actors that support the governance of the European Union's single financial market, notably the European Supervisory Authorities, have the potential to reshape how the European Union engages with international financial governance. It finds that the European Union's effectiveness in influencing international financial governance—and the effectiveness of international financial governance more generally—is likely to strengthen as a result.

Keywords: European Supervisory Authorities, international financial governance

This article considers how the role of the European Union (EU) in international financial governance—regarded as the complex of standards, market access arrangements, and coordination structures that support the global financial market—is changing, the drivers of this change, and the implications. Specifically, it considers how the EU's new supranational administrative structures, which support the governance of the EU's single financial market (the European Supervisory Authorities, or ESAs), may affect change. The single financial market is composed of the national markets of the EU's twenty-eight member states, which are subject to common, harmonized regulation under the EU's "single rule book;" the single rule book also supports liberalized cross-border access by financial actors in one member state of the EU to the markets of other member states. The European Supervisory Authorities were constructed during the global financial crisis era in order to support the financial stability of the single financial market. But they also have the potential to reshape how the EU engages with the institutions of international financial governance, notably the major international standard setters: the Financial Stability Board (FSB), the Basel Committee on Banking Supervision (Basel Committee), and the International Organization of Securities Commissions (IOSCO). The article also suggests that the ESAs are likely to reinforce the effectiveness of international financial governance more generally. By drawing on empirical observation of the new ESAs, and on a composite legal and international political economy literature, the article seeks to contribute to understanding of how administrative ac-

---

Niamh Moloney is professor of financial markets law in the Law Department of the London School of Economics and Political Science.

An earlier version of this article was presented at a workshop at Michigan Law School on International Financial Regulation on May 15, 2015. I am grateful to participants in the workshop for their valuable comments and to the Russell Sage Foundation referees for their comments on the workshop paper. Direct correspondence to: Niamh Moloney at n.moloney@lse.ac.uk, Law Department, London School of Economics and Political Science, Houghton St., London WC2A 2 AE, U.K.

tors interact with and influence international financial governance.

THE EUROPEAN UNION AND THE CHANGING NATURE OF INTERNATIONAL FINANCIAL GOVERNANCE

The EU has long been a significant actor in international financial governance. Prior to the global financial crisis the EU was increasingly imposing its preferences on international financial governance and, in particular, on standard setting and application of standards (Posner 2009). The 2002 adoption by the EU of the International Financial Reporting Standards (IFRS) issued by the IFRS Foundation as the internal financial reporting standard for EU listed companies, for example, became associated with a weakening of the global dominance of the United States' Generally Accepted Accounting Principles (GAAP). This change reflected in part the imposition by the EU of IFRS-equivalence obligations on third-country firms seeking access to the EU financial market (Moloney 2014a, 165–68). Over the global financial crisis reform period (broadly, 2008 to 2014) the EU, sometimes as a loose coalition of member states acting intergovernmentally and sometimes as a more cohesive, supranationally oriented regional bloc, became a significant force in the Basel Committee and in IOSCO as new standards were adopted for the global financial market (Quaglia 2014a). To take another example, EU-U.S. clashes on the over-the-counter (OTC) derivatives market reforms adopted to address the financial stability risks exposed by the global financial crisis became a major preoccupation of international financial diplomacy over the crisis period (Moloney 2014a, 615–20). The extent to which the EU has been able to impose its distinct, collective preferences on international standard setting over the global financial crisis period has been well documented (Blom 2014; Quaglia 2014a). While EU member state preferences have remained of determinative importance during this period, the period can also be associated with the EU's increasingly acting as a hegemonic great power in finance, imposing its political preferences on international standard setting (Mügge 2014). The nature of international financial governance and of the forces playing upon it is changing, however, and reconsideration of the EU's role is accordingly necessary.

The nature of international financial governance is shifting. It has previously been primarily preoccupied with the agreement and adoption of standards governing the international financial system. It is now pivoting to address in addition the achievement of the outcomes sought by standards. It is accordingly engaging more closely with standard implementation and with the management of related divergences, operational supervisory co-ordination and convergence, data collection and assessment, the coordination of enforcement, and regulatory learning and sharing of best practices (Helleiner and Pagliari 2011). Post-crisis international financial governance has similarly been characterized as representing a form of "mutual adaptation" and "cooperative development" (Helleiner and Pagliari 2011). Accordingly, the operational management of divergence and friction in standard implementation, the coordination of supervisory approaches, and mutual regulatory and supervisory learning—rather than the imposition of political preferences on international standard setting—is coming to characterize the dynamics of international financial governance.

For example, international standard setters are increasingly focusing on implementation of standards, the achievement and benchmarking of related required outcomes, and the risks associated with escape from and divergences in standard implementation. The FSB continues to report to the G-20 on progress on implementation of the crisis-era reforms and is undertaking regular and intensive peer reviews of how crisis-era standards are being implemented (Financial Stability Board 2015a). The Basel Committee is carrying out intensive Regulatory Compliance Assessment Programs (RCAPs) of Basel III Accord implementation. Supervisory co-ordination arrangements are being constructed, with attention being trained in particular on co-ordination through colleges of supervisors (Basel Committee on Banking Supervision 2014a; International Organization of Securities Commissions 2013). IOSCO has recently engaged in an intensive review of the range of regulatory tools which can be deployed to support supervisory coordination in the securities markets (International Organization of Securities Commissions 2015a) and has also addressed enforcement, highlighting the tools that should be available to regulators globally (International Organization of Securities Commissions 2015b). The international standard setters are also increasingly focusing their attention on the management, interrogation, and deployment of the massive dataset now emerging for regulatory use, in the wake of the crisis-era reforms, which mandate more intense reporting from a number of market segments, notably the OTC derivatives market (Financial Stability Board 2015b). On a bilateral basis, granular agency contacts are intensifying as the technical details governing third-country market access and reflecting the swathes of new rules imposed domestically and regionally following the global financial crisis are negotiated and coordinated.

Coordinated and optimal operational management of technical difference, supervisory cooperation, the interrogation of complex data, and the sharing of technical regulatory and supervisory experience has accordingly become of central importance to international financial governance. And as international financial governance becomes more outcomes-focused and operational, the administrative actors in international financial governance, primarily the regulators who sit (often alongside treasuries and central banks) on the international standard setters, are, in parallel, acquiring critical importance. How, accordingly, is the EU, which has long engaged with international financial governance by means of imposing national member state and collective EU preferences on standard setting, equipped to engage with a more operational form of governance; and what are the implications for international financial governance and, specifically, for the international standard setters? Will the new administrative apparatus that supports EU financial governance, and specifically the ESAs, provide a means for effective engagement with this changed environment? And how should these questions be situated within the literature?

INTERNATIONAL FINANCIAL GOVERNANCE AND THE EU: SCOPING THE LITERATURE

In assessing the role of the European Supervisory Authorities in providing a new administrative channel through which the EU influences international financial governance, this article seeks to contribute to the composite but rich literature on international financial governance. An influential strand of legal scholarship has recently examined the nature of international financial governance with respect to its effectiveness and to how it achieves outcomes, including through institutional design and legal mechanisms. Drawing on the network theory of international law (Slaughter 2004), this strand explains how and why international financial governance, though primarily based on soft law and on informal networks of regulators operating through the international standard setters, can exercise coercive force (Brummer 2012). In the wake of the global financial crisis this scholarship is increasingly considering the lack of resilience of the structures and products of international financial governance in the face of global systemic risks and intense political intervention (Verdier 2013).

A related body of legal scholarship, which builds on the Global Administrative Law analysis (Krisch and Kingsbury 2006), probes the accountability and legitimacy risks that flow from the soft-law- and network-based nature of international financial governance (Barr 2014). This composite legal literature supports critique of the ESAs as administrative actors in international financial governance given, in particular, their limited coercive ability (discussed further in a later section). But the cognate literature on international political economy provides additional tools of analysis as it examines the power dynamics of how different actors engage with and influence international financial governance and thus can support examination of the context in which the ESAs operate.

An important segment of the international political economy literature probes how different actors and their preferences shape international financial governance. It has traditionally characterized international financial governance as being shaped by the preferences of the "great powers" in finance, classically the United States but increasingly the EU (Drezner 2007; Mügge 2014). But it also probes how "great power" preferences are formed and, with particular relevance for the role of the ESAs in international financial governance, the role of administrative actors (domestic regulators) in shaping and diffusing great power preferences by supporting the "regulatory capacity" of the state: the state's ability to achieve outcomes through the adoption, monitoring, and implementation of rules (Bach and Newman 2007). In particular, the extent of a state's regulatory capacity can be associated with the strength of its ability to influence international financial governance (Newman and Posner 2015) by, for example, imposing third-country access requirements or by diffusing, through technocratically expert national regulators, preferences to the international standard-setting level (Büthe and Mattli 2011). In the EU, distinct member state preferences (which typically diverge to some extent with respect to international standard setting, reflecting the different institutional economic models that characterize the EU's member states; preferences will tend to converge where the distributional effects of international standards are weak), rather than the preferences of the EU as a notional global "great power" in finance, have until recently been the dominant influence on EU engagement with international financial governance (Quaglia 2014a).[1] But the regulatory capacity of the EU, notably with respect to the extent to which the EU can, through its internal legislative and administrative apparatus, shape and implement (and thereby signal the credibility of) international standards and, by means of third-country access rules, impose its preferences on other jurisdictions, has been identified as an increasingly important factor and as strengthening the influence of the EU as a collective actor in international financial governance (Posner 2010; Bach and Newman 2014). Similarly, the EU's regulatory capacity can dictate the extent to which it can delegate to a representative EU actor, typically the European Commission (the EU's supranational executive body), and so through delegation pull the member state principals toward a stronger collective position in the international standard setters (Quaglia 2014a; Mügge 2011).

The nature of the EU's engagement with international financial governance is increasingly receiving attention in EU legal scholarship, particularly in the wake of the global financial crisis and the related framing of the EU reform agenda within the G-20 reform agenda, and given the lessons which the EU's experience in designing legal solutions to cross-border co-ordination problems may hold for the international financial system (Ferran 2014; Amtenbrick 2013). But the ESAs, as new EU administrative actors in international financial governance, have not been examined closely by either the legal or international political economy literature. Legal analysis thus far has primarily focused on the new ESAs' place within the EU's constitutional order and on their impact on institutional governance for the EU financial system (Moloney 2014b, 854–1009; Busuioc 2013; Schammo 2011). International political economy analysis has focused primarily on the member states and on the EU institutions, which are established under the EU Treaties (primarily the European Commission) and through which the member states operate at international level (Quaglia 2014a; Mügge 2014). But legal analysis of the ESAs' powers and their related incentives with respect to international engagement, together with the regulatory capacity insights of international political economy, have potential powerful explanatory force with respect to how the EU's engagement with international financial governance may change. Accordingly, this analysis draws on the composite literature out-

---

1. The EU financial market is second only to the U.S. market in size. Recent analysis by the European Commission notes that as of the end of 2013, EU stock market capitalization stood at €8.4 trillion, 64.5 percent of GDP, and the value of outstanding debt securities was €22.3 trillion, 171.3 percent of GDP. See European Commission 2015a, 10–11.

lined to examine how the ESAs may reshape, through administrative means, how the EU engages with and influences international financial governance.

THE MEMBER STATES AND THEIR PREFERENCES IN INTERNATIONAL FINANCIAL GOVERNANCE

The arrival of the ESAs has led to the construction of a new administrative channel for engagement with international financial governance in the EU. The member states and their preferences have long been the dominant influence on the EU's international financial diplomacy at the international standard setters. International financial relations, notwithstanding the recent changes to institutional governance in the EU and the establishment of the ESAs, remain primarily within the control of the member states and, to a lesser extent, the European Commission (EC, the major EU institution to which collective EU representation is delegated) and, depending on the regulatory issue in question, the European Central Bank (ECB). Although a highly detailed, harmonized single rule book applies to the EU financial system in the wake of the global financial crisis, coordination in the international standard setters can still be loose; the member states and their distinct interests often drive international engagement, and the extent to which the collective EU interest is formally represented and has voting power varies. As discussed in subsequent sections, the ESAs are likely to reshape this allocation of competence and in so doing to strengthen EU engagement with the current and more operational phase of international financial governance.

The EC typically represents the supranational, collective EU interest (where one can be identified, given that the distributional effects of financial regulation are felt differently across the different economies and market structures of the member states). In the Financial Stability Board, for example, the EC, along with the ECB, is a member of the thirty-four-member decisionmaking plenary session along with the U.K., France, Germany, Italy, the Netherlands, and Spain, which are represented by their finance ministries, central banks, or other regulator. In the Basel Committee, the ECB as monetary authority and the ECB as bank supervisor sit along with central banks and national bank regulators from Belgium, France, Germany, Italy, Luxembourg, the Netherlands, Spain, Sweden, and the U.K. as full voting members; the EC is represented but has only nonvoting observer status (Quaglia 2014a, 2015). Similarly, on IOSCO the EC has associate member (nonvoting) status while the national securities regulators of the member states are ordinary voting members of IOSCO. Six EU regulators are permanent members of the thirty-three-member IOSCO decisionmaking body (Conac 2015). Member states are, accordingly, usually independently represented and coordination can be limited. Levels of coordination have varied over time: a high degree of EU coordination can be observed with respect to discussions with the IFRS Foundation, but low levels with respect to IOSCO discussions, reflecting the different interests and incentives engaged in each case (Quaglia 2014b). Similarly the degree of coordination of national and EU positions on the Basel Committee has been mixed, reflecting in particular persistent divergences across member states' banking markets (Quaglia 2015).

A more decentralized model applies with respect to other forms of international engagement beyond participation in the international standard setters, including the negotiation and adoption of supervisory coordination and exchange arrangements by member states (Moloney 2014a). Since the establishment in 2011 of the ESAs, however, the institutional dynamics, incentives, and preferences in play have been changing. The crisis-era reconstruction of institutional governance for the EU financial system was designed to address internal EU challenges with respect to pan-EU risk transmission and the mutualization of supervisory risks and costs. But there have been spill-over effects, notably with respect to the potential role of the ESAs in international financial governance, with respect to the regulatory capacity of the EU, and thus with respect to the different incentives and preferences that shape EU engagement internationally.

THE EUROPEAN SUPERVISORY AUTHORITIES: A NEW ADMINISTRATIVE GOVERNANCE STRUCTURE FOR THE EU

The ESAs represent a new form of administrative governance for the EU single financial market (Moloney 2010, 2013). Prior to their construction, the supervision of the single financial market was for the most part located at national level (although coordination arrangements linking "home" and "host" member state regulators applied), and the EU's capacity to adopt technical administrative rules was limited (Ferran 2012). A significant degree of institutional centralization followed the global financial crisis, which led to a rearrangement of EU-level regulatory and supervisory governance in order to address the catastrophic leakage of risk cross-border in the EU and to support financial stability (Moloney 2014b; Ferran 2012). The ESAs form part of the new European System of Financial Supervision, which was established in 2011 to strengthen the EU's regulatory and supervisory governance and, hence, the EU's ability to contain and manage systemic risk and to support the financial stability of single market. The European System of Financial Supervision is, very broadly, a decentralized institutional arrangement for coordinating supervision and for supporting technical rulemaking for the EU financial system (legislative rulemaking is the prerogative of the EU's Treaty institutions: the EC, which proposes rules; the Council, which represents the Member States and is a co-legislator; and the European Parliament, which represents the citizenry and is a co-legislator). The European System of Financial Supervision is composed of the member states' national regulators, who provide the foundations of the system and are responsible for supervision and enforcement; three sectoral ESAs, which are conferred with an array of quasi-regulatory and supervisory powers (the European Banking Authority, the European Securities and Markets Authority, and the European Insurance and Occupational Pensions Authority); and the European Systemic Risk Board, which is responsible for monitoring pan-EU systemic risks.

The ESAs take the form of independent administrative agencies, funded by a combination of member state and EU funds, and have been established under primary EU legislation adopted by the Council and the European Parliament. Consequently they are not treaty institutions, unlike the EC and the ECB. Decisionmaking is carried out by their respective boards of supervisors, which are composed of the relevant national regulators of the twenty-eight member states. With respect to regulatory governance, the ESAs support administrative rule making by the EC (the constitutional location of administrative rulemaking for the EU under the EU Treaties) by proposing technical rules and by providing expert advice. The ESAs are also empowered to adopt soft law, primarily in the form of "Guidance" with which national regulators must "comply or explain."

Although supervision remains at national level, the ESAs have been given a range of coordination and convergence powers, including data collection, peer review, and participation (on a nonvoting basis) in the different colleges of supervisors required under the EU's harmonized single rule book for financial services. The ESAs can also deploy a very limited suite of direct intervention powers—limited because of the strength of member states' hostility to the ESAs' having powers that could carry fiscal risks for national treasuries. The ESAs can impose decisions on national regulators in three exceptional situations, and subject to detailed conditionality in each case: where the national regulator is in breach of EU law, in emergency conditions, and following a binding mediation by an authority between national regulators. The European Securities and Market Authority has an additional suite of direct powers—reflecting political priorities and conditions as well as the limited fiscal risks posed to the member states by these powers The European Securities and Markets Authority has exclusive supervisory and enforcement authority over credit-rating agencies and the trade repositories that hold OTC derivatives market data (the authority has displaced the national regulators in these areas); specified and exceptional powers to intervene to prohibit short selling in a member state or pan-EU; and specified and exceptional powers relating to prohibiting products and to holding positions in commodity derivative markets in a member state or pan-EU.

Alongside the coordination-oriented EU structures of the single-market-based European System of Financial Supervision are the distinct EU structures that support Banking Union. Banking Union applies to member states that are in the euro area—the Economic and Monetary Union—on a mandatory basis and to other EU member states on a voluntary basis. Banking Union is also institution-specific: with some very minor exceptions relating to group structures it governs only deposit-taking institutions within these member states. Banking Union, a primarily euro-area construct, is distinct from the wider single-market-oriented European System of Financial Supervision. Banking Union is operational, executive, and risk-mutualizing in character; it is not a coordination device, as is the European System of Financial Supervision. Banking Union is designed to address the "toxic feedback loop" which developed over the financial crisis in the EU (relating to the nexus between fragility in the euro-area banking system and the wider sustainability of euro-area member states' fiscal positions and, ultimately, of the euro) by providing for risk mutualization and for pooled support to the euro-area banking system (Moloney 2014b; Ferran 2015a).

Banking Union's Single Supervisory Mechanism brings the supervision of some six thousand banks, directly and indirectly, under the oversight of the ECB. A treaty institution and the EU's monetary authority, now the ECB is a banking supervisory authority. The Single Supervisory Mechanism is concerned with bank authorization, "steady state" bank supervision, and early intervention; it operates under the EU's harmonized single banking rule book for the single market. The ECB is responsible for the functioning of the Single Supervisory Mechanism; has direct supervisory authority over 129 of Banking Union's largest and most systemically significant banks; and has oversight authority (which it exercises by means of rules, guidance, and supervisory protocols, as well as by means of its deterrent power to take over supervision) over the remainder of Banking Union's banks, which are supervised directly by their national banking regulators within the Single Supervisory Mechanism. The Single Resolution Mechanism brings the resolution of Banking Union banks within the control of a new agency called the Single Resolution Board and includes a Single Resolution Fund to support resolution. The Single Resolution Mechanism operates within the EU's harmonized single bank resolution rule book. Both the ECB (within the Single Supervisory Mechanism) and the Single Resolution Board (within the Single Resolution Mechanism) are subject to the ESAs' powers.

THE EUROPEAN SUPERVISORY AUTHORITIES: A NEW ADMINISTRATIVE CHANNEL FOR ENGAGEMENT WITH INTERNATIONAL FINANCIAL GOVERNANCE

Although their primary function is to support the stability and efficiency of the EU single financial market, under their founding EU regulations the ESAs have been given the power to develop contacts and enter into administrative arrangement with international bodies.[2] But the ESAs must use their powers without prejudice to the respective competences of the member states and the EU institutions, so formally the ESAs' representation functions are limited. The more detailed administrative powers with respect to international financial governance conferred on the ESAs in specific EU measures governing particular aspects of the EU financial system relate, for the most part, to supervisory cooperation and coordination, including the facilitation of information exchange and cooperation agreements between member state regulators and third-country regulators.[3] Specific EU measures have also conferred on the ESAs a range of powers relating to the

---

2. For example, Regulation (EU) No. 1093/2010 of the European Parliament and of the Council establishing a European Supervisory Authority (European Banking Authority) OJ (2010) L331/12, Article 33.

3. Such as, for example, the major EU market regulation measures: Directive 2014/65/EU of the European Parliament and of the Council on markets in financial instruments and amending Directive 2002/92/EC and

equivalence-based, third-country market-access requirements that apply to third-country actors seeking to access the EU financial market. The ESAs are usually empowered to advise the EC on whether a third-country legal regime is equivalent to the EU regime. This limited suite of formal powers does not reflect the extent to which the ESAs can extend their regulatory capacity and that of the EU with respect to international financial governance and thereby construct a new administrative channel for international financial governance. A case study of the European Banking Authority, based on empirical observation of its recent activities, is noted in a later section.

Although the three ESAs have distinct incentives and preferences when it comes to international engagement, reflecting their different operating environments, they have others in common. In particular, the ESAs are new administrative actors in EU financial governance, are of ambiguous status, operate in complex institutional environments, and are developing under the "shadow of hierarchy" (Héritier and Lehmkuhl 2008). Although constituted as independent regulatory agencies, the ESAs have little in common with domestic regulators worldwide. They operate under tightly confined mandates and with limited operating powers. This constrained operating environment reflects, politically, the member states' wariness in ceding powers which may lead to incursions into national sovereignty and to fiscal risks, as well as the significant EU Treaty limitations which apply to the construction of EU agencies. The treaty competence that has been used as the basis for the construction of the ESAs (Treaty on the Functioning of the EU, Article 114) remains contested, for example, because of doubts that the competence, which is directed to the approximation of rules for the support for the single market, can be stretched to include institution building. Although the Court of Justice of the EU provided some assurance as to the resilience of the relevant competence in 2014, albeit only with respect to specific authority powers and not with respect to their foundation and their powers more generally,[4] doubts remain given the narrow focus of the Court's ruling. EU constitutional arrangements also prevent the ESAs from being conferred with wide-ranging discretionary powers, in order to protect the institutional balance set up under the treaties between the member states, the EC, the Council, and the European Parliament; strict conditionality accordingly applies to their operation, including with respect to their limited supervisory powers.[5] Similarly, under the EU Treaties the EC is the location of administrative rule making. The ESAs may only propose and advise on administrative rules, and their proposals and advice can be vetoed by the EC, even where extensive market consultation and impact assessment has been undertaken by the ESAs. Finally, the EC represents the EU in trade- and single-market-related matters (Treaty on the Functioning of the European Union, Article 220). The shadow of EC hierarchy accordingly blankets the ESAs. The European Parliament also casts a long shadow. It has long been careful to protect its (limited) prerogatives with respect to administrative rulemaking, in relation to which it, along with the Council, can veto EC rules. It has recently shown some concern to exercise tighter control over the ESAs, including by calling for the European Parliament to have access to internal ESA deliberations on the drafts of the proposals for and advice on administrative rules that the ESAs must deliver to the EC (European Parliament Economic and Monetary Affairs Committee 2015). The operating environment is particularly complex for the European Banking Authority, as it operates under the lengthy and expanding shadow of the ECB within Banking

---

Directive 2011/61/EU (2014) OJ L173/349 (MiFID II); and Regulation (EU) No. 600/2014 of the European Parliament and of the Council on markets in financial instruments and amending Regulation (EU) No. 648/2012 (2014) OJ L173/84 (MiFIR). These measures confer power on the European Securities and Markets Authority with respect to international cooperation and coordination in relation to the matters within their scope.

4. *UK v. Council and Parliament*, Case C-270/12, January 22, 2014.

5. *Meroni v. High Authority*, Case 9/56 (1957–1958) ECR 133.

Union and is facing something of an existential threat (Ferran 2015b).

With this complex and constrained operating environment, the ESAs—as new administrative actors seeking to embed their position within EU financial governance— have considerable incentives to strengthen and assert their institutional position and regulatory capacity, and to reinforce their primacy as technocratic and independent agencies, while respecting the EU Treaties' limits on their powers. International financial governance is likely, accordingly, to have significant appeal for the ESAs. The soft law nature of international financial governance means that engagement with the international standard setters affords the ESAs the opportunity to strengthen their capacity and institutional position with a degree of freedom. As international financial governance and the international standard setters pivot to a more operational orientation, they provide a natural channel through which the ESAs—whose functions and powers are directed to pan-EU coordination and who have a unique set of experiences on how cross-border and regional coordination risks can be managed—can strengthen their capacity and credibility. For example, the European Securities and Markets Authority is becoming increasingly sophisticated in how it approaches the peer review of its member regulators (which is required of it under its founding regulation), having recently upgraded its peer review mechanism and adopted a more robust and granular approach to peer review.[6] It is also increasingly focusing on supporting supervisory coordination and supervisory convergence across its national regulators (European Securities and Markets Authority 2015). Given its practical experience in managing the coordination risks associated with the supervision of securities markets, the European Securities and Markets Authority, although a nonvoting member of IOSCO, can be expected to acquire credibility and capacity and seek influence within IOSCO. As an indication of the movement within international financial governance to operational matters, IOSCO is now subject to requests from the FSB to carry out peer reviews.[7] The opportunities for the European Securities and Markets Authority to strengthen its credibility on IOSCO may therefore be significant, given its extensive experience in this area and given the initial indications that its influence may become significant, if still developing (Conac 2015).

Despite this potential, there are limitations on how much the ESAs can, through international engagement, extend their regulatory capacity and thus the influence of the EU on international financial governance. The structures of national economies across the EU continue to diverge significantly (European Commission 2015a), as is reflected in the EU's current efforts to build a European Capital Markets Union (European Commission 2015b). Accordingly, the national regulators, which, through the different Boards of Supervisors, determine ESA decisionmaking, will often have strong incentives to follow a national rather than a collective position. On the other hand, as international financial governance pivots toward operational coordination and away from standard setting (where distributive effects are likely to be stronger), the opportunities for strong national interests to obstruct European Supervisory Authority decisionmaking may recede. But the ESAs must also often operate in a muddy international environment. The EC, and often the ECB, can also represent the EU interest and they have strong incentives to protect their respective positions. There are, however, indications that the ESAs will intensify their activities in international financial governance—given the potential such activities hold for influence and capacity build-

---

6. On peer review of member regulators with respect to the supervision of best execution see, for example, European Securities and Markets Authority, "Best Execution Under MiFiD: Peer Review," 2015, www.esma.europa.eu/sites/default/files/library/2015/11/2015-494_peer_review_report_on_best_execution_under_mifid_0.pdf; accessed June 10, 2016.

7. See, for example, International Organization of Securities Commissions, "Peer Review of Implementation of Incentive Alignment Recommendations for Securitization," 2014, www.iosco.org/library/pubdocs/pdf/IOSCOPD504.pdf; accessed December, 15, 2015, which followed a request from the FSB.

ing, with a consequent strengthening of both the EU's ability to influence the international standard setters and the resilience of the international standard-setting process, as is discussed further below with respect to the European Banking Authority.

THE EUROPEAN BANKING AUTHORITY: A CASE STUDY

The European Banking Authority has an express general mandate to enter into coordination arrangements and information-exchange agreements with third-country regulators and international standard setters (2010 European Banking Authority Regulation, Article 33). The EU's major harmonized banking regulation measure confers additional administrative powers on the authority,[8] including supporting international coordination and advising the EC on equivalence-related and EU market-access matters. The authority also sits as a nonvoting observer on the Basel Committee, alongside the EC (nonvoting observer), the ECB (voting member), and relevant national regulators and central banks within the EU (voting members).

The fragility of the authority's institutional operating environment gives it significant incentives to engage with international finance governance through formal and informal means. This fragility is a function of the fragmentation between the single market in banking (the remit of the authority's coordination and quasi-regulatory powers) and the euro-area Single Supervisory Mechanism (the remit of the ECB). This fragility generates a number of threats for the authority (Moloney 2014b; Ferran 2015a). Its quasi-rulemaking powers over the single market are threatened by the risk of Single Supervisory Mechanism caucusing with the relevant regulators on the authority's board of supervisors (nineteen of the authority's twenty-eight national regulators are members of the Single Supervisory Mechanism), which could reduce its effectiveness; and also by the emergence of the ECB as a potentially competing standard setter, albeit within the Single Supervisory Mechanism "zone," as the ECB is empowered to adopt rules, guidance, and other protocols for the Single Supervisory Mechanism.

Efforts have been made to address these risks, including through governance reforms (a double-lock procedure applies to authority voting in that decisions must be carried by a majority of Single Supervisory Mechanism authority members and also by a majority of non–Single Supervisory Mechanism members of the authority); and a requirement for the ECB to follow the authority's soft law and other measures. But the risks to the authority's capacity remain considerable, particularly as euro-area membership (and accordingly Single Supervisory Mechanism membership) will grow from the current nineteen (of twenty-eight) EU member states to, over time, twenty-six. Similar risks arise with respect to supervisory governance. The ECB, under the EU regulation that confers on it supervisory power over the Single Supervisory Mechanism, is subject to the authority's soft and hard coordinating powers. But whether or not the authority, a nascent agency established under EU primary legislation and with significant operating constraints, can (and has the incentives to) exert authority over the mighty ECB, which has direct executive supervisory powers over the 129 largest banking groups in the euro area and which enjoys the independence of action of a treaty institution, remains to be seen.

The authority has accordingly significant incentives to seek international financial governance, and in particular Basel Committee deliberations, as a sphere in which it can boost its credibility and regulatory capacity and protect its institutional position. The capacity of

---

8. This regulation is the 2014 Capital Requirements Directive IV, Capital Requirements Regulation, which, inter alia, implements the Basel III Accord in the EU: Regulation (EU) No. 575/2013 of the European Parliament and of the Council on prudential requirements for credit institutions and investment firms, amending Regulation (EU) No. 648/2012 (2013) OJ L176/1; and Directive 2013/36/EU of the European Parliament and of the Council on access to the activity of credit institutions and the prudential supervision of credit institutions and investment firms, amending Directive 2002/87/EC and repealing Directives 2006/48/EC and 2006/49/EC (2013) OJ L176/338.

the EU more generally in international financial governance for banking should accordingly be strengthened. Robust engagement with international financial governance also affords the authority the opportunity to strengthen its relationship with the ECB in a somewhat less contested forum than the EU single market, including on the Basel Committee, where both institutions are represented.

The authority is certainly well equipped to strengthen its capacity and credibility on the Basel Committee (albeit as an observer member) and to strengthen thereby the EU's position, particularly as international financial governance becomes more operational in orientation. It has deep technocratic expertise following its technical support of the construction of the administrative rules which amplify the 2014 CRD IV/CRR legislative rule book. It has valuable expertise in managing operational coordination, including of colleges of supervisors and with respect to supporting supervisory convergence (European Banking Authority 2015a, 2015b); with respect to the latter, for example, it has adopted extensive and granular Supervisory Review and Evaluation Process (SREP) Guidelines, which govern the operational business of banking supervision and amplify the Basel III Accord in the EU (European Banking Authority 2014). Its equivalence-related activities are likely to have a similar capacity-building effect, given the extensive contacts and international network the authority has developed in producing its reports on the equivalence of third-country banking regimes and on the nature of supervisory cooperation between national regulators in the EU and third-country regulators (European Banking Authority 2015c, 2015d).

The authority is also acquiring granular knowledge of the emerging divergences across the member states as to how the 2014 CRD IV/CRR regime (in effect, the Basel III Accord) is being applied (European Banking Authority 2015e), which should further enhance its credibility with the Basel Committee as the committee finesses the regime. Similarly, sitting in the center of a web of bank regulatory disclosures as the EU repository for the FINREP (financial reporting) and COREP (common reporting) reporting disclosures required of EU banks under the 2014 CRD IV/CRR regime (and accordingly under Basel III "Pillar 3"), and as the repository of EU bank stress test disclosures, further enhances the authority's technocratic capacity as the Basel Committee increasingly turns to standard implementation and review.

As against this, the authority may struggle to present a coherent collective position given the distinct interests which still drive the national regulators on its board of supervisors, reflecting the different structures of national banking markets across the EU, which may obstruct its ability to present a collective position. Conflicts of interest may arise between the authority and the EC (also an observer), while the authority must also coordinate with the ECB, which, as a direct supervisor and central bank can exercise voting power (albeit that the Basel Committee tends to operate on a consensual basis). On the other hand, divergences and conflicts are likely to be most acute with respect to standard setting. In more operational matters the authority can be expected to have a clearer space to influence and to impose a collective EU preference.

There is still only limited experience with the authority as an actor in international financial governance and against which its incentives and its growing regulatory capacity and potential as an actor internationally can be tested. But initial indications suggest a potential for growing influence by the authority (and so of the EU), particularly on more operational matters in relation to which it sits on a number of Basel Committee subgroups and working groups (European Banking Authority 2015f; Quaglia 2015). Its incentives to achieve a collective position on its board of supervisors and to seek to influence Basel Committee deliberations can be expected to increase as the ECB within the Single Supervisory Mechanism increases its power, and as the authority becomes more expert on the implementation of the Basel III Accord in the EU, particularly if banking governance internationally continues its current operationally charged trajectory.

This development is likely to strengthen international financial governance in the banking sphere. The authority has significant potential as a "legalization" mechanism (Bach and Newman 2014), which supports the injection of soft Basel Committee standards into binding EU law through its proposal of administrative rules to the EC and which thereby signals the credibility of standards. The authority's soft law can be expected to have a similar effect. Its soft "SREP Guidelines" on how the 2014 CRD IV/CRR/Basel III regime is to be supervised in practice (European Banking Authority 2014) have considerable potential to support the diffusion of global good practice in how the Basel III SREP supervisory process should be carried out and monitored—particularly as the authority is committed to ongoing review and monitoring of the guidelines. The authority also has the capacity to act as a potential corrective agent, and thereby to support the convergent application of Basel Committee standards. International standards, as has been extensively documented, are vulnerable to being reshaped during the national implementation process in order to provide escape opportunities. In the EU the Basel III Accord has been subject to numerous exemptions and derogations in its implementation through the 2014 CRD IV/CRR regime. This led to the Basel Committee's finding, in its December 2014 Regulatory Compliance and Assessment Program review of the EU's Basel III implementation, that the EU was "materially noncompliant" with the Basel III Accord in a number of respects (Basel Committee on Banking Supervision 2014b). The authority, which given its precarious institutional position has much to gain from claiming ownership over the Basel Committee monitoring process, has been robust in warning of the risks that divergent implementation of the Basel III Accord poses and has called for corrective action from the EU's co-legislators in response to specific types of divergence. It has also suggested interim remedial action to be taken by its member regulators (European Banking Authority 2015e). The corrective function that appears to be emerging through the authority augurs well, accordingly, for the regulatory capacity of the EU at least to highlight divergences in Basel Committee standard implementation and to place pressure, accordingly, on its member states, from independent, technocratic regulators operating collectively through the authority, to take remedial action through the EU legislative process.

The authority's engagement may also have the effect of strengthening the accountability and legitimacy of Basel Committee standards, at least in the EU. The mechanisms through which the accountability and legitimacy of international financial governance are supported can be weak but are strengthening (Barr 2014). The strengthening process may be further enhanced by the changes in how the EU engages with international financial governance. Like all the ESAs, the authority is subject to an array of accountability and legitimacy mechanisms under its founding 2010 regulation.[9] These include reporting obligations to the European Parliament and Council, to whom the authority is formally accountable; the design of its board of supervisors (which includes the EC in a nonvoting capacity as well as national regulators); and the many constraints that apply to authority operation under its foundation regulation, which imposes strict conditionality on its action. Any overreaching with respect to international financial governance by the authority will likely be constrained by its board of supervisors as well as by the EC, European Parliament, and Council, particularly where redistributive effects may be significant and national and EU institutional interests are strong.

In addition, the authority, like all the ESAs, is subject to a wide range of consultation obligations under its founding 2010 regulation. These include obligations to consult widely; engage in impact assessment; provide feedback; and have a representative "Stakeholder Group" composed of industry, user, consumer, and other constituencies. In engaging with the Basel Committee the authority is accordingly subject to a range of procedural devices and operates within a constrained institutional environment, both of which should enhance the accountability and legitimacy of EU engagement with international financial governance. The authority is, for example, subject to a more restrictive set of accountability and legitimacy controls than the EC.

---

9. See note 2.

CONCLUSION

The management of operational risks through coordinated action by regulators is increasingly displacing standard setting as the major preoccupation of the international standard setters. Although the EU has typically engaged with international financial governance and the international standard setters primarily through its member states, and although engagement has primarily been in the form of the imposition of national and (less frequently) collective EU preferences on standard setting, it is well equipped to manage this pivot. This article suggests that the EU's European Supervisory Authorities have opened up a new administrative channel through which the EU can engage with international financial governance and the international standard setters. It predicts, from empirical observation of the recent activities of the European Banking Authority in particular and analysis of its operating environment and of the incentives it generates, that the ESAs may gain influence on the international standard setters. The EU's ability to impose its preferences, at least with respect to more operational matters, may accordingly be strengthened. This development augurs well for the effectiveness of international financial governance more generally.

REFERENCES

Amtenbrick, Fabien. 2013. "What Role for the EU in Shaping Global Financial Governance?" In *The EU's Role in Global Governance*, edited by Bart Van Vooren, Steven Blockmans, and Jan Wouters. Oxford: Oxford University Press.

Bach, David, and Abraham Newman. 2007. "The European Regulatory State and Global Public Policy." *Journal of European Public Policy* 14(6): 827–46.

———. 2014. "The European Union as Hardening Agent: Soft Law and the Diffusion of Global Financial Regulation." *Journal of European Public Policy* 21(3): 430–52.

Barr, Michael. 2014. "Who's in Charge of Global Finance?" *Georgetown Journal of International Law* 45(4): 971–1027.

Basel Committee on Banking Supervision. 2014a. "Principles for Effective Supervisory Colleges." Available at: www.bis.org/publ/bcbs287.htm; accessed December 15, 2015.

———. 2014b. "Regulatory Consistency Assessment Program (RCAP) Assessment of Basel III Regulation—European Union." Available at www.bis.org/bcbs/publ/d300.pdf; accessed December 15, 2015.

Blom, Jasper. 2014. "Banking." In *Europe and the Governance of Global Finance*, edited by Daniel Mügge. Oxford: Oxford University Press.

Brummer, Christopher. 2012. *Soft Law and the Global Financial System. Rule-Making in the 21st Century.* Cambridge: Cambridge University Press.

Busuioc, Madalina. 2013. "Rule-Making by the European Financial Supervisory Authorities: Walking a Tight Rope." *European Law Journal* 19(1): 111–25.

Büthe, Tim, and Walter Mattli. 2011. *The New Global Rulers: The Privatization of Regulation in the World Economy.* Princeton, N.J.: Princeton University Press.

Conac, Pierre-Henri. 2015. "The European Union's Role in International Economic Fora, Paper 6: IOSCO." Report prepared for the European Parliament. Available at: www.europarl.europa.eu/RegData/etudes/STUD/2015/542195/IPOL_STU(2015)542195_EN.pdf; accessed December 15, 2015.

Drezner, Daniel. 2007. *All Politics Is Global. Explaining International Regulatory Regimes.* Princeton, N.J.: Princeton University Press.

European Commission. 2015a. "Commission Staff Working Document, Initial Reflections on the Obstacles to the Development of Deep and Integrated EU Capital Market." Available at: http://eur-lex.europa.eu/legal-content/EN/TXT/?uri=CELEX:52015SC0013; accessed December 15, 2015.

———. 2015b. "Capital Markets Union: Unlocking Funding for Europe's Growth." COM (2015) 468. Available at: http://ec.europa.eu/finance/capital-markets-union/index_en.htm#action-plan; accessed June 10, 2016.

European Banking Authority. 2014. "Guidelines on Common Procedures and Methodologies for the Supervisory Review and Evaluation Process." Available at: www.eba.europa.eu/documents/10180/935249/EBA-GL-2014-13+(Guidelines+on+SREP+methodologies+and+processes).pdf; accessed December 15, 2015.

———. 2015a. "Accomplishment of 2014 EBA Colleges Action Plan and 2015 EBA Colleges Action Plan." Available at: www.eba.europa.eu/-/eba

-reviews-work-of-eu-colleges-of-supervisors-for-cross-border-banking-groups; accessed December 15, 2015.

———. 2015b. "Report on Convergence of Supervisory Practices." Available at: www.eba.europa.eu/documents/10180/950548/Supervisory+convergence+report.pdf/9f49ddf9-232f-4062-b34e-ff671d440081; accessed December 15, 2015.

———. 2015c. "Questionnaire on the Assessment of Equivalence with the European Regulatory and Supervisory Framework." Available at: www.eba.europa.eu/documents/10180/1094990/Annex+I+-+EBA+questionnaire+on+regulatory+equivalence_publication.pdf; accessed December 15, 2015.

———. 2015d. "Opinion of the European Banking Authority on Co-operation with Third Countries." Available at: www.eba.europa.eu/documents/10180/983359/EBA-Op-2015-19+(Opinion+on+cooperation+with+third+countries+-+Art+161+(7)%20CRD).pdf; accessed December 15, 2015.

———. 2015e. "Opinion on Credit Valuation Adjustment." Available at: www.eba.europa.eu/documents/10180/983359/EBA-Op-2015-02+(EBA+Opinion+on+CVA+risk).pdf; accessed December 15, 2015.

———. 2015f. "Annual Report on 2014" Available at: www.eba.europa.eu/-/eba-publishes-its-2014-annual-report; accessed December 15, 2015.

European Parliament Economic and Monetary Affairs Committee. 2015. "Draft Report on Stocktaking and Challenges of the EU Financial Services Regulation: Impact and the Way Forward Towards a More Efficient and Effective EU Framework for Financial Regulation and a Capital Markets Union." Available at: www.europarl.europa.eu/committees/en/econ/draft-reports.html?action=1; accessed December 15, 2015.

European Securities and Markets Authority. 2015. "Strategic Orientations 2016–2020." Available at: file:///C:/Documents%20and%20Settings/Niamh/My%20Documents/Downloads/2015-935_esma_strategic_orientation_2016-2020.pdf; accessed December 15, 2015.

Ferran Eilís. 2012. "Crisis-Driven Regulatory Reform: Where in the World Is the EU Going?" In *The Regulatory Aftermath of the Global Financial Crisis*, edited by Eilís Ferran, Niamh Moloney, Jennifer Hill, and John C. Coffee. Cambridge: Cambridge University Press.

———. 2014. "Financial Supervision." In *Europe and the Governance of Global Finance*, edited by Daniel Mügge. Oxford: Oxford University Press.

———. 2015a. "European Banking Union: Imperfect, But It Can Work." In *European Banking Union*, edited by Danny Busch and Guido Ferrarini. Oxford: Oxford University Press.

———. 2015b. "The Existential Search of the European Banking Authority." Research Paper 40/2015; ECGI–Law Working Paper No. 297/2015. Cambridge: University of Cambridge, Faculty of Law, European Corporate Governance Institute Law. Available at: http://ssrn.com/abstract=2634904; accessed December 15, 2015.

Financial Stability Board. 2015a. "Handbook for FSB Peer Review." Available at: www.financialstabilityboard.org/2015/03/handbook-for-fsb-peer-reviews/; accessed December 15, 2015.

———. 2015b. "Ninth Progress Report on Implementation of OTC Derivatives Market Reform." Available at: www.financialstabilityboard.org/2015/07/ninth-progress-report-on-implementation-of-otc-derivatives-market-reforms/; accessed December 15, 2015.

Helleiner, Eric, and Stefano Pagliari. 2011. "The End of an Era in International Financial Regulation? A Postcrisis Research Agenda." *International Organization* 65(1): 169–200.

Héritier, Adrienne, and Dirk Lehmkuhl. 2008. "Introduction: The Shadow of Hierarchy and New Modes of Governance." *Journal of Public Policy* 28(1): 1–17.

International Organization of Securities Commissions. 2013. "Supervisory Colleges for Credit Rating Agencies" Available at: www.iosco.org/library/pubdocs/pdf/IOSCOPD416.pdf; accessed December 15, 2015.

———. 2015a. "Task Force on Cross-border Regulation." Available at: www.iosco.org/library/pubdocs/pdf/IOSCOPD507.pdf

———. 2015b. "Credible Deterrence in the Enforcement of Securities Regulation." Available at: www.iosco.org/library/pubdocs/pdf/IOSCOPD490.pdf; accessed December 15, 2015.

Krisch, Nico, and Benedict Kingsbury. 2006. "Introduction: Global Governance and Global Administrative Law in the International Legal Order." *European Journal of International Law* 17(1): 1–13.

Moloney, Niamh. 2010. "EU Financial Market Regulation After the Global Financial Crisis: 'More Europe' or More Risks?" *Common Market Law Review* 47(5): 1317–83.

———. 2013. "Resetting the Location of Regulatory and Supervisory Control over EU Financial Markets: Lessons from Five Years On." *International and Comparative Law Quarterly* 62(4): 955–65.

———. 2014a. *EU Securities and Financial Markets Regulation*. Oxford: Oxford University Press.

———. 2014b. "European Banking Union: Assessing Its Risks and Resilience." *Common Market Law Review* 51(6): 1609–70.

Mügge, Daniel. 2011. "The European Presence in Global Financial Governance: A Principal Agent Perspective." *Journal of European Public Policy* 18(3): 838–402.

———. 2014. "Europe's Regulatory Role in Post-Crisis Global Finance." *Journal of European Public Policy* 21(3): 316–26.

Newman, Abraham, and Eric Posner. 2015. "Putting the EU in Its Place: Policy Strategies and the Global Regulatory Context." *Journal of European Public Policy* 22(9): 1316–35.

Posner, Eric. 2009. "Making Rules for Global Finance: Transatlantic Regulatory Cooperation at the Turn of the Millennium." *International Organization* 63(4): 665–99.

———. 2010. "Is a European Approach to Financial Regulation Emerging from the Crisis?" In *Global Finance in Crisis. The Politics of International Regulatory Change*, edited by Eric Helleiner, Stefano Pagliari, and Hubert Zimmerman. London and New York: Routledge.

Quaglia, Lucia. 2014a. *The European Union & Global Financial Regulation*. Oxford: Oxford University Press.

———. 2014b. "The Sources of European Influence in International Financial Regulatory Fora." *Journal of European Public Policy* 21(3): 327–45.

———. 2015. "The European Union's Role in International Economic For a. Paper 5: The BCBS." Report prepared for the European Parliament, Directorate-General for International Policies. Available at: www.europarl.europa.eu/RegData/etudes/IDAN/2015/542194/IPOL_IDA(2015)542194_EN.pdf; accessed December 15, 2015.

Schammo, Pierre. 2011. "The European Securities and Markets Authority: Lifting the Veil on the Allocation of Powers." *Common Market Law Review* 48(6): 1879–1914.

Slaughter, Anne-Marie. 2004. *A New World Order*. Princeton, N.J., and Oxford: Princeton University Press.

Verdier, Pierre-Hugues. 2013. "The Political Economy of International Financial Regulation." *Indiana Law Journal* 88(4): 1405–74.